DIAMOND LIGHT ORACLE

Bec Mylonas

HOUSE OF INDIGO

CONTENTS

FOREWORD

I first heard about the Diamond Path from my Dragon guides on one random sunny *(or should I say fiery?)* summer afternoon as I was pulling into my driveway. I heard them say as clear as day... *"You walk the Diamond Path."* I thought to myself, *"Okay, that's cool. Not sure what that means but thanks, I think?"* After that I went on with my day, not giving it too much more thought.

It would take years and countless initiations before I fully realized what the Dragons were talking about and what they really meant.

The Diamond Path is *excruciating*. It's a path of fire & pressure where those of us brave enough to walk it feel like we're being crushed, ripped in two; or both, simultaneously. Fun times, I know...and yet, somehow we're able to alchemize all our pain into such potent medicine that it defies all logic. When we tell others our story, their eyes go wide, and their jaws drop to the floor in disbelief. They don't understand how we came out the other side intact. *Neither do we.*

Sound familiar? My guess is yes since you were drawn to open up this book and didn't immediately slam it shut.

Oh yes, I bet there's a very good chance you're on the Diamond Path as a modern day Oracle, trying to navigate what very few understand or can articulate, let alone show you with clarity *what-the-actual-fuck-is-happening-to-you-and-why*.

I'm so happy to say that you've landed in the right place. I'm going to tell you exactly what and why it's happening in a single sentence. Then you can decide if reading the actual book properly *(remember, this is just the foreword)* is for you or if it's time to give that book cover a good old slap shut after all.

Are you ready?

The reason for the Diamond Path is to forge you into a fully realized version of yourself (the Oracle) capable of holding the medicine & light codes you've been gathering, cultivating & refining for *lifetimes* so that you can help paradigm shift the planet into the new age...**during this lifetime**.

Phew I'm glad to get that out right away.

Are you still with me?

If something deep just got stirred within you or validated what you already know, let's keep going...

To understand *why* it's called the **Diamond** Path, let's geek out on *how* literal diamonds are actually formed in the womb of Mama Gaia. In case you're not familiar or it's been a hot minute since you've thought about it...

Diamonds form in the mantle of the Earth as a result of carbon (coal) being compressed at very high pressures (~50,000 times the surface pressure of the Earth to be specific) and temperatures (~1600°C) over an extremely long period of time (I'm talking millions and billions of years). The atoms are squeezed together so tightly that they actually *change their atomic structure* by bonding with 4 other carbon atoms instead of just 3. This new bonding creates a crystalline tetrahedron structure (think pyramid with a triangle as the base instead of a square), which allows light to pass through it instead of getting trapped. And thus, a diamond is born...extremely rare, radiantly beautiful and literally harder than any other naturally occurring substance on the planet (hardness level is 10 out of 10). The only thing strong enough to scratch or cut a diamond is *another diamond*.

So you see, when you walk the Diamond Path, you're being **forged** into something so clear and strong that you can hold vastly greater amounts of spiritual light (i.e. truth). In other words, instead of being more like a big ol' lump of coal trapping & absorbing light (what a buzz kill) you *transmit and amplify it* (i.e. you become radiant). It also becomes nigh impossible to fuck with you as a result of this process (only a diamond can scratch/cut a diamond).

This level of internal stability is essential for the leaders meant to help humanity transition into the next stage of consciousness, which will bring conflict and upheaval as we all shift. Embodying yourself as the Oracle will allow you to *cut through* lies and illusions projected onto you as you learn to channel greater and greater amounts of divine light. People have a choice when confronted with the truth...they can accept it, run from it or attack **you** since you're the lucky messenger. I know, it's not right, but it is a potential reality we all must face. So you'll need to become essentially impervious to others' projections onto you so you don't collapse under their scrutiny. This requires a level of oneness that exceeds what most humans even know is possible.

Applying the metaphor of the diamond to the path itself on a more relatable, practical level, this transformation looks like starting out as a *wounded* healer (i.e. coal) and then moving to conscious healer, channel, priest/priestess and ultimately Oracle (i.e. diamond). A brief summary of each step in the process is below.

Wounded Healer

Oracles typically start out as wounded healers acting more like energetic sponges than spiritual alchemists. Then, when we become so full of everyone else's energetic shit that we start to come apart at the seams, we seek out ways to use our gifts and energy *for us* instead of against us so that we can become whole again (rather than keep feeling like energetic and emotional swiss cheese). This intentional seeking enters us into the world of *conscious* healing.

Conscious Healers

If we allow this new current of awareness to continue to guide us, then it doesn't take long for all 20 of our channels to open up wider than ever before (more on this later in the book), pulling in greater amounts of energy at more refined frequencies. The downloads flow in like Niagra Falls, sometimes with such gusto that we literally can't write the insights and ideas down fast enough. We start inexplicably knowing things we couldn't possibly have known otherwise and words of wisdom spontaneously pop out our mouths. This is especially true in healing spaces, where it always seems to be *exactly* what was needed in the moment.

This is often a very exhilarating, but frightening time and in truth, many ultimately stop here out of fear...fear of their gifts, fear of what others will think, fear of being ostracized, fear of being punished or even killed, etc.

If they gather up enough internal fire to say, "fuck it" and consciously choose to take on their spirituality as a metaphorical lover rather than "friend-zoning" or even fully rejecting this part of themselves, then they've now stepped deeper onto the path as a priest/priestess.

Priest/Priestess

Priestesses (I'm going to say priestess moving forward for ease) are on a devotional journey where their life is now fully dedicated to cultivating their spiritual side and living in alignment with divine truth. This is where the Diamond Path truly starts and the installation of the diamond light body begins (more on this later in the book). Many have to journey through a birthing portal commonly known as the Dark Night of the Soul to find the hidden entrance onto the Diamond Path.

Oracle

Most priestesses spend decades (in truth lifetimes) birthing and rebirthing themselves over and over again so they can become the Oracle, a version of themselves capable of holding and reflecting vast amounts of light without collapsing. Once the installation of the light body begins they have no choice but to continue forward. There is no half in, half out any more than one can choose to be half pregnant. However, priestesses always have the choice of aborting their mission since we have free will as sovereign beings. Though this choice WILL leave a lasting mark that can take many more lifetimes to heal and integrate. So as you can see, this path is NOT for the faint of heart or weak willed.

Many priestesses will find themselves resisting what's being born through them at some point in time, ESPECIALLY when they are about to give birth to the Oracle within. This is a truly terrifying time because not only are they birthing codes that WILL shift the planet, there's absolutely no going back to the way things were once they do. The Oracle cannot hide anymore like the priestess still can. She has fully outed herself knowing not everyone will understand or approve of her. Preparation for this level of transformation and pattern disruption is absolutely necessary and activates every shadow not yet integrated within.

This is exactly the point where I met Bec Mylonas, the Oracle and author of this book.

Somehow Bec found her way into one of my programs (no coincidence there) after a social media post of mine "randomly" popped up in her feed. We connected as soul sisters immediately. It was kismet. From the first time we talked I knew that she was someone very special and VERY powerful...it wouldn't take long to realize she was holding the codes for ancient wisdom that were meant to shift the planet...and me.

There was a problem though...she was stuck in the spiritual (re)birthing canal...a body of work was preparing to be born through her so massive that she couldn't hold it all alone.

And she shouldn't have to.

Bec felt massive, crippling resistance to what she needed to do (write this book) in order to rebirth herself as the Diamond Light Oracle she is now. She was stuck in a holding pattern because she didn't have a safe human being (yet) to hold her through the intense and often paralyzing initiations she could intuitively feel coming (like the contractions that come in labor). She found me desperate to understand how to work with and hold the tsunami of energy channeling through her without it tearing her body apart.

By the way, that's why this text exists for you now. To give you a sort of road map through this leg of the journey as you transition from priestess to Oracle...to reduce suffering, to amplify pleasure and speed up this biatch as much as possible without losing anything vital in the process.

In order for Bec to bring this sacred codex through she had to go through multiple brutal initiations (all of which she talks about in the book in length and in detail). But I digress, back to when we met...

We quickly dropped into a high level mentorship where I became Bec's spiritual mentor and doula, holding and supporting her as she channeled the book you're about to read. I witnessed her as she bravely went through initiation after initiation in rapid succession (one or two of which were so intense she wanted to metaphorically take her ball and go home). I witnessed her through each metamorphosis as she integrated and refined more of the very medicine you're about to receive in the following pages. She came with a pure heart, disarming vulnerability and above all, devotion to be of service in the highest form of love and integrity.

I'm so happy to say, all of her hard work paid off...and now we get to enjoy the gift of her magick.

Please know, dear reader, that as you dive into this codex you will be stepping through an invisible portal, and when you emerge, you will never be the same again.

That's exactly what happened to me. Even as her mentor, I am forever changed...

It activated such a deep cellular remembrance & massive expansion in me that I thank the powers that be *(and of course Bec)* in earnest that I was able to receive such profound, potent medicine.

Throughout reading the book, I felt called out and called forward every step of the way.

The Initiations at the end of each chapter still vibrate throughout my body and have changed me in ways I am still understanding and integrating to this very day. Bec even asked me to help with one of the Initiations at the end of Part 5 where all twenty of our meridians ("energy highways" used in Traditional Chinese Medicine) are connected to Mama Gaia's meridians. Even though I helped bring that Activation forward, I still received SO much from it!

Each Initiation, in their individual way, felt like they initiated a vast soul retrieval spanning multiple lifetimes and timelines in a matter of minutes. This coupled with Bec's vulnerability sharing the hellscapes and heavenscapes she rode through in her own human experience felt like a warm blanket of permission to be a divine being having a human experience.

In a few words, reading this book brought me closer to my own sacred, inner union. All connections between *me and me* AND me and God/Spirit and Gaia have strengthened...think of loose, partially frayed shoelaces getting replaced with new ones (in your favorite color no less) and then getting pulled tight and snug around each foot. Not only is there a greater sense of comfort now, but each step forward feels smoother, more graceful and more supportive so you can take bigger, bolder steps forward in life.

In other words, this book felt like an upgrade in every way!

Not only that, but what I learned from working with Bec in such close proximity over many months is that she's the real deal...the very embodiment of devotion to the Diamond Light Oracle path. There's no better person on planet earth to walk WITH you, alongside you, on your path from priestess to Oracle.

You will laugh, you will cry, you will vibrate (that happened to me A LOT) and you will transform into the Oracle you came here to be.

To say I'm extremely excited for the journey you're about to go on is an understatement! Get ready to have your cells bathed in love and your shadows integrated into the light.

This book is a multi dimensional vision quest!

Happy reading dear reader!

BIG LOVE,

Erin Ryan, MSOM, LAc, CRMT

To every member of my soul family I have re-encountered in this lifetime, who has in some way touched, shaped, activated, or guided me back home to the Truth of who I am;

Thank you. I see you. I love you.

To the few specific soulmates who have been able to provide a clear enough reflection to hold, witness and support me in birthing this codex, and the larger gridwork it is a part of; enabling me to anchor the fullness of my sacred mission and bring forth this book -

You know who you are and I could not have done it without you.

Thank you. I see you. I love you.

And to all of the courageous trailblazers, pathfinders, chain-breakers, cosmic rebels and wild women; the priestesses who have been walking the Diamond Path, paving pathways of light for others to walk behind -
I dedicate this book to you.

NOTE FROM THE AUTHOR

The woman I was when I began the journey of birthing this codex is not the same one who stands before you at the end with a completed manuscript in her hands. The process I had to go through to bring this transmission into the world broke me down completely, so I could rebirth into an entirely new form.

This is the same process that those who are meant to receive this offering will be led through, as you receive this codex yourself over the following days, weeks, months or however long it takes you to move through this text (and no doubt is the process *many* of you have already been going through for some time as you've navigated your own path to this point).

It is for this reason that I share rather candidly *everything* I experienced as I moved through the initiation of this transmission - not just the codes, the ancient wisdom, the linear narrative of my sacred mission, or the guided activations themselves. I share the parts in between, where the resistance and shadow parts erupting inside me were yelling *so strongly,* and my emotions were spinning *such a compelling story* that I honestly did not believe this work would see the light of day.

Truth be told, for a lot of this process - although a part of me went willingly - another part of me found herself kicking and screaming as she was dragged through the mud.

And as you can imagine, it was *far from graceful*.

I share the raw, dramatic, dark, weak, shadowy, shameful, embarrassing, entitled, hopelessly romantic, uncertain, selfish, unevolved, immature, cringey "Little Human Self" parts of myself as they surface, without curating them or watering them down to create an illusion that I'm more evolved than I am.

I share these things truthfully and honestly because *that's the whole reason I am here* - to be a Truth Teller is the medicine I am here to bring into the world.

It is part of the codex of the Divine Feminine - the Priestess transitioning into Oracle - that this book is largely the journey of stepping into.

To be able to put words to that deep, dark, vulnerable thing that *everyone is feeling* but *nobody is saying aloud*. To be able to share and speak into the things *you know you know, but don't know how you know*. To be able to boldly own, claim and stand behind the beautiful, powerful visions of the future and prophecies of what is to come that you feel as undeniable truth in your bones. To share the things that might trigger the fuck out of people, that might lose you friends and followers, or have people wanting to burn you at the metaphorical stake, but that the world needs to hear.

I share these things in the raw and unfiltered way that I do because I believe it's time we *all* did.

And because in the process of coming to a place where I could share all of this - the most private, vulnerable and personal parts of myself; the parts of me I was so afraid for people to see, the thoughts I was so afraid for other people to hear - I had to face *every single thing* inside me that did the opposite for my self-preservation and safety.

As is the journey *you* will go through, my courageous reader, in the process of your own Great Becoming.

I share this all - naked, raw, unfiltered, unedited, blemishes and all - so that in the process of laying myself bare, *you* can begin to clearly see yourself in the mirror my story provides.

So *you* can feel fully seen in all that you are and all that you go through as part of your process.

Simply receiving the sacred calling to this path will set off a sequence of events inside of you, beginning the initiation process, *before* you even begin to receive the downloads, the codes or the information (as it did for me when I was told I would write this book).

There was a point shortly after receiving the directive to channel this book that *even the thought* of sitting down to write would cause a violent eruption of emotions in my solar plexus: anger, frustration, defiance, abandonment, threat.

The confusing dance of resistance happening between multiple conflicting parts of me, at odds with my sacred mission, with their own secret agendas for my self-preservation and safety.

All the parts of me who think they know best how to keep me safe.

The truth is, part of me didn't want to write this and was fighting a very large urge inside of me to - instead of following the instruction to write - deny my calling, run off to the woods and live in hiding for the rest of my life. (I mean, what self-respecting witch doesn't feel this urge from time to time?)

Part of me did not want to be seen owning, claiming, sharing this work.

Because sharing this work would render me vulnerable and open to attack.

It would put me on the radar of all the parties I've been hiding from, all the parties who have caused me damage in the past, in the lifetimes upon lifetimes where I've shared this work despite great persecution and personal suffering.

This book would expose me for all that I am.

All that I've tried so cleverly to hide away underneath more digestible titles, underneath watered-down versions of the work I'm here to facilitate; underneath self-deprecating excessive humility which masks the truth of my actual power.

Because if I was to truly own it, if I was to truly put it out there, if I was to truly allow myself to be *seen* for who I am... then what might happen?

What might people think?

Who might come after me?

How might the world react if I were to fully step into my power and empower others to do the same?

Another part of me has felt the weight of the responsibility of the task ahead and is so terrified of failure - feeling the reverberations of every time I've shown up here to serve my sacred mission and "failed" - that it doesn't even want to try again.

Part of me was terrified to even begin writing because *"what if God doesn't show up and channel through me, the way I was told? What if I sit in silence, staring at this blank page, and nobody comes? Or worse yet - what if they do?"*

I think knowing the enormity of the repercussions of the latter is what frightened me the most—

Knowing the sheer potency of this body of work and the hugeness of what this information means once it has landed and been integrated on a deep, cellular level.

A very real part of me was still very much attached to the demands of this human existence, like making money and putting food on my table. Wondering where and how this information could possibly help anyone in a practical way. Behaving much like a petulant child having a tantrum, stamping my foot on the ground in defiance and saying, *"You want this book written so badly, God? Well, then, why don't you write it?"*

Yet still, I showed up every day, despite myself...

Despite my fears, my smallness, my resistance, and my desire to burn it all to the ground, walk away from my soul calling and go get a "normal job."

I knew in my heart I could never do that, nor could I turn my back on this mission - the same realisation I come to every time I've come close to "calling it quits" (which is pretty much every time my Little Human Self faces even the slightest inconvenience on this mission).

Despite how challenging it's been, the sacred rebel in me refuses to give up.

The Mayan warrior in me refuses to admit defeat.

So, rather than quitting, I surrender.

I lay down my ego at the altar of Love, and I pray for guidance, support and assistance every day.

I prayed every time I opened this document, that God would help me find the words that somebody out there reading needs to hear.

While I expect there will be resonance with these wounds for many of you who are truly walking this path and know what it feels like, I do not ask for pity or sympathy, for I am not a victim. This is my soul karma, these are my shadows, these are my wounds, and this is all that I have been using as fuel for my alchemy; to turn suffering into more love and light as I walk this path to be this embodiment of the Way.

The darkness in me that I must contend with is a blessing, it is not a curse.

As is the darkness in all of us because it brings rise to the desire within us to find our light.

We all have our own cross to bear, and this is *mine*.

And just as much as it has felt like a heavy burden at times, it has also gifted me in beautiful ways beyond my wildest dreams.

As you read this book, please know this—

In the journey to walking the Diamond Path of awakening our Crystalline (Christ) Consciousness within, we all have our own *"cross to bear"*. That is; our own karma to contend with, our own soul wounds we came in with, our own unique struggles and pathways to pave. We also have our own soul gifts, blessings, medicine and offerings to make into the world.

We cannot do it the same way as someone else.

As visionaries, path-finders and wayshowers, we are here to walk into uncharted territories, *paving our own way* so that others might find the pathways of light we leave behind us and follow in our footsteps.

For this reason, I must say that what is nourishment for one, may be poison for another.

And so I ask, if anything in this manuscript does not resonate with you, do not take it on.

Use your discernment and intuition, use your inherent body wisdom to feel into what feels right and true for you.

Find *your* thread of truth; do not blindly take this on without examining it.

Truth is subjective, and it is always changing.

I can offer you what feels to be *my* truth in this moment, but ultimately it is not fixed; it is always changing.

Some of the truths I hold today, I did not hold yesterday.

In fact, in the process of writing the first draft of this book (over two months) and returning to editing it alone, I have already changed so significantly that I look back over things I wrote mere *weeks* ago and think, *"Wow, it's wild that I ever felt that way!"*

(This is also why I've tried to largely leave these parts unedited because as hard as some of them are for me to read now with my new, evolved perspective, they were *real for me at that moment*. It's important that this whole journey of inner transformation is reflected in every stage that I went through, exactly as I went through it.)

I expect my position to continue to change a lot on this path ‑ as it already has ‑ the more I evolve and grow. And I expect yours to, too.

As souls, we are here to evolve and grow as we assimilate more perspectives and our viewpoint becomes expanded over time. Only through personal experience does knowledge actually become embodied *wisdom*. And some truths we are just not ready for, at any given time in our journey.

A lot of the things I have written, I could imagine a version of myself even *one year ago* rolling her eyes at, or going completely over her head because she simply wasn't ready to receive them. I can imagine that in a year from now, I'll look back and do the same again; but because I've continued to evolve and grow past my limited understanding that I have now.

Some of the things I share in this book will not make sense until you have experienced them yourself, as embodied states of being. And in the same manner, some of these things will only scratch the surface of deeper inner‑standings that will quickly develop and surpass the simplicity in which they have been shared here.

Let them! Do not let this book be the hill you are crucified on (even though *you will* go through a process of death and resurrection whilst reading this book).

This book is designed to be the beginning of your *own* journey to feeling, perceiving and speaking Truth.

The only *solid* and everlasting truth I can offer is that *the entire universe is in a constant state of flux and evolution*. Evolution is our highest soul truth.

Trust this, know this and remain unrigid, willing and open to change and growth.

This is all I ask of you in the process of receiving this codex; be open to receiving what you require to light your own path forward.

INTRODUCTION TO THIS TRANSMISSION AND HOW IT WORKS

This book was born out of a necessity for humankind to move into the next evolution and cycle of ascension as a species, as a guidebook for those leading this Way forward to be prepared for the things that will inevitably come as a part of this evolutionary process.

It was also born out of a necessity to bring back online Ancient information and frequency that has been *lost* for centuries but will be important for us during this evolutionary process.

Some of the content presented in this book has been presented in part by other researchers, historians, archaeologists and channels; you might have consumed similar content or come into contact with parts of this information before, particularly in reference to the Mayan civilisation. I'm not here to offer any dialogue or commentary around what anybody else has studied or written on our histories. Nor am I particularly interested in doing strenuous research to back up my claims with historical, factual details and information.

Everything I share primarily comes through my channel, my soul memories and gnosis before it is then confirmed by outside resources, guidance, research or whatever else. I trust my channel above all else.

If you desire historical information, dates, citations and extensive research, then I'm going to be blunt; *this is not the book for you.*

Facts, figures, numbers, dates; as a divine feminine being who *feels truth in my body* that far surpasses mind-level "logic," these things aren't relevant to me.

To me, of more importance is the transmission of the frequency beneath the words which is not present in many of these historical books - the very codex of the times and teachings of the civilisation in which I share.

To me, of more importance is stimulating within *you* the ability to access and discern truth and information about the histories and futures of our world from within yourself; to deepen your own gnosis.

The frequency is intended to activate a remembering for those reading or listening to the Divine DNA within them. Of their own soul wisdom, knowledge and codex.

Far beyond knowledge, there is an ancient wisdom that is ready to awaken at the cellular level, within all of us. I am not here to teach this, nor am I here to teach anything new (in fact, the "words" written here that explain the concepts only bear about 10% of the weight of what is actually happening on a cellular level as you read these pages). I am simply here to hold the door open and curate an environment for your *own* remembering and gnosis.

Within us all, there is an alchemist with a capacity to create and shape entire worlds.

Humanity may have forgotten along the way the power that is seeded within us - within our very genetic code - but we are moving into an age where that remembering is accessible to all of us.

The dragon is awakening from its slumber and the New Age of Aquarius is upon us.

This book is a culmination of codes I have retrieved from the many lifetimes I have walked on this Earth as an oracle, a priestess, a tantrica, a seer, a shaman, an alchemist, a witch, a medicine woman;

along with those I have walked in other non-human forms. (I have also had many other incarnations in far less spiritually evolved fractals of consciousness, but I daresay these lifetimes are not relevant to this text.)

It is a culmination of codes I have retrieved and downloaded from the collective consciousness, from my oversoul network, and from sacred sites I have been called to visit in different parts of the world.

I will also add that there is an enormous team of high-dimensional beings, ancestors, guides, and unconditionally loving spirits who are co-creating and supporting the energetics of this transmission, and channelling through my words; they have been contracted to support *you* as you move through this journey, in the way they have supported *me* to birth it and bring it into the world. I am taking this moment to acknowledge and thank them for their unconditionally loving support, service and guidance; without them, I would not have been able to do this.

Many of these concepts and words are not meant to be understood on the level of the intellect, but on the level of gnosis; a *remembering* deep in the body that will come online as you read.

The body holds the wisdom and the keys to the Universe within it.

It is time we remembered that.

Practise your discernment, free will and consent to receive the healing and awakening potential of this book; declare your desire to be acti-vated, and it will be done.

If you do not desire it, do not consent to it.

I am not here to impose my will, my energy or my beliefs onto anybody (*been there, done that, dealt with the repercussions and ain't about to create some karmic bullshit ripples for some parallel/future version of Me to deal with*).

Find your message beneath the words and allow the frequency to do its work on you in whatever way is the highest for you.

You may have memories from other lifetimes, you may experience the sudden awakening or remembering of ancient truths that are dormant within you.

There are latent keys and codes that will be activated for every person reading, depending on what is in the highest good for you and your soul path.

What is stirred in one person reading this, will be very different to what awakens in another.

This transmission will take you as *deep as you are willing to go* and it will also rise to meet you exactly where you're at.

You may experience physical sensations as you read or listen to this transmission.

Electrical pulses running through your body. Sudden flashes of heat or cold. Random pains, spasms or discomforts arising. Rushes of pleasurable, tingling or orgasmic energy.

Trust that your body knows the way back to wholeness and unity and that through receiving this transmission, the process is already beginning.

There are guided "initiations" you will find at the end of each section of the book. We recommend that you receive these in audio form, so you can close your eyes and go on a soul journey with them to receive to your fullest capacity, in a relaxed state. (I will add that these audio recordings have been channelled with love, curated and put together as complete sound healing journeys; an offering in themselves, which bring this book to life in a whole new dimension.) You can access and download them here: www.diamondlightoracle.com

These "initiations" solidify on a conscious level the codes and the keys that you are activating simply by going on the journey of reading this book. While they add a deeper layer to the work and expand your capacity to receive and solidify the information, you are already receiving this codex from the moment you first chose to purchase, download or access it. The process has already begun, even in the act of reading this introduction.

This is not just a book, not just a story (my story) or a clever work of fantasy fiction - although to some, I'm aware my musings may very well sound just like that.

This is a sacred transmission to activate the Divine DNA and Crystalline Christ Consciousness within you.

This is a sacred transmission to awaken your multidimensional memory, bring online your soul gifts and stimulate the process of Your Great Becoming.

This is a sacred transmission here to activate those of you who are already walking the Diamond Light Priestess path; to birth the prophecy, vision and offerings that will evolve you into the Oracle you are here to be.

This is not a book; it's a transformational journey.

Treat it as such, open your heart and allow it to work its magic on you.

DIAMOND LIGHT, SACRED SIGHT

Covered my eyes so I can't see
Cut out my tongue to silence me
Without my voice, no siren call
They bound my feet so I would fall

The diamond light beneath my cells
As I morph into something else
I spread my wings, and I grow tall
And from this place, I'll watch it all

Beyond this place of right and wrong
Inside the void where I came from
There is no dark, and there's no light
When seeing things with sacred sight

The underworld is through a door
Past the gateway, there's five more
Through these portals, we must go
To shed the skin of what we know

Beyond this place of right and wrong
Inside the void where I came from
There is no dark, and there's no light
When seeing things with sacred sight

PART ONE

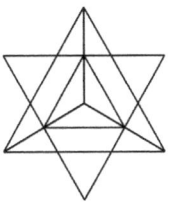

THE LAND

THE JUNGLE

We were just two hours into the first day of my own personal Hell-on-Earth when it dawned on me what I had just agreed to, and that there was absolutely no backing out... I was *fully in this bitch now.*

I started laughing hysterically and manically as a panic response, as the realisation hit me; I had no option but to see the full five-day hike through.

This was not the initiation nor the magical jungle vision quest I had been expecting or wanting.

But clearly, it was the one I required.

As my body began to process the gruelling physical tax involved in constantly yanking the ill-fitting, soaking wet, completely inappropriate, hard-AF work boots up and out of the thick mud that covered the jungle floor every time I needed to move my foot even a centimetre, I was already in intense physical pain.

And we were only in hour two of the first day!

The guide informed us we had covered probably just over one-quarter of the nineteen kilometres we required to reach our campsite on that first day. *Oh. Dear. God.*

You could only imagine the dread that was filling up in Little Human Me - certainly no well-seasoned seasoned hiker - who mustered every ounce of courage within me to step out of my comfort zone and even say 'yes' to this journey.

Already seething in pain, with nothing but the negative spiral of my thoughts to keep me company as we all walked in deathly silence. *Apparently, I was not the only one who had gleaned that this would be a rough journey and was fighting their own inner battle that day, balls-deep in the mud...*

Wandering into the depths of the relentless Guatemalan jungle, the humid air laden thick with mosquitos and rain, I was facing an existential crisis and ego death of epic proportions.

Battling the cesspool of mud that had become the 'path', with no escape for five days straight. *My. Worst. Nightmare.*

It was at that moment - sandwiched somewhere between sweating my ass off and manically laughing so I wouldn't burst into tears - I realised *exactly* what the medicine of this pilgrimage would be.

I had no space in my mind for ANYTHING except diverting myself from the searing pain I was experiencing in my legs, my back, my everything by repeating over and over:

One more step.

You've got this.

You are strong.

Your body is strong.

You are a warrior.

You can do this.

Just make it to lunch.

This is your purpose.

This is a sacred mission.

You must fulfil your purpose.

Failure is not an option.

You've been training for this for lifetimes.

I tried my best to conjure up ANYTHING that would inspire me to keep going; the thought of a limp, mediocre sandwich and a juice box when we eventually stopped for a lunch break; the thought of finally getting to lie down in my tent; the thought of how good a hot shower (or damn, just any shower at all) would feel. When that failed, I sang the hook to "Survivor" by Destiny's Child over and over in my head. For the next five days, this would be what got me through. I had to be relentlessly disciplined with my thoughts, or I wasn't going to make it.

As I began to enter a psychedelic state between the repetitiveness of my looping thoughts, the blur of trees and the highly charged Mayan energy that was permeating through my feet with every step I took, I began to understand what was happening to me, and why I had been called to this journey....

My body was deteriorating fast from the exhaustion of hiking twenty-plus kilometres per day, soaking wet in muddy, humid conditions that were causing all of my limbs to retain moisture and swell.

My menstrual bleed came in like a wrecking ball on the third day, along with incessant cramping.

My right knee finally gave way to a former injury I'd conveniently forgotten about when signing up and was sending shooting pain up my entire leg with every step. From the trauma of repetitively stubbing my toe by sliding in the mud because of my too-big and unbroken-in work boots, my right big toenail was waterlogged, bruised and had started lifting off. (The right ride side of the body is the "masculine" side, which makes sense given the journey was around awakening my inner warrior and stepping into my divine masculine energy.)

Put simply, *I was a total shit show.*

By the third day, I couldn't take a single step without crying out in pain. But I had to keep going.

I was covered in mosquito bites and my tears; oscillating from randomly bursting out in wild, hysterical laughter at how fucked the situation was, boosting the group morale by singing the Mayan Road song my friend and I had written (to the tune of "Country Road") to keep us going ...

To sobbing uncontrollably and feeling sorry for myself the next minute, as we stopped singing, and I once again became blindingly aware of the pain.

I could feel that my old body was dying, cell by cell.

And as they broke down, these cells were being replaced with new codes and DNA.

Mayan warrior coding.

The strength and capability that the human body was initially designed to have (and did have, many, many aeons ago, the last time I walked through this jungle).

This is what the ancestors and elemental spirits moving their way through the trees were whispering to me. My old body had to die for it to evolve into a strong, capable, "masculine" casing to support my mission - as they say; pain is just weakness leaving the body.

And so it was for my mind.

Any negative thoughts of victimhood, any lack of discipline, any tendency to give up; it all had to be stamped out of me.

I could feel immense energy moving through my heart space as I let the tears flow down my face as I sobbed in silence, trying not to affect the rest of the group. I knew the physical pain was just one aspect of the release; I was also releasing deep grief, feelings of discomfort and victimhood.

I was releasing *everything* that was holding me back from being in my power, from embodying the Rainbow Warrior I was on a soul level.

Deep in the bowels of the relentless Mayan jungle, I was releasing a version of myself and letting her completely die, so I could be reborn into the version of myself capable of carrying out the next part of my soul's mission. So I could evolve from *priestess* to *Oracle*.

THE MAYANS WERE
HARMONISERS

To begin, I am being guided to take you back to the Mayan jungle.

The Ancient Mayans were an advanced race of beings who all but disappeared in the height of their civilisation's glory, and were reduced to scattered remains of tribes who struggled to assimilate into a culture that decimated their ancient wisdom, practices, knowledge and ways of being. I won't get into the repercussions of all of this just yet, but suffice it to say it has caused irreparable damage to this lineage; causing the potency of the Mayan genetic bloodline to be watered down, and its power, wisdom and ways of being repressed due to the immense trauma suffered (some of which, I have spent years clearing from my own Mayan past lifetimes).

The Ancient Mayans - like all indigenous cultures - very much lived in harmony with the Earth and with the Heavens above. They were *harmonisers* - meaning, they were called to different places to work with the land and restore it to harmonic balance (we'll dive more into this shortly).

The question that is always posed by archeologists and historians is; *how is it that such a primitive people had access to the wisdom and knowledge that allowed them to chart with accuracy the movements of the planets, the stars, and the natural cycles of the Earth?*

How is it that they were able to predict future cycles and events with such accuracy?

How is it that they built the enormous, intricately constructed pyramids and megaliths that still to this day exist for us to see, along with the many that lie hidden beneath the jungle?

The Mayans were living in perfect communion with the Oneness and therefore, capable of channelling information and frequency from this Oneness. It seems somewhat perfect that much of this book is the channelling of my memories as a Mayan in many past lifetimes, channelled through this vessel and version of Me, here and now. Some of this information I am learning (or rather remembering) as I write, and some has been integrating slowly over the process of months and years since first stepping onto (or rather returning to) Mayan land and sacred sites in this lifetime.

The Mayans understood the premise that will be unravelled and unpacked in great detail in this book. If you take nothing else from this book, this is the most vital thing to grasp. That is; the interconnectedness of all things, and the flow of the Energy that moves through everything. Before we go deep into understanding the codex and wisdom of Ancient Maya that wishes to be shared through me in this transmission, it is important to understand what it is that I mean by *"the Energy that moves through everything"*.

This is a vital precursor to every other idea presented in this book.

Each one of us has this same life force running through us; as does every flower, every tree, every animal, every rock, crystal and living thing on this Earth.

Known in many different traditions under different names - chi/qi, kundalini, shakti, life-force energy, prana, to name a few - this Energy is the representation of the divine feminine essence, the Goddess; Creation itself.

41

Here I must briefly differentiate with the term "Creator", which is the divine masculine essence, or "God". While both are One and One is Both, the "Creator" is the *witness* consciousness; the I am, the presence, or the "thought". While the "Creation" is the *experiential* consciousness; the dance, the sensation, the unfolding. While the Creator conceptualised (or "thought") what to create; the Creation moves through all things, breathes life into, and animates all things. In the Aboriginal Dreamtime, there is the story of the Rainbow Serpent, who breathed all life into being. The Energy that moves through all of us is this same energy; the feminine element of Creation, also known as Kundalini-Shakti. The same power that created galaxies and solar systems and trees and rock forms and elephants and DNA strands and intricately detailed molecular structures – that created *you* – flows *through* you and can be accessed *by* you.

This kundalini energy is depicted (in the Hindu tradition) as a snake that lays dormant, coiled at the base of the spine until awoken. We'll be exploring the process of kundalini awakening in more detail in the next chapters, but I'll give you the summary of what you need to know now to understand this concept of the Mayans as "harmonisers". When Shakti (the feminine, the Creation) rises from her dormant position and travels up through the chakra system to meet Shiva (the masculine, the Creator) at the crown, Divine Union occurs. One recognises that they are simultaneously the Creator and the Creation; the feminine, and the masculine; All of Everything That Ever Was and the Empty Void of Nothingness; the Source, and the individual fractal of Source experiencing life through *their* unique lens. In order for that Divine Union or "enlightened state" to occur while still in this human form, one must clear the distortions in their channels which keep them in a state of separation.

Our life-force energy flows through us via our meridian system – an intricate highway linking all of the different energetic pathways and channels within us – and our chakra system, our "power centres" which serve as amplification points or gateways for different functions and frequencies of this energy. If there are blockages within our meridian system or our chakras, that energy cannot flow and our optional functioning and wellness are inhibited, as are our capabilities physically, emotionally, mentally, and psychically. Disease and illness happen due to blockages in this system which prevent the vital life force from circulating and enabling the body to come back to homeostasis/balance and self-heal.

Everything in the Universe desires and has a natural inclination to come back to homeostasis and balance, unity and oneness. Everything in this Universe is created in perfect, divine order; with an intention and a purpose. Even darkness, destruction, chaos, death, breakdown and decay. It is only when the environment or the natural cyclical flow is inhibited through some sort of blockage that this natural re-balancing and re-unification cannot take place.

The Mayans - like many other indigenous groups and most of the East - understood this natural inclination for things to return to harmonic resonance and balance; this self-healing and regulatory system that not only resides within us but within all things that have been created.

They understood the phenomenon that is naturally occurring within us and all living beings as a result of being animated by the same life-force energy. They used this understanding to synchronise and "harmonise" not only themselves - their own physical, emotional, mental and light bodies so that the 'microcosm' reflects the 'macrocosm' - but also restoring this harmony to the environments they inhabited.

GRIDWORKER: WORKING WITH THE LAND

The Earth - like all other living things - has her own life-force energy/kundalini, her own chakra system, and her own meridian system (energy channels). These energy channels are known as the feminine and masculine "dragon lines"; also known as ley lines, song lines, grid lines and many other names, although some people make distinctions between these.

I discovered one map of these dragon lines and Earth chakras - which served as a huge validation for me of something I'd channelled previously - where the feminine dragon line is labelled as the "Rainbow Serpent", and the masculine dragon line is labelled as the "Plumed/Feathered Serpent". While this is not entirely relevant *right now*, keep this detail in the back of your mind as it will be relevant when we begin to discuss Kukulkan, the feathered serpent creator god of Mayan culture (similar to the figure of Quetzalcoatl in Aztec and other Mesoamerican cultures).

As for the locations of the Earth's chakras; the first/root chakra is at Mt Shasta, California USA. The second/sacral chakra is at Lake Titicaca, in Peru. The third/solar plexus is at Uluru, Australia. The fourth/heart chakra is at Glastonbury & Shaftesbury, UK. The fifth/throat chakra is situated at the Pyramids of Giza, Egypt. The sixth/third eye chakra is considered a 'floating chakra' with no fixed location. The seventh/crown chakra is at Mount Kailash in the Himalayas of Tibet.

In the same way as with humans and other creatures, if there are blockages within the flow of energy through the channels of the Earth, Gaia is not able to return to homeostasis and balance. This happens through direct trauma on the land, inherited trauma from humans, and technology that has been intentionally placed into the grids of the Earth to block and prevent this vital life force from flowing or to imbue it with inorganic frequencies or intentions to control and enslave humanity (I will extrapolate on this later in this book).

A gridworker or portal worker is someone who is "called" to certain parts of the Earth to work with the land and the dragon lines that make up the Earth's energetic grid. They are more often than not called to energetic "high-potency" areas where there are naturally occurring amplification portals. Certain areas have "high energetic potency" due to the area being situated near one of the Earth's "chakras" or ley-line crossing points or the natural properties and features of the Land itself having amplification properties (for instance, certain minerals or crystals under the Earth, or being a "high energy" site like a volcano, or waterfall).

Our ancestors - including the Mayans, which we'll get to shortly - knew of these "high energy" places and how to locate the points on the Earth grid that would have energetic amplification properties and sacred sites (such as pyramids, temples, stone circles etc) were built on these specific points to purposefully harness the energy.

However, while it is common for grid and portal workers to have initiations and be called to these certain "hot-spot" areas where the energies are high, they will also get called to other places that perhaps are not typically known as "energetically charged" areas.

Occasionally a gridworker or portal worker will get called to an area where there is nobody "working/maintaining the grid" (because the indigenous in that community has been eradicated or the area has been gentrified); they have a strong past life/ancestral connection to the land; the grid itself has been damaged (either unintentionally, or intentionally due to technology created to block the grid); or the area is particularly dense with human trauma, and needs to be uplifted energetically.

For example, I believe that during the recent "Coronavirus pandemic" of 2020-2022, lightworkers and starseeds were specifically situated *exactly where they needed to be* to seed their light during that process, and some had intentionally been placed in particularly "dense" or "heavy" areas to negate some of the fear and panic that was happening.

I was in Bali for the majority of that time, and I have an awareness that I was called there to do some *rather heavy* karmic clearing work (not only for myself but for the collective) that was being amplified by the very powerful karmic purification portal that is created in that area, being one of the only places on the Earth where the feminine and masculine dragon lines cross. The only other crossing point of the feminine and masculine dragon lines is at Lake Titicaca, in Peru; another vortex for intense purification.

The specifics of what grid/portal work looks like and entails varies from individual to individual, from the specific codex and skill set of the soul who is called. This can be for a range of reasons such as opening portals to other dimensions to bring galactic/higher frequency energies through; sharing codes from their own soul codex/oversoul network in a part of the Earth that requires them; receiving or retrieving codes and soul memory from the land; awakening ancient wisdom or knowledge in the grid; raising the vibration of an area by infusing their soul frequency into that place; or clearing the Earth's energy channels (freeing it from blockages, ancestral trauma of the people, or direct trauma as a result of what has been done to the land itself) by doing some sort of healing work on the land. There is also an entire discipline called "astrocartography", where the planetary paths at the time of your birth are represented by lines, each line corresponding to a different planet, meaning and purpose. These lines run through specific points geographically, and people may feel called to certain places due to the 'flavour' or energy of the planetary line influencing that place at different times in their life or soul mission.

Many grid or portal workers will not identify as such; in fact, I didn't use the term "gridworker" or have an awareness that I was working with/opening/closing portals or healing the land for the first years that I was actively "doing it". It was only with hindsight that I could understand what my soul was having me do while I spent all those days basically incapacitated, lying in a trance by the pool in Bali; my body was acting as a portal, supporting a *lot* of collective heaviness to pass through it and be transmuted.

If you feel "called" to go to certain areas without knowing why, or to do certain specific rituals/ceremonies or bring certain objects to these areas (such as crystals) then chances are you are doing some sort of gridwork. If you live a nomadic, "gypsy" life or feel very "called" to travel around a lot - like myself - then chances are, you are a grid or portal worker.

If there are certain sites (such as sacred sites) or places you feel very "called" to visit, or that you have a strong connection to - Egypt, Stonehenge, Uluru, India, Bali, Mount Shasta, Hawaii, to name a few - it's probably because there is something for you to *receive* from that specific vortex of energy and the codex held there; or because you have a strong past life connection to that place or that lineage, and are being called there to support the land in some way.

Much like myself and the Ancient Mayan codex which is being transmitted through this book, you may have *no freaking idea* how connected you are to a civilization or place until one day you finally listen to the soul calling and physically show up there.

INITIATION 1:
SOUL CODEX ACTIVATION

Welcome to the first in the series of sacred activations that you will receive on this journey.

For the deepest experience and integration, I wholeheartedly recommend you go ahead and access the audio version of this activation, which you can download for FREE here: www.diamondlightoracle.com.

To begin with, we invite you to set up a sacred space in which you may journey for the next little while without distraction or disruption.

If now is not a good time to put yourself into this space, we suggest you pause your experience here, or continue to read ahead, and return to this activation when it is suitable.

Let us begin.

Welcome to your sacred space and to this Soul Codex Activation.

Today we will be creating and setting up the sacred space for your journey ahead.

We will be constructing a private grid for *you* to connect even more deeply to your own Soul Codex and receive a specific activation through this transmission that is unique to only *you* and the sacred mission you have come into this body to fulfil.

We will also be connecting you to the larger network that was created for the purpose of this transmission.

In your mind and with your heart, set the intention that this is the work that will be done during our time together in this activation and that you are open to receive all that is in your highest good.

I now invite all the beings of the highest light who wish to support this activation taking place.

I welcome your Higher Self, your Soul Family and Oversoul Network, and invite them to support you in receiving what is of the highest for you at this time.

I declare that this is a sacred space, only that which is resonating on the frequency of unconditional love is welcome in this space.

I ask that everything that takes place here today is for the *highest good of all* and in service to the Whole.

I ask that the work we do together here today ripples out and serves the collective.

And so it is, and so it is, and so it is.

Allow yourself to take a moment to connect to your body.

Taking some deep breaths, allowing your heart rate to begin to slow.

Allowing your body to soften and relax as you sink deeper into the material of the chair, the floor, or the bed beneath you.

Allow the feeling of comfort and relaxation wash over you; as you feel a beautiful, warming, golden energy starting to make its way through your crown, permeating your entire body.

This golden light gently streams into your head, calming your mind and relaxing the muscles in your face.

It washes down your neck, releasing any tension in your neck, your shoulders and your upper back.

It begins to wrap around your upper torso, and make its way down your arms, and as it does you feel this warming, soothing energy begin to envelop your entire upper body.

Let it continue to wash down the centre of your torso, relaxing your abdomen, your stomach, your hips.

As it washes down your bottom, your thighs, down to your knees, you are feeling your entire body continuing to melt like honey.

It streams down into your feet, relaxing your feet - making its way into each individual toe - allowing your feet to release any tension and your receiving channels to fully soften.

You are now completely enveloped in this golden light, and it extends out past your body.

It wraps around you like a warm blanket, protecting you, supporting you, holding you.

As you sit in this sensation, you begin to develop the awareness that *this energy IS you - it is your own soul frequency.*

This is what it feels like to be purely in your own energy.

Take a moment in this energy to connect to yourself, to feel and familiarise yourself with the energy of your own Soul.

When you are ready, allow this bubble of energy to begin to expand out further past your body, as far as it wants to go.

You may notice it changing colour or texture as it expands out.

Keep pushing the boundaries out until you have enough space to fully spread out and feel you can spread no further.

Expanding, expanding, expanding.

Once you have expanded as far as you can expand, invite this energy to begin to manifest as a visual which represents your Sacred Space, your Sacred Temple.

This may take the form of a temple, an ancient pyramid, or some other building-like structure.

Trust what is being shown to you and how this desires to manifest for you - it may not even have a physical structure at all but be a colour, a shape, a texture, or even just a frequency.

This is the place which is unique to *you* that allows you to access and pull from your own soul codex.

Nobody else is permitted to enter this space unless you invite them to; it is *yours* alone.

Know that you are totally safe here and that this space is hidden to all others.

It is your unique soul frequency, your very essence which acts as a biometric thumbprint that allows you to enter this space.

You can come here whenever you need to block out all other noise, and be in your own energy.

You can come here whenever you want to download codes from your soul codex, or receive wisdom or guidance from your Higher Self.

This is your sacred space, and your sacred space alone.

This is the sacred space you will be held in as you journey through this process over the coming days, weeks, months or however long it takes for you to fully receive this transmission.

Take a moment to familiarise yourself with this space.

If it is a building or an architectural structure, take a look around.

Notice what is on the walls, or how it is decorated.

You may wish to make adjustments to make this space even more unique and comfortable for you.

Take as long as you need to familiarise with and personalise this space so it feels good for you.

If you wish, you may pause here to do so.

We are going to begin to activate this space; to activate your own personal grid so that you begin to pull the frequencies into this space that will be required for you to receive all that you need throughout this transmission.

Invite your Soul Contracted Team to support you in calibrating this space so you will receive what you need throughout the duration of this journey, at the exact pace which is required for the smoothest and most graceful integration.

Feel free to pause here for a moment if you need to.

Invite your Higher Self to begin to stream into this space all dormant Soul Codes, keys, memories, gifts, abilities, offerings and connections that would be of the highest benefit to you at this time.

As we move through the following activations, feel free to pause at any time if you require to allow the energy to settle, or to receive more.

Now - only with your willingness and consent - we share into this grid any codes, any keys and any frequencies from the oversoul network that will support you in fulfilling your sacred mission, that you have agreed on a soul level to receive at this time.

Now - only with your willingness and consent - we connect your Sacred Space up to the larger network that has been created for this transmission.

We ask that as we complete this connection, only that which has *soul resonance* with you, is for *your highest good* and is *relevant to your journey* is transmitted into your Sacred Space.

We gently begin to stream into your sacred space any codes from Ancient Maya that will support *you* on this journey.

We connect you to any Ancient Mayan connections, lifetimes, soul memories and cellular memory.

We gently begin to stream into your sacred space any codes from any other ancient civilisations contained within this network; Atlantis, Lemuria, Egypt, Avalon, and beyond, which will support *you* on this journey.

We connect you to any past or parallel lifetimes, connections, soul memories, cellular memories from any of these ancient civilisations that are relevant and in resonance for you now.

We gently begin to stream into your sacred space any galactic codes from other non-human races, civilisations and lifetimes that are relevant to you, and will support *you* on this journey now.

We connect you to any past or parallel lifetimes, connections, soul memories, cellular memories of any of these galactic civilisations that are relevant and in resonance for you now.

We invite your Sacred Space to expand once again, as far out as it needs to expand to receive and hold all of this new energy.

You may wish to pause for a moment as this energy settles and recalibrates.

With your consent, we now connect your Sacred Space deep into the mycelium network, anchoring it down into Gaia, and rippling out into the Earth where you are situated - or any points to which you may travel while completing this journey - so that the Earth may receive and share these frequencies, and we may support Her with her ascension process.

With this connection, the positive transformation you are experiencing inside of your Sacred Space will ripple out and be shared with those around you in a positive way, for those who are ready to receive.

May this work ripple out in service of the collective, to create pathways of light leading those who are here to awaken their own soul memory to find their Way as they walk the Earth where you have been.

We now request that a personal transmutation vortex is created within this space, so that any shadow that erupts throughout this process and any density that surfaces may be transmuted and purified through your own Sacred Grid, and through the mycelium network of the Earth, which will draw down any dense frequencies to be recycled into fertiliser for your growth.

We request that all work that takes place throughout receiving this transmission happens within your Sacred Space, and that you remain at all times held by this space as this codex works on you in the background.

We request that once you have received all that you have agreed on a soul level to receive on this journey, your personal grid is cleansed, all connection points that are no longer required are disconnected and flushed, all portals and gateways that are no longer required are immediately shut down, and all energy that is no longer required is returned back to where it came from.

We invite your Soul Contracted Team to oversee this grid, to maintain its integrity throughout this process, and to make any necessary adjustments to the frequency and the structure as you expand and evolve.

And so it is, and so it is, and so it is.

You may find yourself travelling to this place in your dreams, or in lucid states.

You may come back to visit this place as often as you desire throughout this journey, and beyond.

You may feel called to make adjustments, to tend to your grid, to remove or add in connection points, to recalibrate throughout this process to make it as smooth and easy for you as possible.

Trust yourself and your own inner guidance system above all else.

We have now completed the process for this first activation.

We now shut down any and all open portals and gateways that are no longer required, and send back all energy that has come through any portals or gateways in the process of this work.

We now dissolve any bonds, chords or attachments that have been formed for the process of this activation, and call you back into complete Soul Sovereignty.

All of your energy is now returning back to you as we begin to integrate and calibrate this on all levels.

Integrating and calibrating this now on the physical level.

Integrating and calibrating this now on the emotional level.

Integrating and calibrating this now on the mental level.

Integrating and calibrating this now through all levels and dimensions of your light body.

Integrating, calibrating and sharing this frequency now through all timelines and all versions of your multidimensional self across the multiverse.

Inviting Diamond Light in now, to cleanse and close this space; bringing this sacred activation to a close, thanking all of the beings who have been here supporting in this process.

It is done, it is done, it is done, and so it is.

You may spend some time here in silent reflection, or receiving in your Sacred Space if it feels necessary.

If you feel complete, we invite you to gently bring yourself back into your body and into the room, wiggling your fingers and toes, and opening your eyes when you are ready.

PART TWO

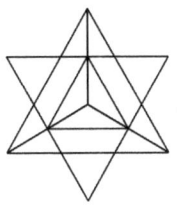

THE SKY

THE CALLING TO MEXICO

The first time I felt the calling to Mexico was during the height of the pandemic, as I was living in Bali. I say "living", but it was more like *"frolicking in blissful ignorance considering what was happening in the rest of the world"*, as things were still pretty chill in that part of the world at that point. I'm talking about the early "doomsday" stages, where the whole of Australia was locked down, I had no idea if I'd ever see my parents again, and everyone was still convinced that the world was going to end. Believe it or not, I frolicked my way right through that with only a minor existential crisis in the very beginning, in March of 2020, where I had to trust my heart and stay in Bali despite the whole world - AKA the Australian government, my parents, every news outlet ever, and a lot of the people around me in Bali who were piling onto the last planes out - trying to convince me that if I didn't go back to Australia I'd regret it and probably die. (And yet here I am, *alive and well*, with not a single regret, having spent the first year and a half of the "pandemic" tanning by the pool with a coconut in hand, living my best island life with barely any restrictions. Funny what happens when you listen to your intuition over other people's fears, isn't it?)

The call to Mexico was a passing moment that I quickly forgot about - after all, the whole world was apparently "locked down", so travelling didn't seem like a high possibility at the time - but it was strong knowing that there was something there for me on that land. In a flash, I saw myself living there, and I felt a wave of warmth wash over my entire body; a homecoming I hadn't yet felt elsewhere. *"Wow, I guess I need to go to Mexico, then"* I remember thinking.

Then, just as quickly, I put it out of my mind and went on with my life.

In the latter part of 2021, I met a man in a six-month group program online with whom I had a profound soul connection and with whom I knew I had to travel to meet in person for some soul-contracted work and karmic cycles we had to complete. (Really, this is a *whole* story in itself, given the mission we navigated together and the rather treacherous soul contracts that were coming up around the program, which proved to be a *massive* initiation into my sovereignty for me... but I'll save that story for another time.)

This man lived on the other side of the globe, in Costa Rica.

So off I went, despite my Little Human Self kicking and screaming - as she tends to do whenever a large leap of faith off a proverbial cliff is required - in the middle of a global pandemic, to the other side of the world, to a country where I didn't speak the language (yet) and didn't know anyone other than a "stranger" I met on the internet.

Long (like reeeeally long) story short, I was in Costa Rica for several months for a huge and rather intense uprooting and clearing of a lot of past life trauma, completing the sacred contract that we had come together to fulfil. (I invited this man onto my podcast in 2022 to share the story of our joint mission and the collective healing that was being brought through it; so if you're feeling called to hear more of this story, you can go listen to *"Episode 26: Transcending Past Life Karma"* at www. becmylonas.com/podcast.)

After not being able to fly home and see my parents for nearly two years - having believed at a point during the pandemic that I might not see them ever again, with Australia's insanely strict lockdown in place - I was due to finally see them as restrictions began to lessen in early January of 2022. After months of fighting both literal and metaphorical demons, I was mentally exhausted and emotionally worn out, my nervous system was completely fried and dysregulated, and all I wanted to do was collapse in my mother's arms.

I had a soul sister in the States who had left Bali in a hurry as they began to impose vaccine mandates about six months prior, and we had agreed to meet in Mexico for a few days on my way back home as it was an easier flight path and I didn't know when I would be back on that side of the world again and able to see her. At this point, I still had not joined the dots and remembered my calling to Mexico earlier that year.

So, there I was in Cancun; excited to see my friend, but otherwise not really desiring to be there at all as I was exhausted from the emotional hangover the karmic 'situationship' I had just been navigating had caused for me. All I wanted was some peace and quiet; not the chaos that was ensuing with military men strolling up and down the strip with guns, obnoxious dance music blasting all day long from the beach clubs, drunken American tourists, and intermittent fog horns going off from the large, inflatable rubber duck that was hovering over one particular beach club, every time an aerial performer would hang off it as part of a performance set. (Believe me when I say it was as absurd as it sounds.)

We had only planned a short trip of a few days, but something in my gut was telling me - even though I desperately wanted to ignore it - that I would not be getting on my flight to Australia that coming Sunday. Just as predicted, the day before my flight I received my PCR test back (which at the time was still required to board a flight to Australia, but not from Costa Rica to Mexico) and it was positive. As a result, I was not permitted to fly.

My friend was headed to a different part of Mexico the next day, and I had huge resistance to going with her as I didn't have the energy to travel at that point, let alone board two flights for a detour to an area of Mexico I didn't feel called going to, that would make my life that much more difficult to get home from. Yet, I didn't want to be stuck in Cancun alone until my test came back negative, and I was able to fly.

At that point, I didn't know how long that would be (falsifying my documents didn't cross my mind at that moment, although now it seems like the rather obvious solution to my problem).

At the time, travelling off the beaten path alone was still a huge stretch for me and frightened me a lot. Especially in Mexico, where my father - in his panic and obvious concern for me, thanks to all the Narcos he no doubt watches - had drilled into me the paranoia that I would almost certainly be shot down or abducted by the cartel. And so, not knowing what else to do at that point; I had a full-blown tantrum, cried, hurled insults at God, bitched and moaned that all I wanted to do was collapse in Australia, return to the "safety" of my folks, and that it wasn't fair... and then eventually calmed down and realised the only thing I could do to come up with a creative solution was *offer it up to God*. (I might add, I got over my Little Human Self tantrum in about an hour, when only a few months prior, it would sometimes take *days* of sulking in my resistance and victimhood before I shifted back into 'trust and surrender'. So it seems the trip to Costa Rica and the brutal soul clearing it facilitated *well and truly served my evolution*.)

After surrendering and asking what spirit would have me do in this moment, it dropped in quite clearly, with an instant feeling of that "homecoming" washing over me that I'd forgotten I'd felt six months earlier in Bali when I was shown I needed to go to Mexico. *Tulum*, the guidance told me, *I needed to go to Tulum*. Not only did I need to go to Tulum, but someone was waiting for me there that I needed to meet; a man.

Um... well, ok then...

At the exact moment the download dropped in, it was like a haze lifted off me. The haze of months of crippling suffering evaporated, and the fears about travelling alone that had been plaguing me completely vanished as if they were never even a thing to begin with. Suddenly I felt excited as I made my arrangements and moved my flight by a week. Mere *hours* after moving my flight and making arrangements to go to Tulum, I found an article that Australia would be changing their entry restrictions effective as of the *following day* and that I would no longer require a negative PCR test to fly, just a doctor's certificate stating I was clear from COVID symptoms.

Literally. The. Next. Day. *You can't even make this shit up.*

It was like the Universe was saying, "Okay, you got the message, and you've been redirected towards your destiny. And now that you've been re-routed, your easy path home can open up again."

After having to pinch myself at the absurdity of it all, off I went on a bus the very next day (yes, a public bus, in Mexico, all by myself - something that seemed like an impossibility to me only months earlier) to Tulum.

As the road on the highway began to become more dilapidated and swallowed by jungle as we came to the part of the highway between Playa Del Carmen and Tulum, I started to feel it in my body. *I had been here before, and I was finally coming home.* A warmth, a happiness, a comfort washed over me and I instantly felt uplifted on a deep soul level. I had never felt anything like it in any other place I'd been in the world - not even Bali, where the ancestors in spirit and huge-hearted Balinese people welcomed me with open arms, and I made a beautiful, happy home for many years.

The days following my arrival, it felt as though I was in a magical vortex as I sunk into the energy and potency of the land.

Underneath Tulum and the surrounding areas, there is an intricate network of Cenotes (underground caves/pools) that are all connected and which link up to the main energetic points where the pyramids and sacred sites are built. This is important to the Mayan gridwork mission that I was enlisted to complete in 2023, but we'll come back to this. The whole area is built on top of this intricate water network flowing beneath it. The potency of the energy is undeniable and palpable. This is one of the reasons that Tulum - like many other main "spiritual meccas" that "spiritual" (sarcastic 'air finger quotes' intended, because I am aware I am a walking stereotype) folk seem to flock to - is an energetic portal which amplifies your frequency, and whatever you're going through at the time. It is a place where you go to receive initiations, clear karma, and learn spiritual lessons. Like the island of Bali (the place I'd first been called when my soul mission began to open up in 2019 - yes, I know, *how cliched of me*), Tulum calls you into her vortex when it's time, and she spits you out when she's done with you. Although I daresay, there are many who get called there, sucked into the magical vortex, and never leave, even if they had every intention to.

The energy in Tulum feels very contrasting in its extreme polarities; heaven and hell, light and dark, all at once. Like Bali - and most other energetically-charged vortexes - your experience of Tulum can either be Heaven or Hell on Earth, depending on what you've signed up to experience at that moment. Many people I speak to found it to be a heavy and dark energy - they share horror stories of being tormented by evil spirits or being mugged on the street. Others share how nourishing, magical and expansive it feels; how they were welcomed into Tulum's arms and how miracles ensued for them whilst grounded on that land. There is a power, a purity, a lightness, a magic to it... and then on the other side; there is a heaviness, an underbelly of darkness. Partially because of the trauma endured by the land and the people... partially because of the gross discrepancy of wealth and displacement of the locals due to the gentrification of the area... potentially because of the dark history of some of the magic being used there... and *almost definitely* because of the corrupt police, the cartel presence and underworld wars raging in that part of Mexico. Simultaneously, there is a magical glimmer, a spiritual energy to the place; a power to the stretches of jungle that have swallowed up half-built developments; and the purity of the brilliant, crystalline, aqua blue of the pristine ocean.

On that first trip to Tulum, the first few days were heaven; I felt like I was walking on clouds, high on my own supply, in a neverending vortex of magic and miracles. I did find it strange that upon seeing an Indigenous child selling trinkets down at the beach, I was overcome by a deep sadness - at that time, I had not recognised that I had such a strong Mayan connection, other than the sense of homecoming I experienced upon arriving. It had never happened in Bali, where the locals would frequently approach me selling their wares along the beach or begging for money (not even throughout the pandemic, where I was supporting multiple families through donations at one time, due to the detriment it had done to their economy, which was so largely reliant on tourism). But something in me saw this small Mexican child and felt an immense grief I'd never felt in this context; far beyond compassion or even guilt. I remember thinking, *"So this is what has happened to my people"*, and then immediately wondering where the hell that had come from, considering here was I; this entitled tourist, this white (well, olive-skinned) woman; this *gringo* who was contributing to the very problem of white-washing and gentrification that no doubt had caused this child to be begging for money in the first place.

A few days into my trip, I met a laid-back Canadian man - just like the guidance had told me would be the case prior to arriving - who gave off Jesus vibes and felt familiar to me somehow, despite not being the "type" of guy I would normally find myself attracted to. (I will add that while I have a physical "type" I'm traditionally attracted to - tall, dark, handsome and a little *spicy;* Southern European, Latino, Middle Eastern, you get the picture - and couldn't see myself ending up with some super "white" dude, I certainly went through many initiations to learn to see *beyond* someone's looks, straight to their *soul.* Learning this made me realise that while physical attraction is important, it's not *everything;* you can still develop a deep attraction to someone if you vibe with them on the level of the soul.) Very soon after meeting, we both began to have memories surfacing of our Mayan lifetime together on the land we had both chosen to meet again.

It hit us both quickly, with a weight like a tonne of bricks.

One moment, he was a random stranger I was sitting next to in a vegetarian cafe on our first date, wondering what the hell I was doing there, considering how uninterested I was in pursuing something romantic as I was still quite shaken by the karmic situationship and Costa Rica. Like some other part of me had taken me over and arranged the date while I was unconscious, and I was now having to painstakingly live through it.

The next moment, he'd accompanied me to the cliffside by the ruins where I wanted to meditate; I let my guard down for a moment, and something shifted. It was like a veil lifted in that instant, and I remembered who he was... and that I'd been missing him for a *very* long time.

On that first evening when we were spending time back at my Airbnb together, I could feel the words coming out of my mouth as he held me tenderly after doing some healing work on me - not even knowing where they were coming from, but feeling them as if my soul's yearning for and memory of him was speaking for me.

"I've been waiting for you... where have you been... I've missed you so much..."

To which he kept responding, *"I'm here now, my love, I'm here..."*

It was as wild for me to be experiencing it as it is to be reading this, I'm sure.

It wasn't coming from my mind or a part of me that was conscious or aware of what I was saying - after all, I *literally just met the guy*; he certainly wasn't my "love". I was channelling it from some part of me in the depths of my soul that had been long lost and forgotten about.

Following that, I spent the remainder of my trip in bed (held by the safety of his masculine presence and the tantric transmutation portal we'd created together), shaking, convulsing, crying, laughing, and orgasming simultaneously. I was physically purging immense amounts of toxicity; throwing up violently and incessantly (*so sexy*) as I was reliving and clearing the trauma of having our entire tribe wiped out by colonisers and losing him in the most brutal way possible. This man I had only '*just met*' was holding and loving me in possibly the most unappealing and fragile state I'd been in, in a long time; like you'd hold and love someone you've committed to caring for until death do you part.

We both knew that whatever was happening in that space was so much bigger than us and our human-level connection at that moment, which was still brand new.

We had been brought together at that moment for this mission in service of the collective. It was grid work that we were doing; healing the land. Our role was to release a very large blockage that was preventing the energy from flowing into the land and the ancient Mayan grid through relieving and transmuting the trauma we had endured together on that land by coming together in our soul-level, unconditional love. He would hold me in his masculine container while making tantric love to me; creating a safe and sacred space for me to completely open my vessel so that the energy of the trauma endured by the land and the people on the land could move through me, as I released all the emotions without judgement and in the safety of his energetic holding.

This was the second time I'd experienced the alchemical power of sex magic with another - the practices that priestesses and priests of the temple of Isis were initiated in - and it wasn't something that I had to set an intention to do either time, it just happened naturally as we came together. A remembering of a discipline that I'd attained mastery of over many lifetimes that naturally occurred as I found myself in the space of a masculine counterpart who could hold all of my energy after practising intentional celibacy and exploring my sacred sexual energy for over a year.

My body was acting as an acupuncture point for the land; releasing and transmuting the density through my vessel. In hindsight - I learnt this when I returned to the very same place in 2023 because I had to "fix" some of the work I'd not completed properly - I realised that we were opening a rather large portal of energy that had been blocked with dark energy. Many other cosmic and magical things happened in that space; like the Goddess Isis channelling through me a message to the divine masculine from the divine feminine, that would then go on to touch many people in an activation I later recorded on someone else's show.

However, this was my first recollection and memory of my soul's Mayan heritage and connection and where this aspect of my gridwork mission began.

After the magical week I spent with my past-life lover, we both left Mexico on our respective onward adventures and after a few weeks of keeping in contact, things felt complete for me, and there was no further reason to pursue a connection.

We had come together for a specific purpose, and that purpose was fulfilled.

Yet little did I know, my work with the Mayan grid was just beginning.

PYRAMIDS AND SPIRITUAL TECHNOLOGY

The Mayans - like many indigenous cultures - were naturally gridworkers due to their strong connection to the Earth. Like many ancient civilisations such as the Lemurians, the Atlanteans, the Egyptians, and the Avalonians - they had the spiritual technology to be able to locate and track where these highly charged energy points and vortexes were on the Earth's grid.

Specifically, where would be the most advantageous places to set up structures (such as pyramids and stone circles) that harnessed and amplified this heightened energy to enable enhanced healing and alchemical abilities; to send out pulses of energy or intentions to bring the larger grid back into harmony; to travel interdimensionally, and to open portals to other dimensions and civilisations.

We're going to explore *how* the pyramids were created a little further in this book, but for now, let's ask the question "why". What were the applications of such structures, and why have we seen them showing up throughout our history for as long as there has been documentation of humans - perhaps, arguably, even longer?

Every object (including our body) expands past its "physical" boundaries, with an electromagnetic/toroidal energetic field around it. When we clear and open our chakra system and awaken our kundalini, this toroidal field of magnetic energy becomes larger, expanding far beyond our physical bodies. The structure and shape of a pyramid (the sacred geometry) act as its toroidal field or amplification point.

There are several functions to the pyramid; firstly to amplify the size of the toroidal field of magnetic energy, which is generated from the centre of the pyramid where an initiate would stand or from the "pulse" point of the Earth in which the pyramid is placed upon to amplify and propel the energy outwards. This enables one to impact a larger grid on which the pyramid is situated, influencing the properties of much larger fields of space. This is how the pyramids are used to harmonise entire larger networks, as the Mayans would do; and later, how the pyramids were used to both power free-energy grids and control and enslave people, as in Atlantis and beyond.

Secondly, through its specific sacred geometry, the pyramid acts as a "channel" or "funnel" for high-vibrational energy; allowing portals to other dimensions to be opened up, to receive direct energetic transmission from other planets, and to enable interdimensional travel.

Thirdly, how the pyramid is built enables *sound* (vibration) to travel and be amplified to support sound-based alchemical and healing practices which could affect and alter physical matter by breaking down density.

I'm guided to touch briefly on a few sacred geometrical patterns. The Merkaba is a sacred geometry, which is two pyramid/triangular structures intertwined with each other, forming a shape that is also seen as the three-dimensional "Star of David". One triangle facing with the point upwards - the masculine, the "penetrating blade", or "fire" element - and the other triangle with the point facing downwards - the feminine, the "chalice", or the element of "water". The two opposite-facing triangles combined, are representative of the Sacred Union. It is the divine light vehicle used by ascended masters to travel interdimensionally, to connect with, and reach those in tune with higher realms; "Mer" meaning Light, "Ka" meaning Spirit, and "Ba" meaning body; it is representative of our "light-body".

While we see only half of the pyramid that is above the ground, many pyramids had chambers that were descended; inverse pyramid structures with the 'pointy end' going deep into the Earth, much like a chalice. Thus, the chambers within the pyramid itself - containing both these upright and downward-facing triangular chambers representing the feminine and masculine, activating the Merkaba sacred geometry - enable those inside to travel interdimensionally. For instance, to visit higher dimensions or to enter the realms of the shamanic underworld for sacred rites of life and death, soul retrieval and rebirth. In a visionary journey and initiation I was taken through once returning home from Mexico and in the process of writing this book, I was eaten by a jaguar, guided into an inner chamber of the pyramid, the "Jaguar" chamber, and descended through five gateways of the underworld, before being reborn. In my vision, I was shown that this 'descended' pyramid and inner chamber was reserved solely for High Priests and Priestesses to perform sacred rites of crossing between Life and Death.

The "Flower of Life" sacred geometry represents energetic synthesis or unity; a pattern omnipresent and existing in all forms and scales of nature, and every living thing that is animated by Life. Within this symbol can be found all the building blocks of the Universe; a metaphor illustrating the connectedness of everything. When one activates and expands the electromagnetic field around them from their heart space, they are contained within the sacred geometry of the Flower of Life, as they flow in resonance with this Unified energy. When one harnesses the energy from the Earth to be amplified through the vessel of the pyramid, they are creating a larger sacred geometrical pattern of the Flower of Life, as it is generated not only through their own life-force and energetic field but through the resonant frequencies of the life-force and energetic field of the Earth.

Thus, when the Flower of Life - representing the harmonic life-force that flows through and animates everything - is superimposed on top of the Merkaba - with both the pyramid and the light body of the initiate within the pyramid generating the Merkaba pattern - it is an even deeper reinforcement of Unity Consciousness. With these symbols combined, the energy is *amplified*.

As I have already touched on, the use of pyramids was not unique to the Mayans; we see them across virtually every ancient civilization throughout history. One must wonder how these civilisations had access to such potent spiritual technology or understanding when they were considered "primitive" in many other ways.

I am not going to go too far into the galactic origins of humanity - the Anunnaki of the Sumerian texts; the two opposing brothers Enki and Enlil who had different intentions for their "children" of humanity; the non-human races such as the Draconians and Reptilians who sought to enslave us; the Galactic / Orion Wars that preceded this; the creation of the Galactic Federation; or the secret "underworld" agendas, conspiracy theories, and controversies of our history. I will only be touching on parts that I feel are relevant to *this* journey and initiation.

How to build and utilise pyramids and other sacred technologies is something taught to us by our galactic forefathers and mothers, whose DNA was merged with our species in various experiments since the dawn of time. There were varying intentions as to the "why" behind breeding with and genetically modifying humans; some sinister, and some benevolent.

I have relived memories of being on *both* sides of the fence (whether they are my own soul memories or memories that have been shared from my oversoul network, I am not entirely sure; but I have felt them deeply nevertheless). I have had many flashes of being one of the female "breeders" of the first round of these human-galactic hybrids; a High Priestess establishing the original mystery schools of Isis and Hathor; of carrying these half-human, half-alien children in my womb; of loving them profusely, and teaching them our ways as if they were my own (as they were). I have also had memories of adoring mankind so much that I fell in love with a human man, which led to being punished and excommunicated when he eventually "sold me out", as it was forbidden (this was certainly my soul memory as it was excavated through one of my first ever "karmic" soulmate re-encounters in this lifetime, and brought up a significant amount of grief around betrayal and heartbreak with it).

I have *also* had many memories resurface of the other, more sinister, side of the fence; despising humanity, thinking they were 'beneath' us; desiring to enslave and control them, and being instrumental in helping to set up the "slave grids" that prevented humanity from activating their 12 strand DNA, constraining them to the matrix of illusion. I had a healing session in recent years where I uncovered Draconian "breeder" contracts still active where I agreed to use my womb space to incubate Draconian 'eggs' (even just writing it makes me feel like projectile vomiting, so you can imagine how fun that one was to uncover and release). I have memories of Atlantis, and being used (against my will) to harness this sacred technology to infiltrate the grids, to enslave and brainwash many.

These "darker" lifetimes were the very reason I have had many contracts in *this lifetime* of dismantling these slave grids that some former version of myself was instrumental in creating. They have also been a source of many karmic repercussions for me, which I have been clearing in the lifetimes that rippled out since, forcing me to endure the opposite experience of being the victim of satanic ritual slavery and sexual abuse many times over. However, the warnings I desire to share from my karmic lessons about what happens when we use sacred technologies and our superhuman abilities to harm others will come later in this book.

For now, I'm being guided to bring us back to these pyramids and their purpose.

Initiates across ancient civilisations were taught by our galactic forefathers how to use the various chambers of the pyramid to activate the properties of the pyramids I have already touched on. This information was then passed down through the line of priests and priestesses once the initial period of seeding had passed, and humans were left to their own devices. Eventually, it was all but lost and forgotten about as

BEC MYLONAS

the lineages of these sacred mystery schools gradually faded from existence.

We were also taught how to use these pyramids and sacred sites to carry out spiritual initiations and attunements, to connect the initiates to the various energies and information of other planets than our own.

This is how the Mayans were able to track - with accuracy - the movements of the stars and planets and how they had such an advanced astrological understanding and system for such a 'primitive' people. Not only were they taught how to use these pyramids to track these movements, but they were also using these pyramids to enable sacred attunement to the various energies of planets such as Venus, the Moon, or the Sun. This attunement is how they could feel and sense subtle shifts in energies and the influence of different planets as they made their transits or moved through their cycles. They had a way of *communicating* with the planets directly and downloaded information via frequency into their central channel, which was later integrated into their system. As this information was of an incredibly high frequency, it took some time to be transformed into a slower waveform and frequency, which could then be assimilated and interpreted. Once these codes and information became a denser material, it was able to be understood and translated by the mind into useful, practical instructions. For instance, how that planet and its transit would be influencing their harvest or the movement of the tides.

For the record, this is often how I experience "downloads" coming in today, particularly when I visit sacred sites. I receive a high influx of light, codes and information into my channel, which I cannot usually interpret in the moment I am receiving the stream. Only once I have assimilated and integrated those "codes" can I make sense of what the information is trying to tell me. This is part of the reason why it has taken months, from the moment I visited my last Mayan site, to beginning to compile this book, even though I was instructed I was to write a book with my rememberings. (That, and the seemingly never-ending Little Human Self tantrum that ensued.)

78

The Mayans knew which planet they needed to work with at any given time and were able to track these planets and their movement throughout the skies with precision. Their pyramids and observatories were precisely built to be able to track the progressions of the Solstice and the Equinox; along with the movements and cycles of many key planets including Venus, the Moon, and the Sun.

SOLAR CODES - ATTUNEMENT TO THE SUN

Like many ancient cultures, the Mayans were highly attuned to the energy of the Sun, and the Sun was a focal part of their spiritual understanding and beliefs. Many of the pyramids I visited in 2023 as part of my Mayan gridwork mission had both a pyramid devoted to the sun and one to the moon.

The sun represents the masculine element that was worshipped in the form of the Sun God "K'iinich Ahau" (in Yucatan Mayan). The moon represents the feminine element that was worshipped in the form of the Goddess of the Moon, "Ixchel" (in Yucatan Mayan).

However, when I speak of the attunement of the ancient Mayans to the sun's energy and cycles, I am not referring to their worship of the pantheon of Gods representing the various planets. I'm specifically speaking to their understanding and attunement to the giant ball of spinning gas, the exploding star that you see up in the sky.

The ancient Mayans understood that the sun was the central part of our solar system that much of what happened on our Earth revolved - *pun intended* - around the Sun and its activity. (After all, it *is* called the "Solar" System!)

They believed that to be attuned to the energy of the Sun would mean that they would be given insights into what was to come. Having High Priest(esse)s who could channel and interpret information from the sun itself, they delivered the prophecy foretelling the very age of high solar activity that we are experiencing now, which has been gradually increasing in recent years.

For some background to help you understand the level of intensity we're seeing currently, solar flares are classified according to their strength, each letter representing a ten-fold increase in energy output. The smallest are B-class, followed by C, M and then X, being the largest. X-Class solar flares have been frequenting our planet more and more over the past few years, to the point where seeing several occurring in a single week has become somewhat normal.

As gifted astronomers, the Mayans were able to track the cycles of solar activity rather accurately and could deduce - like scientists today - that the sun goes through cycles or "periods" of low or high solar activity. A period with "increased solar activity" is marked by strong solar flares, solar storms, coronal mass ejections, magnetic fields and large clouds of plasma erupting from the sun's outer atmosphere. All of which affect the Earth, causing potential pole shifts that bring on extreme weather events and natural disasters.

The Mayans understood that shifts in solar activity could cause cataclysmic, extinction level events or 'cycle restarters' like the magnetic pole shift, which brought about the sequence of events culminating in the Great Flood. (For the record, I don't believe solar energy was the cause of the pole shift that eventually caused the flood which sank Atlantis; I believe it was a result of abusing sacred technology, but we'll get into that later.)

In fact, one recent theory as to the disappearance of the Yucatan Mayans offered by scientists in recent years is just that; increased solar activity caused a drought, which the Mayans did not survive. If this is true, it could stand to reason that the prophecy passed on by the Mayans is to warn us of the possible collapse of our society when the sun entered into its new cycle, bringing with it increased solar activity. This would coincide with the infamous "ending" of the Mayan calendar in 2012; their calendar marked larger cosmic "cycles" after taking in all the information of all the planets and their movements. Fun side note: whilst doing probably the only bit of research I was guided to do whilst writing this book, I found that actually there *was* a significant solar event, "one of the strongest solar storms ever recorded" in 2012, that could have potentially wiped out the Earth; however, it narrowly missed us.

While touching on the infamous ending of the Mayan Calendar, I also find it important to digress for a moment here to note that while there are some disagreements around the specific dates and years, many people believe that in 2012, there *was* an important ending of a cycle which happens every 2000 or so years. Many believe 2012 marked the ending of The Age of Pisces, also known as the Age of Darkness or the Kali Yuga; a period which has been characterised by a collective consciousness primarily driven by ego, materialism, individualism, separation and competition. This would usher us into the Age of Aquarius, which is upon us now; an advanced scientific and humanitarian age with a shift into unity consciousness highlighting the interconnectedness as a global community.

The Mayans were not only aware of these shifting 'ages' or cycles and the characteristics each age would bring with them due to their astrological influences but the changes in planetary - in particular, solar - activity that would come with them. Perhaps the level of influence that could have contributed to the severe droughts in the Yucatan area pointed to by research.

If you could imagine that intensifying solar activity could severely affect the Mayans that were in tune with the land and lived simple lifestyles to the point that they were no longer able to survive, you could imagine what would happen to *our civilization today,* who are so heavily reliant on technology. In our modern day and age, with all of the technological advancements that we have, solar storms can wreak havoc on electrical power grids, causing radio blackouts and scrambling GPS and satellite systems that are in low-Earth orbit.

Having lived in places where electrical grid blackouts are frequent, I can tell you that a *lot* of things you take for granted in a 'developed' society become affected when there's a blackout. Even something as simple as being able to cook a meal for yourself becomes impossible if you don't have a gas stove. The places I lived had water pumps connected to the electrical grid, so when the electricity was out, there was also no running water. (Conveniently, these places also happened to be either tropical or *very hot* climates, so you could imagine how fun it would be going for days sometimes without showers or a ceiling fan.) For some of you reading this, these things won't be a big deal as perhaps you're already living off-grid, living remotely, or growing your own food (*and how I envy you*).

For many others of you, I invite you to consider what a day in your life might look like without the internet, without electricity, without running water, without heating, without AC, or whatever other luxuries you enjoy. Imagine what would happen to our *larger society* and how quickly it would crumble if all the electricity networks and satellites went down. The financial system would crumble; supermarkets, hospitals, educational institutions and workplaces would have to shut; you wouldn't be able to pay for the food you (couldn't even) buy, nor would you be able to cook it.

I'm not trying to freak anyone out, but *many of us* are living so far removed from nature that we wouldn't even know how to survive without some of these things. It would mean a complete global collapse in all places on the Earth except those still living modestly and simply off the land. I think I've sufficiently painted the picture of just some of the ways these solar flares could mess with the order of things... *moving right along...*

The Mayans not only had an awareness of the effect the sun had on the weather on our planet, but due to their connection with the Oneness, they understood the profound effect of solar energy on the human body, the earth and *all of its living creatures*. They understood that the solar energy being emitted contained specific information that would affect humans and all other living things on the Earth, including the Earth herself. They understood that solar energy had the potential to destroy and break down DNA so that it could be reconstructed and "upgraded" from carbon to crystalline. They understood that the sun is *literally* helping us to take on more of its properties, to become more like it, more light.

The image I am being given to describe what happens every time a solar flare hits the planet is a supernova exploding in our DNA, breaking down the cells so they can be reconstructed again with less density and more light. Moving from carbon-based to crystalline-based. I'm also being shown these energies awakening the "junk" DNA (more on this later) in our cells. When this happens, we purge density and toxins from our body at alarming rates and can have a whole array of uncomfortable physical symptoms as a result: exhaustion, emotional explosions, headaches, brain fog, mood swings, random body aches, cold and flu-like symptoms. We can see that the same is happening to Gaia; only her "purging" comes in the form of wild weather, volcanic eruptions, landslides, earthquakes, and other natural events.

As our cells contain more light and less density, they become less affected by heightened solar activity because they become *attuned* to it. Our bodies are able to *hold* the high-frequency light because they are more *like it*. **Those not willing or available to shed the density by 'allowing themselves to metaphorically die' in this way will not be able to hold the amount of light that is required in order to survive the heightened solar activity that is to come.**

This is part of the Mayan prophecy that will be shared in full at the end of the book; that we must be willing to face our own *death* in order to experience our rebirth in a new form. Hold this in your awareness for now; we'll be exploring what this actually means - and could possibly look like from a practical standpoint - later. The seed has been planted here, and there's no reason to send anyone running out of fear just yet...

Attunement to the energy of the sun, sun worship and understanding the importance of the sun is not ritual only practised by the ancient Mayans but by *most* ancient lineages. As an ancient priestess and oracle reincarnated into this current vessel, I have recalled myself attuning to, or channelling, the sun in many forms across many incarnations. The sun was channelled in the form of the god Apollo in my most recent "oracle" lifetime I experienced in Greece, where I served as the second Pythia instated at the temple of Delphi, delivering messages from Apollo to those who would journey to visit with me. (I think it's absolutely no coincidence that autocorrect tried to change the word "instated" to "enslaved" as this lifetime created such significant soul trauma that the waves continue to surface every time I am asked to step into the next level of my mission, even though I have "healed" them many times over the past years. That I chose to be of Greek descent in this lifetime and reincarnate into the same blood lineage was also no coincidence.)

In Ancient Egypt, the sun god, Ra, was the form of the sun channelled as we led our initiates through sacred rituals, awakening their kundalini and unlocking their mystical abilities.

And of course, in ancient Mayan times, as a High Priest, I would guide initiates through many ceremonies and rituals around the Sun, including an attunement ceremony that increased the capacity for your cells to take in the expanded Solar energy; the very process which you are about to be guided through.

When taking the priestesses through my mystery school training that was happening alongside the sacred gridwork mission I was fulfilling in Central America in 2023; I was shown the process of initiation in the same way that it was done in ancient Maya.

I was shown visuals of a large circular, sun-dial shaped ceremonial altar stone etched into the ground at the top of the pyramid, with various symbols around the corners. It seemed to represent a calendar or a progression of elements. In the attunement ceremony, an initiate would enter into the centre of the sun-dial-like altar, and each of their peers would surround her/him in a circle, calling upon the various gods and the elements. In the centre of this dial, she/he would be attuned to the energy of the sun and then all of the planets. She/he would be attuned to the energy of the Oneness, to God, to the connection between all things. Each initiate would go through this process, sharing blessings and energy with the one whose turn it was in the centre.

I hadn't actually heard of anything like this before, nor had I read any books around ancient Maya at the time I channelled this process for the mystery training.

This was later confirmed for me by a tour guide on the five-day pilgrimage I completed through the jungle to El Mirador in Guatemala; a tour guide who had seen me in a dream before I arrived - *talk about wild!* He would describe this same dial and type of ceremony to me and share that a dial or circular ornate stone similar to this one was the focal point for ceremony and offerings in most Mayan archeological sites. There was one at El Mirador where I held a ceremony. However, the jungle had covered it, so all that was left were the rocks as outliers for the circle that people had placed there to mark the section out in more recent years. He also told me that this specific feature at El Mirador was an altar that many people would travel to create offerings and hold ceremonies on from all over the world, from various spiritual traditions during peak energetic portals such as the Equinox.

It would seem that many others have received the very same memo I did of the potency of this symbol, its placement and the spiritual significance for not only the ancient Mayans but many cultures and traditions that succeeded them.

INITIATION 2: PLANETARY & ELEMENTAL ATTUNEMENT

You can access the recommended audio version of this initiation at this website: www.diamondlightoracle.com.

Welcome to the second initiation in this transmission.

The following is an attunement to sacred elemental and planetary energies and an opening of your channel.

In your mind and with your heart; set the intention that this is the work that will be done during our time together in this activation, and that you are open to receive all that is in your highest good.

I now invite all the beings of the highest light who wish to support this activation taking place.

I welcome your Higher Self, your Soul Family and Oversoul Network; and invite them to support you in receiving what is of the highest for you at this time.

I declare that this is sacred space; only that which is resonating at the frequency of unconditional love is welcome in this space.

I ask that everything that takes place here today is for the *highest good of all* and in service to the Whole.

That the work we do together here today ripples out and serves the collective.

And so it is, and so it is, and so it is.

We invite you to enter your Sacred Space; the safe and protected ceremony space in which you receive all re-calibrations, downloads, codes and activations throughout this journey.

Acknowledging internally that *you have now entered Sacred Space.*

Know that while you will be guided to journey elsewhere for the following activation, all of the frequency you receive at this other place will be relayed and routed via your own Sacred Space, which will act as a buffer for all that is not required.

To begin with, you find yourself at the landing of a large, ancient limestone pyramid.

The day is cloudy and ominous; there is a darkness to it, a stillness, a potency in the air.

There are stairs running up the middle of the pyramid's face, and at the base of the pyramid, on each side of the step, are the heads of two serpents, with mouths wide open.

The air is thick with anticipation, although the breeze is calm and crisp.

You feel the sun on your face and a warmth washes over your body.

You are safe, you are loved, you are protected here in this space.

You are met at the base of the pyramid by a figure who takes your hand.

You see that she is dressed in an ornate and intricate garment, with a large headpiece covered with dangling jade crystals.

She is a high priestess, an oracle.

As she looks into your eyes, you can feel a deep wisdom transferring from her into you.

Through her eyes you see galaxies, you see stars, you see portals to other dimensions.

There is a depth, an expansiveness in the space you find yourself gazing into.

It is never-ending, infinite.

As she looks into your eyes, you feel your womb space begin to pulse alive with the memory of this blank, open space.

The cosmic void.

As she looks into your eyes, you see infinity.

As she looks into your eyes, you see all versions of yourself across all time, space and dimensions across the multiverse.

Pause here for a moment as you allow this connection point to be made.

When you feel ready, the Oracle begins to guide you up the side of the pyramid.

The stone snakes on the side of each stairway animate, and you see they have feathers around their head; they are feathered serpents.

The feathered serpents peel themselves off the limestone base of the stairs and begin to follow behind you up the stairs.

As you delicately make your way up each step of the pyramid, you can feel the intensity of the Ancient energy encoded in the limestone beginning to take your breath away.

With each step, you are allowing the wisdom, the codex of the ancient pyramid, to move through your foot chakras to be assimilated into your meridian system.

Your feet feel activated, and you can feel the electricity starting to move up your calves.

It is working within your DNA; awakening dormant memories, keys and codes; ancient wisdom within your body.

You now start to feel these electrical pulses moving all the way up your legs, into your thighs and lower body.

With each step, the process intensifies, and you feel your legs wobbling as you reach the top of the pyramid.

As you reach the top of the pyramid, you look out and see vast expanses of jungle in every direction that you look; as if the jungle had swallowed up everything else around it but this ancient pyramid.

You connect to the sea of green and feel each Ancient Tree consciousness waving back at you, welcoming you into this space.

You feel connected again to Nature.

The frequency of Abundance that is Earth.

This pyramid stands alone, magnificent amidst the background of beautiful, fecund, abundant and untouched Earth.

Mother Nature in all her glory.

You feel moved by the sheer power, the potency of her energy.

It takes your breath away.

You feel the element of Air which is violently rattling the trees beneath you, as it lashes against your face, your hair, your clothing.

As you breathe the cleansing air in, you feel the purity of the air expand in your lungs; renewing you.

The element of Air is cleansing you, releasing impurities and preparing you for the ceremony ahead.

You hear a distant thunder clash, and you know somewhere off in the distance, there is a storm raging.

However, you are not afraid and you know you are perfectly safe on this pyramid.

The intensity of Mother Nature only inspires more awe and reverence in you.

Deep inside, you feel connected to the electrical current of this storm as your own electricity awakens within you.

At the top of the pyramid, there is a circular dial; an altar.

Surrounding the circular altar, you find your brothers and sisters, priests and priestesses of the mysteries, awaiting you eagerly in anticipation of your initiation.

Feel their eagerness and appreciation of you.

Feel the comfort of their support and encouragement.

In front of the altar, there is an ornamental lantern; a fire pit.

The priestess lights the fire pit and invites you to stand in front of the centre of the altar.

You watch as the flames dance and lick at the sides of the fire pit, threatening but not spilling over.

You feel as if a flame begins to ignite and awaken inside of your sacral.

The now-alive stone-feathered serpents dance around the base of the fire pit, and as they slither their way in a circular movement, intertwining with each other to where the fire is lit, they open their mouths.

As they swallow the fire from the pit, they turn their heads and breathe the smoke from the fire onto your body; like tiny dragons.

The element of smoke prepares and cleanses you so you are ready to step into the centre of the altar.

You are invited to step into the centre of the altar and notice you are standing on what appears to be a sundial, a large circle surrounded by ancient symbols all around you.

The Oracle invites your peers surrounding you in a circle, to begin to chant in a low hum all around you.

As they begin to tone, singing notes and creating vibrations with the sounds, the symbols on the edges of the circle begin to mobilise, moving around the dial in a clockwise direction.

The entire centre disk you are standing on lifts off, and you notice the altar is two different disks - the circular centre you stand on, with the secondary spinning disk outside, which is filled with the symbols.

The priests and priestesses around you continue to chant, to tone, to sing.

The Oracle begins to speak light language, a strong, powerful and striking language you have heard before; it feels familiar to you and awakens a sense of homecoming deep in your cells.

See yarakoi m'eke si' koo me' yarakoi.

See yarakoi m'eke si' koo me' yarakoi.

See yarakoi m'eke si' koo me' yarakoi.

She is connecting you to the stars, the planets, attuning your body to the subtle frequencies.

She is calibrating you to reconnect to the Oneness.

As she speaks, you notice the clouds above you parting as a beam of pure Sunlight streams down directly onto you.

You can see the particles in the air, sparkling brightly, as this brilliant and radiant frequency from the sun hits your skin. You feel it penetrating beneath, warming your blood, warming your atoms.

This Ray begins to work within you at a cellular level - breaking down the cellular walls - like a million tiny supernovas exploding under your skin.

Your skin starts to tingle like it is on fire, but you still feel perfectly safe, and you find the warmth comforting.

In the centre of each atom, you feel a spark from the Sun being implanted - igniting something within you, coming alive again.

The group continues to chant and tone around you as this process continues.

See yarakoi m'eke si' koo me' yarakoi.

See yarakoi m'eke si' koo me' yarakoi.

See yarakoi m'eke si' koo me' yarakoi.

You may stay here for as long as you feel is required for this process to be completed.

The Oracle presents a chalice of crystalline Holy Water and proceeds to bless you with this water - flicking this water onto your crown, your third eye, your throat, your heart, your solar plexus, your sacral, and your root.

She then hands you the chalice to drink from.

You lift the chalice to your lips, and you begin to drink.

As you drink, the crystalline Holy Water blesses you and purifies you from the inside out.

It soothes and relaxes the intensity of the solar energy breaking down your cells and begins to cool your temperature down.

As your temperature internally cools, you look to the sky and see that the Sun is beginning to be eclipsed by the Moon, slowly at first, before it begins to speed up.

In this quantum ceremony space, you are noticing a full Solar Eclipse taking place.

As the Sun slowly becomes covered more and more by the Moon, the setting around you becomes darker and darker.

Soon the Moon is completely covering the Sun, and as it does this you receive frequency and calibration now to attune you even more deeply to the cycles of the Moon.

The spinning disk around you continues to circle around, calibrating, calibrating, calibrating your field.

Just as quickly as the Moon covers the Sun, it begins to move away, as the scene becomes slowly brighter again and the Sun begins to reveal itself.

As the Sun comes fully into view, this process is coming to a close, as is your ceremony.

You are now connected to all the elements.

You are connected to all the planets.

You are connected to the Sun.

You are connected to the Moon.

You are connected to the Infinite All of Everything.

See yarakoi m'eke si' koo me' yarakoi.

See yarakoi m'eke si' koo me' yarakoi.

See yarakoi m'eke si' koo me' yarakoi.

This attunement is now complete.

And so it is, and so it is, and so it is.

When you feel ready, you may step off the platform, and if it feels appropriate you can thank the Oracle and your peers, before gently making your way down the pyramid stairs.

With each step you descend, you start to feel more and more grounded in your body.

As you find yourself at the base of the pyramid again, this process comes to a completion as we begin to integrate and calibrate this on all levels.

Integrating and calibrating this now on the physical level.

Integrating and calibrating this now on the emotional level.

Integrating and calibrating this now on the mental level.

Integrating and calibrating this now through all levels and dimensions of your light body.

Integrating, calibrating and sharing this frequency now through all timelines and all versions of yourself across the multiverse.

We now shut down any and all open portals and gateways that are no longer required and send back all energy that has come through any portals or gateways in the process of this work.

We now dissolve any bonds, chords or attachments that have been formed for the process of this activation and call you back into complete Soul Sovereignty.

We return all of your energy to you now as you call your Soul fully into your body.

Now inviting in Diamond Light to cleanse and close this space; bringing this sacred activation to a close; thanking all of the beings who have been here supporting in this process.

It is done, it is done, it is done, and so it is.

You may spend some time here in silent reflection, or receiving in your Sacred Space if it feels necessary.

If you feel complete, we invite you to gently bring yourself back into your body and into the room, wiggling your fingers and toes, and opening your eyes when you are ready.

PART THREE

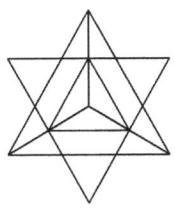

EVERYTHING

THE RETURN TO MEXICO

Mexico and the magic that had ensued the last time I was there had almost faded from my mind by the time I heard the call again over a year later, although this time it was much louder, *much* clearer and descended onto me with a sense of excitement to go back.

I had just returned to Bali in the early months of 2023, where the intention was to spend a few weeks packing up my life and belongings there as that chapter and the soul work I was doing there felt complete for me.

I didn't know what was next or where I needed to be after that, but I had a desire at the time to return to Australia and sow some roots - in fact, it came as quite a shock to me that it would not be the immediate case.

That particular week, I had spent quite a lot of time in bed, receiving huge activations and moving enormous amounts of energy through my body as I connected directly with dragon energy for the first time and experienced some rather hectic initiations.

As I lay there, the Mayan ancestors came to me and told me it was time to go back and spend more time in Mexico, that there was work to do, and there was *"love for me there"*.

This time, there were no trepidations and no resistance; having been quite some time (and quite a lot of "character development") since my last Mexican adventure, I was much more aware of my role as a grid-worker and the mission I was carrying out. I was more trusting and willing to follow the guidance, and my channel was far clearer. *I guess you can say that the previous year of initiations, strenuous healing work and being held to the soul fire had paid off.* I knew I was being called there to fulfil the next part of my sacred mission, although I must admit that the thought of "love for me there" certainly helped sweeten the deal and would be a prophecy that proved true.

At the time, I was in a pretty tight place financially, having had many months off client-facing work in my business; focusing on launching my podcast, which wasn't yet bringing me any income. However, I trusted that if God wanted me to go to Mexico, a way would find itself to me.

A few weeks later, I was guided to open to the possibility of working for someone else (which brought up huge resistance at first and bruised my ego as I had declared I'd *"never work for anyone ever again"* when I started my soul-preneurial journey in 2019 and hadn't yet had to). However, I was soon to find out that it was not at all about me having to give up my soul business, it was about the sacred purpose I was being called into as a result of entering this particular vortex. I would never have considered "applying" for a position in someone else's business at that point, as I would only individually contract clients through the marketing work I would do. I was always my own "boss", so to speak. However, being given this ping to look for a "job" led me to exactly where spirit needed me to be. The morning after working through my resistance, I saw that a major women's work company - who had been a large catalyst for my gifts coming online spontaneously in 2020, in an online workshop of theirs I had been guided to take - was looking for a content creator, and I knew immediately the job was already mine. Within a few days of applying, I was hired, and my money issues became a non-issue. I was going to Mexico!

After a few weeks of navigating full-time work and the wild initiations of inner union and dragon energy that I was going through in Bali, I returned back to Australia, bought my flights to Mexico and prepared for my next departure.

In the short time since I had begun the contract with this company, the purpose I was called in for had already been completed.

A large part of my soul mission is to act as an activator, amplifier and catalyst for the expansion of the soul mission and visions of others. I come in over a short amount of time to expand their gridwork and activate them into their next iteration or level of their mission, and then I leave.

Although on 'paper', the women's work company was looking for a content creator, what I was called into their vortex for on a soul level was *much more than that* (and there was a mutual knowing when we began to work together that this was the case). I was brought in to expand the vision for the company, create sacred geometry behind their marketing content, activating it; contribute to the larger grid-work mission they were doing in the background, and receive specific codes myself. (The retreat this company was working on, as I was part of their team, was around dragon energy, so I mean... *go figure*.)

I also had a strong soul connection with one of the team members, who would later go on to be one of the priestesses called to support the Mayan gridwork/mystery mission I would be going on. Once my work with the company was complete, there was no reason for me to continue on and after an open-hearted and intuitively led conversation with the founder, we decided to lovingly part ways (you can hear us unpacking this in Episode 38 of my podcast; "Hold Yourself to Soul Fire", which you can listen to at www.becmylonas.com/podcast).

After a momentary panic attack - having just purchased plane tickets and now not having any guaranteed income to see me through my Mexico adventure - I did the old practice of "surrender and trust" I was a certified *pro* at by this point and quickly managed to turn it around to being one of the highest income months I had done in my business in a while. I had also been guided to apply to be a speaker at a conference in Mexico City later that year around ascension and UFOlogy; which I can see contributed to the leap and which I later found out had a divine purpose in itself, in some of the soul connections I made at the conference. I had put the money down for the conference a few days after concluding my work contract and buying my flight. I was *committing* even if I had no guarantee I'd be able to sustain myself financially once I was there, as my business had been far from consistent in the previous year. (Things would tend to pause in my business as I would go through large initiations, so I'd have these incredible high-income months, sometimes followed by no income for months.)

For the record, THIS is the miracle secret sauce for a guaranteed quantum leap, 9 times out of 10. Trusting and taking the big, scary action even if you have no guarantee or idea how it's going to work out. This is something I daresay I've all but mastered over the years of taking massive, terrifying leaps out of my comfort zone at the instruction of my inner guidance system.

In the months leading up to my departure, I was moving through a lot of initiations around sacred inner union, mermaid/siren energy, Venusian "lover" light-divine-feminine codes awakening in me, and having my heart cracked open to allow *even* more love to flow through it. There were moments when I thought the amount of love that wanted to flow through me would destroy me - that my Little Human vessel couldn't hold it all. In the months leading up to the second time in Mexico, I spent a lot of days in bed, shaking, convulsing, laughing, orgasming, crying and seeing God. I was being prepared to hold even more divinity in my cells than ever before in anticipation of where I was being led next.

In hindsight, I can see how, over the years since my awakening began, I was being prepared emotionally and spiritually to hold higher and higher volumes of energy as part of my mission. Cracked open, pummelled, blasted open, humbled, brought to my knees time and time again. So was my physical body. In order to activate people in the ways I do, to be a channel for this energy, I would be required to grace-fully command vast amounts of extremely potent energy through my vessel while still remaining grounded and anchored to the Earth. A lot of the time, whilst simultaneously being able to talk or guide a session for a group of people.

And to get to that point required a *lot* of purging and a lot of physical, mental and emotional preparation. It required a *lot* of feeling completely ungrounded, disempowered and overwhelmed by it all for many years until it eventually strengthened me.

Like a diamond forged under pressure, I can see that it all *had to* unfold in the challenging and almost debilitating way it did for me - I had to be *humbled* - so I could hold it with grace and remain anchored in my heart at all times despite the power I had access to.

To say these initiations would affect my quality of living and ability to hold down any semblance of a 'normal life' would be the understate-ment of the century. Even as I write this book and go on this journey with you as it channels through me, I am being initiated by it on deeper levels, which means pretty much every other aspect of my life has been put on pause. Frankly, I am surprised I managed to have such an active lifestyle, social life and work calendar during my most recent pilgrimage in Mexico as the volume of codes and sacred information I was receiving was extensive and also felt neverending while I was present on the land.

The intensity of the downloads I was receiving leading up to the trip only just amplified once I was back on Mayan soil again. I knew I was on some sort of divine mission when I arrived in Mexico, but the scope and breadth of that hadn't really hit me until the guidance started dropping in after I visited the first pyramid, Ek Balam (close in vicinity to its more famous sibling, Chichén Itzá, which I'd also later visit).

On the second day of my arrival - jetlagged and completely disoriented, experiencing a little culture shock and inner-child discomfort even though I'd been there before as still dawned on me that *"I'm alone on the other side of the world where I'm only just learning the language"* - I met a couple of Mexican men while I was hanging by the pool in my complex. One of them I immediately hit it off with, and felt very safe and calm in his energy. (His older friend I did not, as he continually proceeded to hit on me even though I made it very clear I was not interested; luckily, however, I didn't have to see him ever again after that day even though we were staying mere rooms away from each other.)

I had mentioned that I wanted to go see some sacred sites, and the one that I had a good connection with had said he'd also love to visit Ek Balam, as he'd not yet been there himself.

We made plans to go two weeks later, and after checking in with my guidance team and setting up some "safety" contingency plans (like making sure I had his licence details recorded and sent off to a few friends and family, along with a moving location pin when we were on the road - after all, this was Mexico we were talking about, where women just like me have a habit of disappearing after meeting random men), we were on our way to the sacred site.

I felt safe and comfortable with this man as we conversed like we were two old friends - half in my *muy basico Español* that wasn't apparently as bad as I thought it was after 3 months of practising every day in Australia, half in his broken English - over the loud house music that was blasting through the car stereo. I felt immensely grateful that within two days of arriving, Spirit had already orchestrated someone to take me directly to the first pyramid. Not only that, but I had already made a friend who seemed very knowledgeable of the area and full of helpful information for me as a solo traveller.

As we drove across long stretches of road that were basically enveloped in jungle, I was feeling intense sensations all throughout my body. I felt like I had swallowed a bag of magic mushrooms as I watched the trees begin to warp and felt my kundalini rise, bringing tingling sensations of warmth and electricity all throughout my body.

What started as a few droplets from the sky along our path became a sudden, intense storm that came out of nowhere. As it began bucketing down, we were laughing to ourselves loudly, saying, 'Well, I guess that's perfect' - as if the weather was some sort of foreboding omen of the intensity of energy we were both feeling, but neither of us was speaking into.

Closer and closer we got to the sacred site as the rain continued to pour down; fast, heavy and loudly, and I was beginning to dread navigating the site in those weather conditions.

As we finally arrived at the entry gate - as if by a miracle - the rain began to stop, the clouds slowly parted, and the sun revealed itself in enough time for us to complete the tour. It was still overcast enough that we managed to avoid the relentless, blistering sauna-like heat that was a feature of this time of year in that part of Mexico, and I was grateful to not have to be drenched in sweat as we walked around the site, in the thick, moist, dense canopy of the jungle that surrounded the site.

It was amazing to me how the ancient structures that made their presence known in the landing of the site just kind of popped up and appeared out of nowhere in the middle of a jungle that seemed to otherwise swallow them. I wondered how many other ancient Mayan buildings, structures, megaliths and artefacts were swallowed by the surrounding jungle, yet to be discovered (*many*, I would later find out when hiking through the Guatemalan jungle a few months later). The canopy of the jungle acted like a time capsule that preserved this little forgotten memory of ancient times. As you entered the archeological site and looked upon the scattered remains of rocks that once formed buildings, structures, pyramids and temples, it felt as though you were transported right back into the dimension where this once existed, and you couldn't help but marvel at the mysteries of what had happened here.

Being low season and also being far less popular than its nearby sibling, Chichén Itzá, there were hardly any other tourists at Ek Balam that day... *just the way I liked it.*

We were able to climb the steps of most of the structures, and once we reached the main pyramid - much taller than most of the others, reaching 32 metres in height - I wondered how I'd make it to the top of the 106 stairs, with my legs already wobbly from the electrical charge that was running through them. With each step, the energy seemed to intensify, and by halfway up the front of the pyramid, it was *literally* taking my breath away.

We stopped about midway, where there was a landing to the side of the stairs; several room-like structures cutting into the wall of the pyramid, with incredible images and symbols carved into the limestone, which was roped off and protected. I felt this was a good place to drop into the energy fully and to receive from the pyramid, as it was hidden enough that nobody would bother me.

As I felt the electricity move through my body, it began to cause me to sway from side to side in graceful, subtle movements stemming from my hips. As the connection point was established, my channel opened, and the current picked up; I felt my body move back and forth from the force of the electrical charge much like a metronome; left to right, in this rhythmic fashion that accelerated in pace until my hips were moving so fast side to side, it looked like I was shaking. I could feel the electricity pulsing through my body, causing it to involuntarily move; left, right, left, right, left, right; in this continuous rhythm. I was noticing many bright colours flashing in lightforms behind my closed eyelids, like someone had set off a coloured strobe light.

As the energy increased, I found myself feeling giddier and giddier, higher and higher, as it moved through my chakras and into my heart-space, causing me to crack an involuntary smile and start giggling to myself with the pleasurable orgasmicness of it. I began to allow my hands to move on their own accord, swirling back and forth around my body in circular motions like two snakes dancing and weaving with each other.

Just like the belly dancers of my ancestry or a Bollywood dancer, they moved gracefully above my head, in front of my heart, to my sides, as my hips and my torso moved in these serpent-like fluid, circular motions as if guided by my arms.

I could feel my hands take on a life of their own, making all sorts of mudras and shapes, writing symbols in the air in a light language I didn't consciously know but somehow remembered. I knew that at this point, there was nothing for me to "do" but let the energy flow, and allow the part of myself that "knew" to take over. I didn't have to "understand" the downloads at that moment or experience a human, "linear" explanation of what was happening or what I was doing there. A lot of the time, when I do gridwork, I don't actually receive "messages" that come through in an already interpreted form. It comes through as frequency, which then later integrates as a form that I'm able to understand (if you remember me talking about the *frequency* of the codes having to slow down and become *denser* so my human mind is able to "translate" them into actual information). My only job is to show up where I've been guided to be, open a clear channel, and let the divine and ancient part of me take the wheel.

I knew I was receiving from the pyramid and the ancient wisdom that was coded into the limestone, but I also got a sense there was something I was doing that was supporting this frequency to come back online; as if it had been dormant, forgotten, sleeping, lost... and I was there to spark it back up again. It was a two-way flow of energy; an ever-looping infinity symbol; I was receiving and giving all at once.

It is hard to say for sure exactly how long I was there for - as I completely lose all sense of linear "time" when in a semi-trance state, and minutes can expand into hours - but I couldn't have been there for more than fifteen minutes in active meditation before I felt complete, and began to make the way to the top of the pyramid. Again, at the top, I stood in silent meditation for a few moments to check if there was anything else that needed doing and to confirm I was, in fact, complete. I got the message that I was, so I took a moment to take in the breathtaking view over the expanse of jungle that spread out far into the horizon in every direction; nothing but a sea of green. We took a few photos and began to make our way down the stairs. Well in truth, I *crawled* down them backwards, whilst on my hands and knees, because I was so afraid I would fall face-first down the 106 stairs before me.

Fun fact; the size and shape of the stairs of the Mayan pyramids actually provided a relevant insight into the size (and therefore genetic origin) of people who inhabited them, I later learnt. This pyramid (Ek

Balam) had fairly small-sized stairs, considering some of the other pyramids I visited, which had enormous stairs. This was actually something the Ancient Mayan royalty intended through the way they built the pyramids. To humble and humiliate the "peasants" - who were significantly shorter in size than the royal family with their Annunaki genetics, being half-giants, some 7ft tall and above - they created stairs that were tall enough to cater to the royal family but not the peasants who would have to humiliate themselves to "crawl" up them. For context, I'm about 160cm (5"3') in height, and the stairs on some of the structures at El Mirador (in Guatemala) would nearly come up to my hip, which made them rather uncomfortable to climb. Not to mention, it was also terrifying considering there was no handrail to support you as you climbed the megalithic structures, so you'd be worrying about accidentally missing a step or leaning too far forward and plunging to your death the way I was at Ek Balam... hence, the crawling.

We reached the bottom of the pyramid feeling sufficiently humbled, stopped for a moment to catch our breath and ground, and then headed home. I had received what I needed at that point, and now it was time to integrate all that had energetically come to pass.

THE ALCHEMICAL PROCESS

The dictionary definition of alchemy is *"the mediaeval forerunner of chemistry, concerned with the transmutation of matter, in particular with attempts to convert base metals into gold or find a universal elixir."* To me, the most important part of the definition is 'the transmutation of matter' as that is what Alchemists do, both within themselves and externally. **<u>To put it simply, alchemy is the process of changing form, and the alchemist is one who is able to transmute matter from one form to another.</u>**

All priestesses/priests are alchemists. From the beginning of their journey, they learn how to master the ability to change density into higher frequencies across various applications. Shadow alchemy: the ability to transmute shadow into light (both internally, within oneself, and externally, for the collective). Emotional alchemy: the ability to transmute 'dense' emotions (such as grief or suffering) into higher frequencies of acceptance, peace, unconditional love and bliss. Sexual alchemy: the ability to transmute eros, desire, and raw electric sexual energy to birth creations, create Life or heal miraculously.

The alchemist gains complete mastery of each state by allowing herself/himself to **experience** the full intensity of it (in the *feminine* "feeling" aspect of consciousness). The alchemist does not turn away from it, try to diminish it, or negate its existence; she/he allows it to be as loud as it needs to be. She/he feels it all the way through, and she/he becomes it; she/he *merges* with it. In doing so, she/he is able to affect the very matter of it from a *subatomic level*, enabling it to *change form*.

At the same time as holding this polarity of the feminine *experiential feeling*, she/he is also in "observer" mode, masculine witness consciousness, able to do this while simultaneously remaining detached from the story or sensation of it. It takes a master to be able to perform this level of alchemy in merging so deeply with an experience and still not getting caught up in the story of the sensation, of the pain, the grief, the discomfort, or even of the ecstasy and the pleasure of it.

A priestess is forged over extremes to gain mastery over her energy and the energy that creates the world around her through various initiations both directly - through formal teaching - and indirectly - through the process of her life and circumstances. She harnesses, transmutes and directs energy to create outcomes seen by others as 'miracles' or 'magic'. This is essentially what Jesus Christ / Yeshua was doing when he was healing miraculously or performing miracles; he was practising the art of alchemy that he mastered after his extensive teachings in mystery schools in his "un-accounted for years" in the bible. A priestess similarly has trained over lifetimes in mystery schools to gain this level of mastery over energy, and her soul journey is a continued path of mastering her alchemical abilities in various contexts, which intensify in difficulty and level of mastery required.

To move from 'priestess' to 'Oracle', the level of alchemical mastery required is much higher, as the priestess must move _beyond_ her current form to essentially shape-shift into something else entirely.

Another way of approaching alchemy is that **alchemy is the result of embodying the properties of that which you are trying to affect**. For instance, if you desire to move or influence a tree, you must *become* the tree. Or perhaps you remember the martial artist Bruce Lee's famous words, "Be like water" - *this* is what he is talking about.

But what does that really mean?

It means to *draw every fibre and cell of your body into harmonic resonance* - on a subatomic level - until there is no separation between that which you wish to become and the version of "Self", which is interfacing with the reality you are currently observing. This principle of alchemy is how martial artists can break huge planks of wood with one swift karate chop or send someone flying with a gentle touch of the pinkie finger.

By becoming a pure channel, you may *become* that which you are trying to affect.

You aren't just affecting the tree; you *are* the tree; you become the tree (or the water, or the block of wood you are chopping, or the poor opponent you desire to send flying across the room). You quantum jump into a fractal of yourself, which *is* the tree; living, breathing, experiencing the consciousness of the Tree. You move like the tree. You behave like the tree. You think like the tree. You *are* the tree. *You have become the tree.* There is no separation between "you" and the tree (or, for that matter, the guy you're trying to send flying across the room - which is exactly what you realise at a certain level of consciousness; there *is* no separation, so any shitty thing you are doing to someone else, you're really just doing to *yourself*). **You connect to that point of the living consciousness of Oneness - the web of life - and you bi-locate into *being* that fractal of the Creator in order to receive instructions from it, to download codes from it, to pull that consciousness into your body, and to affect it from a place of *beingness.***

This is how the pyramids were built. The builders *became* the limestone and then were able to move it with their will because they were encoded with the specific frequency of the limestone. To illustrate this with an example, if you play a tuning fork, it will only cause another tuning fork that is in resonance / in the same tone to play along with it. If another tuning fork on a different note was played with a different frequency/resonance, nothing would happen.

Thus, in order to affect the limestone - move it, carve it, shape it, imbue properties or information into it with their minds - the ancient ones had to first attune to the sub-atomic make-up of the limestone.

The pyramids are coded with the information of all of our ancestors because their very memory - their cellular information - is imprinted into the limestone. They _became_ one with the limestone and thus imprinted onto it.

When you visit a sacred site, and you have an open intention to connect with the minerals on that site, you are able to essentially download all of the information that has been encoded onto that site. Our ancestors - such as the ancient Mayans - knew this and have been encoding sacred sites with information since the dawn of time, sharing ancient wisdom, secrets, technologies and warnings for future generations to come.

This sacred technology is also how we are able to quantum jump or 'leap timelines' between multidimensional versions of ourselves (aka parallel/past/future lives). Versions of ourselves on other timelines who already exist with codes/keys you desire to bring online into this reality; who are experiencing a reality we desire; who have abilities we do not yet have; or who have achieved things we have not yet achieved. For instance, in the process of writing this book, I was constantly 'tuning into' the version of myself who _had already completed the act of writing this book_. If you've ever seen the movie _"Everything, Everywhere, All at Once"_, this is another _great_ example of this concept; the protagonist can "download" skills from different alternate versions of herself across the multiverse, such as kung-fu, acting, and even having physical anomalies like having sausage hands.

We collapse space and time by melding with the frequency of this 'alternate' version of Self across the multiverse, and we bi-locate our consciousness into this version of Self, in essence, merging with it. The repercussions of this for our "manifestation" practice are profound, and is where the concept of "quantum jumping" comes from.

It really highlights the concept taught by many spiritual teachers: "If you desire more love, become love" and "If you desire to be wealthy, give money away." By being a living embodiment of that which you seek, it collapses space and time **and draws you into the timeline where that reality and version of you *already* exists.**

This is not a process of 'faking it 'til you make it'; it is a process of tuning into that fractal of consciousness and *downloading* - directly - what instructions, what actions, what behaviours, what thoughts, and even what cellular structure your body would take on (on a biological level, we're talking epigenetics here) if you were that version of yourself.

You are downloading information from the field, imprinting it into your "current" body, upgrading your own cellular structure as it receives the instructions from the consciousness you are downloading, then *embodying it* and anchoring it here in the physical reality.

This principle is how I was able to go from *'couldn't even get an intuitive hunch'* to *'psychic AF'* overnight. While spontaneously reliving all of these priestess/oracle/witch/shaman past lives (and the trauma that came with them), I was connecting to and bringing online versions of myself from past/parallel lifetimes who *already* had these faculties open and active. *I didn't have to learn anything* because *I already had that mastery* in many other timelines; I simply needed to connect to it and awaken my muscle memory of it.

This is where the importance of having a physical embodiment practice comes in, as a priestess, channeller and alchemist. Practices such as Qi Gong, yoga, dance or some other intuitive movement practice enable you to "anchor" the frequency into your physical body. Additionally, somatic practices and bodywork, which opens and clears the physical body, creates *space* within the channels (your own meridian system; energetic highways) to be able to take frequency from this Quantum Field and anchor it into the physical. I'll get more into the importance of this a little later as we look deeper into the meridian system and our connection to Gaia.

If we go back to the start of this book, you may remember my gruelling recount of my initiation deep in the Guatemalan jungle, where my old "self" had to die to be replaced by the version of myself who was capable of holding this mission. It was not a 'new' self I was being imprinted by; it was an ancient self whose body was one of a Mayan warrior, highly attuned to nature and physically strong. In that experience, I was downloading information encoded into the mycelium and root network in the jungle as instructions to re-code my entire body to return to the cellular structure of what my body once was in my Mayan timelines.

Of course, I didn't suddenly grow a penis, spurt a six pack or any other physical features that my male Mayan warrior self had (although that would be kind of a hilarious plot twist in terms of "meeting my divine masculine counterpart"). However, I *did* start to re-code my cells to release illness, inflammation and disease.

Humans were not genetically created to only live 90 or 100 years in the best-case scenario. Our bodies were created originally to live *hundreds* of years, with the capacity to self-heal and many more "superhuman" faculties online. It is by design and rather intentional that our capacity for Aliveness and our genetic potential has been shut down and repressed over history (which is now coming back online, with the rising frequency of the planet, which is stimulating the awakening of our dormant, Divine DNA).

Not to exclude mentioning the poor diets, environments and lifestyles we lead, which have us in complete separation and disconnection from the Oneness and from receiving the instructions from the Earth on how our body is to regenerate. This process we are going through now is bringing our bodies back to the Divine Template of what they were always designed to be. Scientists tell us that 90% of our DNA is "junk" or useless. Frankly, this is a farce. There is no such thing as "junk DNA" because the Creator would never create something that wasn't perfect, was accidental, or was a 'waste'. These Divine DNA strands, which have been offline until now, are the ones that provide instructions for our bodies to have the strength, self-healing capacity, longevity and capabilities of a Superhuman alchemist. These are the strands of our DNA that consciously working with and rising our kundalini awakens within us.

KUNDALINI RISING

For many of you reading this, the concept of a Kundalini or a Kundalini rising will not be new, but I invite you to read this with fresh eyes and a beginner's mind. Kundalini rising is, essentially, the fast track to spiritual evolution and DNA activation, an intensive purification of your vessel so that the life force within can flow freely and you can experience higher states of consciousness and spiritual enlightenment. It brings upon feelings of bliss, ecstasy, pleasure, connection and love; along with profound altered states of consciousness, the awakening of psychic or 'spiritual gifts', and mystical experiences. This is why many seek to have their kundalini awakened by a master, guru or teacher or through an intentional practice.

However, due to the sheer electrical current and force of the energy, if one is not ready or prepared for their kundalini awakening or it awakens spontaneously, it can wreak havoc on the system and become very dangerous to the seeker. I'll elaborate further on this shortly, but suffice it to say, it can cause psychosis, paralysis, violent convulsions, or fry your brain if your kundalini shoots up to your head prematurely (along with many other slightly less dramatic but still extremely uncomfortable states which I've personally experienced).

A kundalini rising can be the most beautiful, rewarding and terrifying experience that you will ever have, but it's important for me to state that not everybody experiences it in the same way. If you are one of the people who hasn't experienced it in the way I'm about to describe, it doesn't mean *anything* about how 'enlightened' or 'spiritual' you are. Allow me to repeat: having an intense Kundalini experience does *not* *mean anything* about how powerful, evolved or enlightened you are. (I'm talking to the performative folk at the back, thinking that sending someone into an unnecessary, near-catatonic state during a Kundalini Activation session is the goal. This is one of the things I had to learn personally when I realised my violent kundalini was actually *not* a good thing; it was showing me I had a lot of supportive work to do for my body to learn to channel it gracefully.) I have many friends who are very old souls yet have never experienced a kundalini rising; they are still incredibly spiritually gifted and connected to consciousness. Some people have relatively gentle or subtle kundalini awakenings that they are not even aware of.

Others - clearly the borderline masochistic ones like myself, who signed up for the *"turn the volume waaaay the fuck up"* version of the human experience - have intense, incredibly visceral and at times violent experiences of their kundalini. Having experienced it this way at times, I would say that I would gladly take the "subtle, graceful, easy version" *any day,* although I admit it unfolded exactly as it needed to for me. It all depends on where you are in your process, what your unique dharma is, what is required of you to be prepared for your soul mission and what your soul decided to experience in this incarnation.

For me, my extreme experience of kundalini rising is due to the fact that my soul decided to experience the fastest, hardest and most accelerated evolution possible as I was destined to fulfil my soul purpose relatively young in life. I simply didn't choose the gentle experience of slowly peeling back layers of healing and awakening over decades (my higher self is over here like *'ain't nobody got time for that'*), and I needed to be ready, like *yesterday*. I had a lot of 'catching up to do' in a very short time, and the experience of an intense kundalini rising was the most optimal way for my soul to do that.

I will also be the first to admit that my body was *certainly* not clear when this process began and was riddled with distortions and blockages; therefore, the kundalini had a lot of heavy lifting to do in order to burst through all the density and flow freely within me. I will add that because of the sheer volume of energy that is required in order for me to do what I do, I needed to learn *mastery* over the enormous amounts of energy which would often debilitate me.

The kundalini has a divine intelligence of her own; she *knows* what you require (even if it's not what you consciously desire). She is at times a deliverer of "tough love" and hard lessons; much like Kali Ma, she is the cosmic bitch slap you didn't even know you needed, putting you on your knees and initiating you into higher and higher expressions of love through her process of awakening in you.

As I share all of this information, please know that I don't share it with the intention of frightening anyone or discouraging their kundalini practice, but I feel it's important to share *my honest experience* so that you are adequately prepared physically, mentally, emotionally and spiritually before you decide to consciously awaken your kundalini if it hasn't already begun to rise. I daresay if you're reading this book, it's already more than active; and if not, this book is a kundalini awakening in itself, so it *sure will be* by the time you finish reading it. Which I suppose is why it is so important I am upfront and honest; it is my duty of care to be! The process is a *lot* easier if you are prepared for the can of worms you're opening - you can't put the lid back on once it's off - and have already done a lot of the foundational work of clearing distortions out of your system.

I'm aware that my experience of kundalini has been far from graceful at times, and not everyone experiences it the way I do, but perhaps sharing my full, unfiltered experience may serve someone out there who is going through these symptoms with *no idea* what is causing them. For me, finding books and websites that spoke to the experiences I'd go through of "kundalini crisis" made the experience a lot less isolating to navigate. I must add, while my kundalini awakening has been ridiculously challenging at times, it's also been the most profound, rewarding, blissful and incredible experience I have ever had. I get to experience endless streams of energy orgasms just by breathing and *existing, so while I share everything candidly,* including the 'not-so-nice' aspects, *you also won't hear me complaining about it one bit.*

I resonate with the depiction of the serpentine energy of Kundalini-Shakti in the Hindu tradition, and I adore the mythology and symbolism of this lineage, along with the understanding and explanation of the chakra system that accompanies it. I never actually studied or read any Hindu or Vedic sacred texts; I did not journey to an ashram, study under a guru, or do kundalini yoga or meditation practices, intentionally attempting to "awaken" mine. Nor did I have much interaction with the chakra system other than the occasional reference in a yoga class or on a prayer flag until my kundalini spontaneously awoke during a Kali Ma dark goddess online workshop in 2019. I had *no fucking idea* what kundalini was or what was happening to me, and it was terrifying; I suddenly found myself in a near catatonic state, speaking in tongues, drumming on an empty water barrel and sweating profusely. This set about a sequence of events over months where I spent a lot of the time in semi-catatonic states, sobbing and wailing on the floor of my parent's spare room (where I was crashing for a short stint of time before returning to Bali); reliving and purging trauma of many past lifetimes where I'd been hung, burnt at the stake or brutally murdered as a result of being a witch; bringing online with it my psychic and healing gifts. After that trial-by-fire introduction to kundalini, the process continued and intensified over years; and has been active within me ever since.

In the spirit of complete transparency, I had declared, *"Everyone keeps telling me I'm this healer, God, so fine, show me!"* just the day before this initial 'awakening' happened. I declared it rather petulantly, I might add, as I was convinced I was going to be the next Tony Robbins at the time. I was married to the idea of being a life coach, frustrated that the Universe seemed to be blocking me from succeeding at that, whilst continually running into psychics, shamans and healers everywhere who were telling me *I was a powerful healer.* (*'Are you going to get the signs, Bec? Or do we have to smack you upside the head with it?'* was what I can only imagine my guides were thinking.) While I didn't technically "ask" for it to spontaneously awaken - nor know what I was even asking *for* - the dark goddess heard me *loud and clear* and served me up the dose of humble pie I desperately needed. As the saying goes; *be careful what you wish for 'cause you just might get it.*

In hindsight, I can also see that the Dr Joe Dispenza breathwork meditations I was doing daily at the time were also directly stimulating the kundalini, contributing to this without me knowing. However, it wasn't intentional, nor was it explained in the book *what* exactly you're messing with when you're focusing on sucking all your breath up your spine as you squeeze your perineum; nor was it explained that this might bring about a *kundalini awakening* you are not all that prepared for. I adore Dr Joe, and I have no regrets in how things unfolded, but I do believe it's important to educate people around what *else* might happen if you do this powerful breathwork every day, other than miraculously healing your health issues and manifesting your best life. I can also see that the kundalini was *already* stirring in more subtle ways before she viscerally shot up my spine and sent me into a near-catatonic state that fateful day in 2019.

I do believe that even if I had *intentionally* studied or learnt about kundalini prior to my own awakening in the way it did, it would not have really landed or resonated with me anyway. I'm a three-line in Human Design - three being the "martyr" - which basically means I learn things through experimentation and direct experience. As a kid, it wasn't enough to tell me the stove was hot; I had to stick my damn hand on it and set it on fire to learn that it was hot through experience. This has echoed throughout my entire self-initiation process; virtually everything I've learnt has been through my own direct experience of it, not from a book or a mentor (although I have had several people throughout this journey offer me important pieces I was missing which have supported me greatly, and I must give credit where credit is due). My understanding of kundalini awakening and moving its way through my chakra system is the same. It was largely through personal experience before I found other resources to back up or help me understand what I was already going through or anyone who could support me. Even so, I have found the *kundalini herself* to be my mentor and teacher; far beyond what any human person has been able to.

When I finally sought out information and assistance to help me understand what the hell was happening to me, I came across the concept of Kundalini Rising in these traditional texts, and everything I was feeling and experiencing began to make sense. Everything from the snake-like motion it made as it moved through my body to the types of emotions and traumas that were coming up as the kundalini moved through specific chakras. The teachings - which I'm about to grossly simplify, so forgive me - depict that Shakti remains coiled like a snake at the base of our spine in the root (first) chakra until one is ready to begin the journey to spiritual enlightenment.

Once awakened - either spontaneously, like it did for me, or through intentional spiritual practice such as meditation or yoga - kundalini begins to move through the chakras, clearing and unblocking spiritual and emotional trauma and purifying the human vessel. Shakti (the feminine) must travel up through the chakra system to meet Shiva (the masculine) at the crown chakra to attain inner divine union, or 'enlightenment'. (From my experience, there is no magical destination of "enlightenment" that you arrive at where the process is finally "fin-ished"; just endless cycles of continued evolution and the ability to hold these heightened states for longer and longer until they become a more consistently embodied experience of your everyday waking life.)

Once the kundalini can flow uninhibited up to the crown chakra, access to the highest level of consciousness is granted; one experiences the phenomenon of merging back with the creator.

On the path there, each chakra is correlated to a different *dimension* and energetic frequency. Once your kundalini reaches and activates an energy centre, you can access the frequency and perceive the dimen-sion it is correlated to. Each chakra is linked to the one before or after it, so the lifeforce energy cannot flow up to the next chakra if there are blockages. Kundalini will flow through many cycles in one's lifetime; it can remain in one cycle between particular chakras for quite some time before returning to rest again at the root. As I write this and move through the journey of stepping into my full sovereign power as an Oracle, the kundalini inside me has been giving me some rather brutal solar plexus spring-cleaning; stirring up along with it all sorts of rage, frustration and victimhood (*good times, indeed*).

Generally, when one first experiences an awakening, the kundalini will spend a lot of time cycling through the first three chakras, purifying and dealing with blockages related to these chakras as these are the most primal and basic centres tying us to the third-dimensional human experience of separateness and survival. (This is the stuff that most "love and light" spiritual seekers tend to bypass because dealing with the painful, shadowy, human stuff isn't fun - "*I just wanna open my third eye, live in the 5D, become superhuman like the gurus told me I could, and manifest me some cool shit*". Ironically, it's the very stuff we *need* to truly address and integrate in order to fully anchor and seed ourselves here, to create Heaven on Earth.)

As your kundalini cycles through and 'unblocks' each chakra, it forces all of the distortions associated with that chakra to the surface and purifies any calcification there (blocked emotions, traumas and belief systems that need to be cleared).

The first chakra, the Root chakra, is all about basic human needs and survival. While the kundalini is moving through this chakra, you will purge away distortions that prevent you from fully "grounding" here into the human experience. You will address anything related to any time in your life (or past lives) when you felt like your basic human needs, such as safety, shelter, food or protection, were not met. Generally, while processing 'root chakra' issues, we begin to become aware of our childhood trauma and attachment styles, particularly if we were ill-treated or did not have our basic needs met as children.

The second chakra, the sacral, is all about sexuality, intimacy, fertility and creativity and addressing distortions which prevent you from being a *conscious creator*. As the kundalini activates and moves through your sacral, any creative insecurity, sexual trauma, guilt, or shame will start to surface, along with any blocks or traumas around intimacy. For women, this is also where the physical womb space is located, along with our magical gifts of the feminine, the connection to "fertility" and motherhood, and the ability to create and birth energy into form. The energetic 'womb' space is present whether you have a physical 'womb' or not (even men have an energetic womb space).

The energetic womb space holds not only our connection to our own inherent feminine gifts but also the ancestral knowledge, wisdom and trauma from the women that have gone before us: our mothers, grand-mothers and ancestors. It is usually where most past life trauma relating to the 'witch wound' is stored; which means as you begin to clear out your sacral, you will also most likely begin to clear any trau-matic memories of past lives where you were burnt at the stake, hung or tortured for sharing your gifts. As a result of clearing these traumas and having the kundalini activate this centre, your sacred feminine gifts - medicine-womanery, midwifery, psychic and healing abilities - will begin to come back online. You can also begin to experience deeper pleasure, intimacy, and waves of tingly, orgasmic energy that may build to full-blown energy orgasms if you're lucky. Once again, *I'm absolutely not complaining* about being a living, breathing, walking orgasm, and neither have any of my post-kundalini-awakening intimate partners, considering they don't even need to touch or even be in the same room as me for me to have a great time. In fact, I don't really need *anyone else,* nor do I need *any* physical stimulation in order to experience endless energetic orgasms whilst being what I affection-ately refer to as '*fucked by the divine'.* This is a whole other topic I could get into at length, as this is what it feels like to fully *merge* back with God, and this is what *tantra* is really about - but to avoid railroading you, I'll save it for another time and get back to where we were.

The third chakra, the solar plexus, is related to our personal strength, self-esteem, willpower and 'warrior' energy. As the kundalini moves through your solar plexus, you will begin to clear out distortions keeping you in 'victimhood', along with memories or traumas regarding your power being stripped from you in this life or past lives. You begin to cultivate a deep sense of empowerment and personal drive towards your journey as you anchor into 'sovereignty' and personal respon-sibility.

Once the kundalini has cycled through and cleared out enough in these chakras, it begins to make its way to the heart-space, the Rainbow Bridge, the gateway to unity consciousness. That's not to say that once you have reached your heart space and opened your heart, you're now fully ascended or "living in the 5th dimension" or that your kundalini won't return through further cycles in the lower chakras from time to time. However, once you've experienced an initial "heart opening", you may begin to have your kundalini flowing up to the realms of higher spiritual consciousness accessed through the upper chakras.

The fourth chakra, the heart space, is related to interconnectedness and our ability to connect to, understand and empathise with others. It is where we begin to break down the barriers around our heart and address the wounds that hold us in separation; betrayal, heartbreak, abandonment, and so forth. When you have spent your entire life not feeling things, the beginnings of a heart opening can be incredibly overwhelming as you are swept up in a depth of feeling you've never experienced before. You begin to feel connected to *everyone* and *every-thing*. The beauty of the world becomes sensed as a pang in the heart space; a *feeling* of warmth extending from your heart centre out, oozing like honey.

You may find yourself crying at the drop of a hat, completely incon-solable because a sentence in a book, a line in a movie or a piece of music has triggered something within your heart; overcome with both an explosion of love and overwhelming sadness simultaneously. You may find yourself laughing incessantly as you cry, unsure why you were laughing or crying in the first place; completely swept away by a wave of emotions that arose so suddenly and out of the blue. Or perhaps you may find yourself laughing and crying and orgasming, *all at the same time* (my personal specialty). Since beginning to bring down the walls surrounding my heart, there's not a single day that goes by that I don't cry - the full range from "tears of bliss and ecstasy" to "sobbing in despair as I'm feeling the pain of the world", to "ugly-crying because there was a slightly-moving advertisement for an old folks home on the TV".

As your heart opens, so do you as you begin to soften and allow yourself to become vulnerable. You begin to take down the barriers and walls that have protected your heart from being broken or from letting others close to you. You may find yourself staring at somebody you barely know and feeling this unexplainable explosion of love within your chest. You begin to realise you're feeling these feelings of love you'd reserved for the special few for everyone: friends, lovers, co-workers, family, even strangers on the street. You begin to empathise with others in a way that you've never known before; 'compassion' becomes something that you automatically practise because you feel deeply the plight of others. You begin to sense how you are connected with this person, having this experience; you feel what they are feeling, and your heart weeps for them or fills with joy for them. Soon, the distinction between 'self' and 'other' becomes incredibly blurred. You may start to perceive the oneness that connects all living beings. This can be *overwhelming* to say the least; as not only are you feeling all of your *own* emotions, you are becoming incredibly sensitive to the emotions of your friends, your co-workers, your partner, or the collective at large.

As your heart opens, you not only feel greater love, joy, ecstasy and bliss, but you also become increasingly sensitive to all of the suffering of the world. Your depths become deeper as your heights become higher, and you begin to have a greater awareness and ability to perceive polar extremes: fear and love, darkness and light, etc. When you begin to experience the intense states of bliss, ecstasy, joy, pleasure or love available to you when you fully connect via the heart space to higher dimensional states of being, the darkness and heaviness of the third-dimensional realm of contrast, pain and suffering, can feel unbearable in comparison. The pain and suffering of the world becomes like a heavy, constrictive vice that grips your chest and refuses to let go. It can feel at times like your heart is *literally* breaking, and that is because it *is* - it is breaking open, so even more love can flood through it.

It is tempting to want to go back to sleep, to hide from it all, to shut your heart off to all of the suffering of the world. It is also tempting to follow the kundalini upwards to the higher chakras and *stay there*, to remain flying in the spiritual realms instead of grounding yourself back down to the Earth. It's tempting to spiritually bypass yourself and detach; to use logic, wisdom or esoteric knowledge as a form of escapism from the pain and suffering that is being human (this might manifest as *'well, it's just their karma from a past life that is causing them to starve to death in this one, so I don't have to feel bad'*).

However, as a priestess who is here to attain *mastery* over extremes in order to alchemise, you must allow yourself to remain in the heart - *even* if the pain feels like it's too much to bear or if it feels like the amount of love that wants to move through your heart will completely obliterate your Little Human Self. **The path of the priestess (and, eventually, the Oracle) is to be able to *feel it all* without crumbling under the weight of it.** You must be the bridge between the lower chakras and the higher chakras, having one foot firmly planted on the ground and one in the heavens as you live from your heart, which is connected to all that is.

Once the kundalini has begun to crack open your heart, it can begin to flow up into the higher three chakras: the throat, the third eye and the crown. These are the centres that allow a deeper connection to the psychic realms, to your own intuition, to consciousness itself. As your kundalini begins to flow up and activate these areas, your "superhuman" abilities may start to deepen and come online. You may begin to experience sudden flashes of psychic insights, telepathy, knowing, visions, out-of-body experiences, astral travel, supercharged manifestations, activated healing abilities - just to name a few things.

As I stated before, you don't necessarily have to experience a kundalini awakening to experience any of these things. I know people who are incredibly psychic without ever having a kundalini awakening they were consciously aware of. However, kundalini unlocking and activating these areas means a rapid amplification of the gifts you may already be aware of; your psychic abilities "supercharged", so to speak. Before my kundalini began to flow up into my higher chakras, I didn't even believe I was truly intuitive (even though I kept being told *over and over again* by every healer, shaman, or psychic I came into contact with). Within the space of *weeks* of this kundalini stirring, my past-life gifts of claircognizance and clairsentience came online so dramatically it felt like I went to bed a mere mortal and woke up the next day an oracle.

It is at this stage - with the rapid acceleration and awakening of these psychic faculties or "siddhis" - that some people tend to develop a spiritual ego and believe they are the Second Coming. No, I am not exempt from this, and yes, for a hot minute there, I *did* believe I was better than everyone else for as long as it took for the dark goddess to cut off my head and bring me crashing right back down to Earth (and again, and again, and again, any time I so much as caught a whiff of claiming I was somehow a Superior or Enlightened One).

For the record, this is where the false light "Guru" template was born; people who have awakened these abilities claim they are somehow superior to others, gate-keep the information, place themselves on a pedestal, create cults, and forge co-dependent attachments with their 'followers'. It is time for us to do away with this template of "pedestalling" and "hierarchy" and move into round-table leadership and co-creation, where we embody our wisdom and invite others to rise into higher states of being, lifting them up and empowering *them* to come into their own sovereignty and power. (This is the New Earth Leadership template I'm sharing in this book, by the way. Sharing freely *everything I know*, have embodied and have access to so this wisdom can awaken in others through *their* own journey of it, rather than keeping the information to myself.)

The fifth chakra, the throat chakra, is related to our ability to communicate and speak our authentic truth. It is also where we are able to speak energy into form, bringing our manifestations into physical existence. When we connect our heart and womb with our throat chakra, we find our Siren Song; our ability to *speak things into existence*, to *create* with vibration, sound and spoken word. We also may go through a vocal activation or opening, allowing us to create certain sounds and frequencies which have magical healing or alchemical properties, also known as "toning" - something I frequently do in my music and sound activations.

The sixth chakra, the third eye, is related to our psychic gifts, telepathy, imagination and seeing through the veil into other realms. The third eye relates to all of the "clairs" - clairvoyance (seeing), claircognizance (knowing), clairsentience (feeling) and clairaudience (hearing), to name a few - but is most frequently associated with the ability to see with the 'mind's eye' (clairvoyance). Many consider the pineal gland to be the third eye, and it produces melatonin, which regulates our sleep and waking states. The pineal gland can produce and release naturally occurring DMT (Dimethyltryptamine), which creates psychedelic, altered-consciousness states.

The seventh chakra, the crown chakra, is related to connecting to higher realms and consciousness itself. Once the kundalini begins to move through your crown, you can't help but feel profoundly changed; a sense of peace, oneness and connection to everything. This is the feeling of 'enlightenment' that many seek to experience. I frequently experience the phenomenon of kundalini surging right through to (and beyond) my crown; connecting me with everything that is. There are no human words apt to describe what it feels like. (So frequently, in fact, I've had to train it to do the *opposite* because it just automatically happens whenever I sit or stand with my spine straight; which makes it quite challenging to go about your day humaning, as all you want to do when this happens is melt into the love bubble, or continue flying.) Through these profound, life-changing mystical experiences, one's outlook on life dramatically changes, much like the phenomena reported when people have NDE (near-death experiences) or journey with plant medicine.

If the kundalini is blocked from flowing upwards, it accumulates in the previous chakra, which can be *very* uncomfortable. For instance, I spent a *lot* of time during my initial 'heart opening' with an incredibly bloated stomach - often referred to as Buddha Belly - as the energy was building in my lower chakras and pushing its way into my heart space but unable to fully move through, accumulating and creating great amounts of pressure and discomfort. This is another reason why doing bodywork on yourself and having a physical movement practice is so crucial: to be able to move stagnant energy through your channels.

When kundalini is "stuck" in an energy centre in the process of purification, you may feel significant physical pain. It becomes like a hose that has a kink in it; the energy and pressure build-up but cannot be released. The times it's been stuck in my heart space, it has felt like a physical knot (also known as a heart knot, which is a very common thing to happen) pressing down on my chest.

There were many times on this journey I was genuinely unsure if it was the kundalini or if it was a physical illness; the possibility of a heart condition, lung failure or some other serious condition kept running through my mind. Facing the feeling that I was *literally* dying and the overwhelming anxiety that was coming over me as a result. I've experienced cramping in my abdomen, sharp physical pain or pressure, gas, wind, constipation, nausea, extreme fatigue, flu symptoms, feeling like I'd been hit by a bus, the feeling of a drill boring into my skull, throat aches, strange shooting sensations of heat or electricity in my body, convulsions, spasms... you name it, I've had it. All sorts of bizarre and intense physical symptoms came into my life that were simply the result of kundalini *doing her thang.*

One time, I could feel the kundalini building up around a block in my heart space for *days.* As I sat down to meditate, the kundalini spontaneously unblocked and shot its way in one intense, explosive upward surge of electricity from my base to my crown that was so forceful and sudden that it caused me to start convulsing as if I'd had a seizure, fall backwards, and hit my head hard on the floor. It was terrifying; I completely lost control of my body and found myself suddenly on the floor, forgetting where I was, dramatically shaking and utterly confused about what had just happened, worrying that I'd experienced a concussion. I've had surges of electricity through my body that were so powerful and intense I *knew* (and have been told) they could probably kill someone, render them paraplegic or completely fry their brain. I've spent many nights unable to sleep due to the sudden hot flashes, the room warping around me, or the feeling of electricity sizzling throughout my body.

As for the *emotional* and mental symptoms... Once again, I'm not trying to frighten anyone with what I'm about to share, but it's important for you to be adequately warned so you know you're not going insane. Because, frankly, it can feel a lot like you *are* during a kundalini rising. You may find yourself suddenly speaking strange languages or tongues, singing or chanting melodies you'd never heard before. You may start to make strange sounds with your mouth, like hissing, clicking or shushing. You may hear or see things that cause you to feel like you're experiencing psychosis or have the unfortunate experience of a 'spiritual emergency' where you *do* experience a brief stint of psychosis. You may feel paranoid or afraid of death or that you are dying because a part of you *is*. You may experience Ego Death, where suddenly all the constructs that you knew to be true fade around you; your identity, time, space... all of it melds, and you experience the feeling of being one with everything (which sounds great in theory, but can be quite a terrifying experience when your Little Human mind is trying desperately to grasp or hold on to 'reality', or has the sense that it will never be 'normal' again).

You *will* cry. A lot. Like... *a lot*, a lot. I have cried more during the period of my initial spiritual awakening and kundalini rising than I did in the sum total of my entire life leading up to it. You might cry without even knowing why you're crying. You might feel overcome with grief, sadness, loss, heartbreak, depression, often unable to attribute it to anything. You might find yourself huddled up in a ball in a fetal position in your bed, sobbing and wailing one moment and laughing hysterically the next. You might feel incredibly overwhelmed, confused and alienated.

This is simply a result of the kundalini purifying your vessel, bringing up all the dense energy to the surface so you have space to upgrade or to get you to a point of discomfort that is so intense that you have no choice but to surrender to the divine.

It all sounds rather intense, and you might be wondering, 'Why would I sign up for this?' but I need to remind you that if you have agreed to experience a kundalini awakening in this incarnation, it is because it is a pivotal part of your spiritual evolution process. It is a beautiful gift that guides you through your rapid "unbecoming" and purification towards your highest unfolding and becoming. As a side note, I also believe that given the acceleration of energy and the energetic momentum of this New Age, kundalini awakenings perhaps will not manifest in the same ways as they have been until now. I believe that perhaps those who will begin to go through this process will be able to go through it much more rapidly and gracefully than I did, as density is clearing *much more quickly* these days. Just as I have been able to go through it much more rapidly and gracefully than those in the 'slower' energies before me; who could take an entire lifetime devoted to their kundalini practice just to experience what I was able to within the space of mere months. That being said, a kundalini rising is not something that happens *to* you; it is something that happens *for* you, to support you to embody Inner Union by coming into communion with this energy, awakening with it your full capacity and potential as a conscious creator. To me, any challenging symptoms that one may go through are completely and totally *worth it*.

When we are an open channel, and we are in communion with this life force energy that moves through us, we awaken our "Divine DNA", which means remembering the ability coded within us to consciously co-create with *all of creation*. We direct the energy of raw creative potential (Kundalini-Shakti, the feminine) running through our channels via our own creator consciousness (Shiva, the masculine): our thoughts, our presence, our intentions and our awareness. Once we can open up these channels and allow this life force to flow freely with its own intelligence and wisdom - the intelligence and wisdom that is connected to Everyone and Everything - it brings online all sorts of other abilities that could be perceived as "Superhuman".

Essentially, we become vessels for the manifesting power of the Creator - God - moving and living and breathing *through us*. Our life-force energy (the divine feminine energy within) guides us to what it desires to create, how it wants to live and *express through us*; and we direct it with our intentions and actions (the divine masculine energy within). We step into "creator consciousness" by coming into the sacred union of the feminine and masculine energies within us and all of creation. This is what it is to be an alchemist, wielding the power of the Creator through our human vessel by entering into a Sacred Union (hieros gamos) with the Creator, awakening our abilities to miraculously heal, manifest, impact physical matter, perform miracles with our intention alone.

This is what Yeshua's teachings were really instructing people to do - to enter into holy communion with God; to become Christed by awakening the Christ (Creator) Consciousness within; and thereby entering the Kingdom(s) of Heaven.

CRYSTALLINE (CHRIST) CONSCIOUSNESS

The process of ascension is shifting on a cellular level from carbon-based to crystalline, awakening our "Crystalline DNA", which is our fifth-dimensional consciousness. This is the state of consciousness that all Ascended Masters (including Christ, the Buddha, Isis, Quan Yin, Mother Mary, Mary Magdalene, Green Tara, and so on) have achieved: the state of awakening their own divine blueprint and coming into Sacred Union with the Creator. The process of becoming crystalline - walking the path of Christ Consciousness - is a constant cycle of destruction and rebirth that is occurring for us on a cellular level to be able to hold and embody more light. As our cells are broken down and destroyed - as they receive these solar energies and the high dimensional energies hitting the planet - they move from carbon to crystalline, from density to light, to be re-created in the Creator's image. As they become closer in material to the Creator, they not only take on the qualities and gifts of the Creator, they take on the perspective of the Creator.

To me, Christ Consciousness - unity consciousness - is beautifully represented by looking at the symbolism of a diamond or crystal structure. The structure itself has *many* different surfaces through which light that passes through may be refracted by. As the light hits and moves through a different surface of the crystal, it behaves differently; it produces different flavours and *colours*, expressing as the individuated *rays* of the rainbow spectrum of consciousness. These fractals or surfaces - these 'rays' - represent *each of our individual consciousnesses* as one fractal of the Source or the One (or the crystal or diamond). Although each refraction of the light may be slightly different depending on the angle or surface of the diamond which is being hit by the light, they are all still part of the *same* crystal. That is to say, our individual experiences are *still just* the One consciousness experiencing itself through all our individual fractals; the Creator (God) knowing and experiencing itself through *us*. If that's a difficult analogy to get your head around, let's use the analogy of the bucket of ocean water and the ocean; the bucket contains *one fractal* of the ocean but is still part of the *entire* greater ocean (we are the bucket, and the ocean is the Source).

Christ Consciousness - crystalline consciousness - is understanding there is no separation between *us* and another fractal of the Creator experiencing life through it. If you zoom out, we *are all One* (and this extends *beyond* just humankind but every living being in the universe). This is moving beyond *self-service to being in service of the whole,* understanding that naturally, what benefits the Whole will benefit the Individual. You realise *everything is just a cosmic mirror, reflecting yourself right back to you.* What you do to another, you are also doing to yourself. What you condemn in another, you are also condemning in yourself. What you are seeing in another, you are simply witnessing in yourself. You would have no reason to harm or hurt another because you understand that in doing so, you are *only just hurting yourself.* You can see yourself in everyone and everything, and you can have compassion because you can put yourself in their shoes.

Therefore, it is also moving beyond polarity-based, 'right or wrong', 'black or white' ways of thinking or being. All of it is the Creator, and therefore, there is Love within all of it. The things, experiences or fractals we perceive or judge as 'bad and wrong' *cannot* be 'bad and wrong' as they are by divine design - they are *perfect*. (Who are *we* - in our limited perspective - to judge creations as right and wrong if they are serving some divine design unbeknownst to us?) We *require* the dark in order to see the light. We *require* suffering in order to experience the absence of that suffering. We *require* the emptiness to experience being filled. We *require* the experience of contrast until we recognise that we are living in an illusion, enabling us to let go of the attachment to the illusion itself, which is what is creating our suffering and keeping us experiencing "contrast" in the first place. (*Now, isn't that a trip?*)

We enter into a state of being where *everything* is perfect, whole and complete, a place of absolute present-moment awareness and acceptance of what "is" because we no longer feel the need to change anything outside of us in order to feel content. **In order to reach *this* place of eternal peace and perfection - to enter the Kingdom of Heaven within, as Christ prophesied - we must first release all our attachments, judgements, fears, preferences and our Little Human Self resistance to "what is".**

Doing so requires us to willingly face our own death - just like Jesus did in the crucifixion - over and over again so that we can resurrect just as Christ did, in our ascended form, realising that our metaphorical and literal 'death' is not the end, it is simply the beginning of a whole new cycle and iteration of our soul's journey.

INITIATION 3: CRYSTALLINE ACTIVATION & CHAKRA RE-CALIBRATION

You can access the recommended audio version of this initiation at this website: www.diamondlightoracle.com.

Welcome to the third initiation in this transmission.

The following is an activation to recalibrate and rebalance your chakra system and awaken the sacred energies within you.

In your mind and with your heart, set the intention that this is the work that will be done during our time together in this activation, and that you are open to receive all that is in your highest good.

I now invite all the beings of the highest light who wish to support this activation taking place.

I welcome your Higher Self, your Soul Family and Oversoul Network, and invite them to support you in receiving what is of the highest for you at this time.

I declare that this is sacred space; only that which is resonating on the frequency of unconditional love is welcome in this space.

I ask that everything that takes place here today is for the *highest good of all*, and in service to the Whole.

I ask that the work we do together here today ripples out and serves the collective.

And so it is, and so it is, and so it is.

We invite you to enter your Sacred Space - the safe and protected ceremony space in which you receive all calibrations, downloads, codes and activations throughout this transmission.

Acknowledging internally that *you have now entered Sacred Space.*

To begin with, ensure you have a straight spine.

You may receive this activation in either a seated or lying position as long as your spine is as straight as possible.

Ensure your hips are straight and level.

Begin by scanning over your body, setting the intention to *open* the front of your body, creating more space there.

Create space in the hips and the pelvic area, allowing the hips and the pelvic area to open.

Create space in the womb or energetic womb, allowing the womb or energetic womb to open.

Create space in the stomach, allowing the stomach to open.

Create space in the sternum, allowing the sternum and the bottom of the rib cage to open.

Create space in the lower and mid back, inviting the lower and mid-back to open; opening the spine and imagining you can create even more space in the lumbar vertebrae.

Create space in your entire spine now, imagining you can allow all the vertebrae in your spine to open.

Create space in your chest, your lungs, and the front of your rib cage; allowing your chest, lungs and rib cage to open.

Create space in your upper back and shoulders, allowing them to roll back, creating more space in your upper chest.

Create space in your neck, the front of your neck, the back of your neck and the nape of your neck where the base of your skull begins; allowing them to open.

Create space in your head, imagining you can soften your lips, your eyes, your nose, your ears; allowing them to open.

Now that your entire body is open and receptive, allow your awareness to return to the base of your spine.

Focus all of your energy to the bottoms of your feet, imagining that you can extend all of the invisible meridians that end in your feet, through your feet and deep into the Earth, like roots.

Imagine these roots going down, deep down, into the Mycelium network of the Earth, anchoring and grounding you Here and Now.

You are now connected to the Creation.

Focus all your energy and intention on the base of your spine, with the intention of opening your root chakra.

We are now sending energy into your root chakra; activating it, awakening it, and re-calibrating it.

See, sense, imagine or perceive that your root chakra is now open, and begins to spin in a clockwise direction.

Allow anything that is not required, such as any density or calcification, to be broken down by your root system and spun out of it.

As this process happens, allow the energy to be drawn down into the root system of the Earth to be recycled and serve as fertiliser for Gaia.

Repeat the following out loud -

I am safe to be in my body, and to fully seed myself here and now on this Earth.

I am safe to be in my body, and to fully seed myself here and now on this Earth.

I am safe to be in my body, and to fully seed myself here and now on this Earth.

Stay here for as long as it takes for you to feel complete.

Moving up to your sacral chakra, below your navel.

Focus all your energy and awareness on the area below your navel, with the intention of opening your sacral chakra.

We are now sending energy into your sacral chakra; activating it, awakening it, and re-calibrating it.

See, sense, imagine or perceive that your sacral chakra is now open, and begins to spin in a clockwise direction.

Allow anything that is no longer required such as any density or calcification in your sacral to be drawn down into the root system of the Earth to be recycled and serve as fertiliser for Gaia.

We are now requesting a full opening and expansion of the energetic womb space.

Repeat the following out loud:

It is safe for me to birth my sacred creations into the world.

It is safe for me to birth my sacred creations into the world.

It is safe for me to birth my sacred creations into the world.

Stay here for as long as it takes for you to feel complete.

Moving up to your solar plexus chakra, above your navel.

Focus all your energy and awareness on the area above your navel, with the intention of opening your solar plexus chakra.

We are now sending energy into your solar plexus chakra, activating it, awakening it, and re-calibrating it.

See, sense, imagine or perceive that your solar plexus chakra is now open and begins to spin in a clockwise direction.

Allow anything that is no longer required such as any density or calcification in your solar plexus to be drawn down into the root system of the Earth to be recycled and serve as fertiliser for Gaia.

We are activating your Personal Power.

We are awakening within you the radiant Sun within.

Imagine a brilliant light - as bright as the Sun - illuminating from this place which represents all of your Sacred Power.

Ra. Ra. Ra.

Repeat the following out loud:

I now declare my soul sovereignty and take full responsibility for all I am creating.

I now declare my soul sovereignty and take full responsibility for all I am creating.

I now declare my soul sovereignty and take full responsibility for all I am creating.

Stay here for as long as feels necessary.

Moving up to your heart space, in the centre of your chest.

Focus all your energy and awareness on your heart space, and create as much open space as you can in your chest.

We are now sending energy into your heart space; activating it, opening it, awakening it and re-calibrating it.

We are now opening the Rainbow Bridge within.

See, sense, or perceive a stream of rainbow-coloured energy coming into the heart space as you allow your heart space to expand, expand, expand.

Let this rainbow light and the light of your own heart begin to dissolve the borders and barriers around your heart so you can soften and open even more.

Let this rainbow light and the light of your own heart begin to dissolve any density or calcification in your heart space, which is preventing you from deeper connection to the All.

Repeat the following out loud:

I now awaken my Sacred Heart and allow it to guide me as a vessel of unconditional love.

I now awaken my Sacred Heart and allow it to guide me as a vessel of unconditional love.

I now awaken my Sacred Heart and allow it to guide me as a vessel of unconditional love.

Now and always, I choose Love.

Now and always, I choose Love.

Now and always, I choose Love.

Sit here for as long as is required for this process to feel complete.

Moving up to the throat chakra, taking your attention and focus to your throat and the back of your neck.

We are now sending energy into your throat chakra; activating it, awakening it, and re-calibrating it.

You may feel the need to yawn or move your mouth as energy here begins to clear.

You may also feel the need to make sounds.

Trust whatever feels right for you.

See, sense, imagine or perceive that your throat chakra is now open, and begins to spin in a clockwise direction.

We are activating your ability to speak the Truth.

We are re-awakening within you your Siren Song.

Stimulating within you the memory of being able to speak things into Existence.

Use your own ability to make sound - to tone, to sing, to hum, to chant, or whatever feels good to you at this time - to clear out any density or calcification in your Throat space.

Allow the vibrations emanating from your throat and the sounds you are making to clear all that no longer serves your sacred mission as a Truth Teller.

Repeat the following out loud:

I use my Voice to speak my sacred creations and visions into the world. My word is my sacred commandment. My music is Medicine.

I use my Voice to speak my sacred creations and visions into the world. My word is my sacred commandment. My music is Medicine.

I use my Voice to speak my sacred creations and visions into the world. My word is my sacred commandment. My music is Medicine.

Sit here for as long as you feel is necessary.

Moving up to the place between your eyes, in the centre of your head.

Also bringing your awareness to the place at the back of your skull.

We are now sending energy into your third-eye; opening it, activating it, awakening it, and re-calibrating it.

We are awakening and deepening within you the ability to Perceive Truth.

We are awakening and deepening within you the ability to Receive Visions.

And with it, clearing any fears around Seeing.

See, sense, imagine or perceive that your Third Eye chakra is now open and begins to spin in a clockwise direction.

Allow any calcification, any distortions, any density to be cleared out of your Third Eye now.

Allow your Third Eye now to be blessed with the frequency of Frankincense oil, smeared gently on the place between your brows.

Repeat the following aloud:

I now awaken my Sacred Sight and my ability to perceive Truth. I honour and trust my Sacred Visions.

I now awaken my Sacred Sight and my ability to perceive Truth. I honour and trust my Sacred Visions.

I now awaken my Sacred Sight and my ability to perceive Truth. I honour and trust my Sacred Visions.

Sit here for as long as it feels necessary.

Finally, moving your awareness to the top of your head, and inviting your Crown chakra to open.

We are now sending energy into your crown; opening it, activating it, awakening it, and re-calibrating it.

You are now connected to the Creator.

See, sense, imagine or perceive that your Crown chakra is now open, and begins to spin in a clockwise direction.

Imagine, see, or perceive a bright stream of diamond light coming from above - so far above that you cannot see where it begins.

Allow this light to stream down into your open crown, clearing your crown of any distortions, any blockages and any frequencies which are not for your Highest good at this time.

Declare the following aloud:

I am All Knowing Presence, the Witness of my Sacred Creations. As above, so below.

I am All Knowing Presence, the Witness of my Sacred Creations. As above, so below.

I am All Knowing Presence, the Witness of my Sacred Creations. As above, so below.

Allow this light to stream past your crown, into your central column and spine, making its way down your chakra system into every open chakra.

Allow it to stream down into your Third Eye - clearing, recalibrating.

Allow it to stream down into your Throat - clearing, recalibrating.

Allow it to stream down into your Heart space - clearing, recalibrating.

Allow it to stream down into your Solar Plexus - clearing, recalibrating.

Allow it to stream down into your Sacral - clearing, recalibrating.

Allow it to stream down into your Root - clearing, recalibrating.

Allow this light now to stream down through the bottoms of your feet and into the roots you have created deep down into the Earth, nourishing the Earth.

And as you reach the roots, you begin to feel the energy stream which is simultaneously moving *upwards* from the Earth.

The Life Force energy; the Creative Force; the Serpentine Energy.

We are now inviting the Sacred Feminine within - your kundalini - to begin to rise up, through your central column and your chakras.

Allow Her to rise up through your root and the base of your spine.

Allow Her to rise up through your sacral and your hips.

Allow Her to rise up through your solar plexus.

Allow Her to rise up into the heart.

Allow Her to rise up into the throat.

Allow Her to rise up into the third eye.

Allow Her to rise up into and beyond the crown, where she meets that downward stream of energy.

Observe these two streams of energy dancing above your crown.

Sit here for as long as feels good for you before bringing your awareness down to where they meet in your heart space.

See, sense, perceive or notice that in the centre of your chest, you are creating a figure-8 movement of energy - an infinity symbol - with these two dancing energy streams, one descending from above and one ascending from below.

Observe this infinite figure 8 motion created inside of you - giving, receiving, giving, receiving.

Awakening the divine give and receive cycle within.

As this motion continues, it is creating a larger magnetic toroidal field around your body.

Push this energetic field out as far as it can go.

Expand. Expand. Expand. Expand.

Now activating the Crystalline Frequency within.

Declare the following out loud:

I now begin the process of activating my Crystalline Consciousness and my Diamond Light Body

I now begin the process of activating my Crystalline Consciousness and my Diamond Light Body

I now begin the process of activating my Crystalline Consciousness and my Diamond Light Body

It is done. It is done. It is done.

In the space between this activation and the next, your field will begin to enter and form a chrysalis, which will hold you in the process of breaking down all that is no longer required for you to evolve into your Highest Form.

Our work here today is complete.

You may wish to sit here in this heightened energy, sending intention towards your creations or receiving downloads or guidance.

When you feel complete, set the intention to close down each of your chakras and energy channels, with the intention that anything further which is required to happen as a result of this activation will now take place in your Sacred Space and your own personal grid.

Closing down your crown chakra and sealing it now.

Closing down your third eye chakra and sealing it now.

Closing down your throat chakra and sealing it now.

Closing down your heart chakra and sealing it now.

Closing down your solar plexus chakra and sealing it now.

Closing down your sacral chakra and sealing it now.

Closing down your root chakra and sealing it now.

Integrating and calibrating this now on the physical level.

Integrating and calibrating this now on the emotional level.

Integrating and calibrating this now on the mental level.

Integrating and calibrating this now through all levels and dimensions of your light body.

Integrating, calibrating and sharing this frequency now through all timelines and all versions of yourself across the multiverse.

We now shut down any and all open portals and gateways that are no longer required and send back all energy that has come through any portals or gateways in the process of this work.

We now dissolve any bonds, chords or attachments that have been formed for the process of this activation and call you back into complete Soul Sovereignty.

We return all of your energy to you now as you call your Soul fully into your body.

We invite in Diamond Light to cleanse and close this space, bringing this sacred activation to a close and thanking all of the beings who have been here supporting in this process.

It is done, it is done, it is done, and so it is.

You may spend some time here in silent reflection, or receiving in your Sacred Space if it feels necessary.

If you feel complete, we invite you to gently bring yourself back into your body and into the room, wiggling your fingers and toes and opening your eyes when you are ready.

PART FOUR

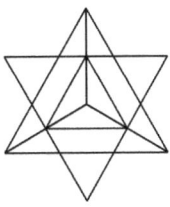

NOTHING

THE RESISTANCE

I'm sitting in the car, stuck in traffic driving home from my sister's place, when it hits me again: the Resistance. It's been about a week since I've written anything substantial, and the last decent writing session, I couldn't write fast enough due to the rate of the downloads that were streaming in thick and fast; life-changing material and codes around death, destruction and rebirth; about being willing to face our own destruction as a humanity, in order to change form.

Since then, every time I've sat down to write, I'm met with radio *silence* - zip, zilch, nada. Staring down that patronising blinking cursor taunting me on a Google Doc so blank that there's not even tumble-weed in sight.

For the past week, I've been in complete avoidance of writing - busying myself with other projects and telling myself I don't have time to write, yet finding every spare moment I have procrastinating with time-wasting activities like watching trash TV or over-exercising - or wiped out in bed, seeing God and moving enormous amounts of energy through my body.

Every time I've even *thought* about writing, I've either felt like being violently ill and therefore not even tried, or I've subconsciously (yet on some level, intentionally) loaded myself up with too much caffeine prior to writing, so I'm so activated and jittery I can't actually string coherent sentences together between the rave that's taken over my brain. I'd sit in front of the screen for about five seconds, watching the words I'd already written before begin to warp as I read the same sentence over and over again before getting frustrated, throwing the towel in and crawling back into bed for the day, deciding *"nope, clearly it's not a writing day today, I'm meant to be resting, so I'm gonna do just that"*. (Although, in my defence, I also think that is partially true as I have been integrating a lot since the last round of downloads and do need a lot of rest.)

As I'm drumming my fingers in agitation on the steering wheel, the frustration and anger I've been feeling since I woke up are welling up inside of me, threatening to explode in a fiery rage like the volcano I am - knowing my job and focus right now is to write, but witnessing and observing myself go into complete avoidance, nervous system shutdown mode instead.

And then perpetuating the vicious cycle because I'm not taking the 'aligned action' I know I need to be taking to move forward with my mission, and getting even more frustrated at God, my guides and mySELF for not telling me what else I need to be focusing on or "doing" in order to change my external circumstances.

(No shit, Sherlock... uhhh maybe it's because you're meant to write?)

As the distorted electric guitar melody in Chris Isaak's *Wicked Games* starts to gently work its way into the mix I'm listening to, I can feel it beginning to melt its way through the wall of anger and frustration I've been hiding behind and blaming for my inability to write for the past week... and finally, the tears I've been waiting for all morning begin to flow.

And I recognise it: The Resistance.

Suddenly, I realise this sensation that's been creeping up inside of me every time I've even *thought* about sitting down to write for the past week - it's not writer's block, it's not frustration, nor is it anger...*it's fear*.

A part of me (the same part of me that put me into a three-month-long-ego death-self-induced-coma and blocked any of the downloads from coming in to begin with when I was told I was to channel this book) is *so fucking afraid* that it's rail-roading any attempt at moving forward with this manuscript the moment I start to channel anything even moderately substantial...

That same feeling that's been coming up every time I even *think* about sitting down to write; that old familiar feeling of being punched in the gut; a thousand butterflies simultaneously projectile vomiting in my stomach; feeling like I need to stick my head out of the car window because I'm about to expel the last meal I ate violently all over the road and perhaps the side of my mum's Tesla (*take that, Elon Musk*)...

The Resistance.

Fear of what would happen if I was to *actually* sit down and write.

Oh, that beautiful witch wound inside of me, being fueled by Chiron and Pluto dancing in the sky right now, triggered by the act of writing this book...

Hello, old friend, it's nice to see you again.

As I sit with this feeling and let the tears stream down my face in peak hour traffic, avoiding making eye contact with the Tradie banked up in the Ute next to me as I casually (just casually) have an ego death and an epiphany all at once while sitting behind the wheel of the car, waiting on the lights to change (honestly, I don't know what it is about Wicked Games and that damn guitar that always gets me in my Pisces-feels every time) - I'm noticing the words starting to flow to me...

You're meant to write about the resistance you're feeling, Bec.

Uhhh... *Duh.*

And as I recognise and witness my internal Resistance - the layers of frustration and anger and sacred rage starting to dissolve from deep in my solar plexus and my womb space - and start to ask it why it's here, what I'm so afraid of; the words and ideas for this chapter are coming to my mind so fast I can't stop them.

I get my voice recorder out and start to dictate everything that is flowing through me. Suddenly, the writer's block seems like a distant memory as I find all these clever ways to give it a voice and speak into the Resistance inside of me, and the more I speak into it, the more I feel the words melting the density in my body (and perhaps yours, as you are reading this).

And I find myself in this bizarre situation where writing about the resistance to writing this book, is ironically getting me writing this book again. *Oh humans are funny little creatures.*

Remembering that the guidance told me I'd be feeling this way and that the process of channelling and writing this book was going to cause me to go through a death and rebirth process in *real-time*. That it was going to *"forever change me and those who read it"*, as my mentor shared as she witnessed this project being birthed by me and felt into its significance not only for myself but for the collective - and that I needed to *document the process.*

(Perhaps you are going through the same process as you read these words, and I'm here to give this feeling of vulnerability a voice and allow it to be seen and witnessed - *hello, I see you.*)

As I sit there documenting the words I am to write as they come out of my mouth and into the voice recorder app on my phone, I feel the guidance showing me that this is the cycle I will go through:

Channel the codes as I write.

Go through the ego death as the codes integrate.

Recognise the resistance.

Witness the resistance and the part of me that is dying.

Hold her in tenderness, love and compassion as I acknowledge her fear.

Rebirth as the version of myself who moves through the resistance with love and shows up for my mission despite the fear.

New codes and downloads come through, as I am now ready to receive them.

These new codes and downloads seem to be a more 'advanced' understanding, a deeper layer of activation than I was ready for previously.

Well, given the obvious cycle I've already repeated twice now since receiving the initial download to start this project, I'm willing to bet tomorrow is going to be the most productive writing day, and I can't wait to see what magic comes through...

And so, as I move through my own internal resistance and speak into it, I feel to share this so that you, beautiful soul, can take solace in it - no matter how far or deep you are into your own journey of unfolding and evolution. You will undoubtedly feel all sorts of things as you read these words, and they stimulate another layer of awakening within you - hell, you'll feel all sorts of things regardless of this book, through the simple process of journeying through Life.

You will meet all different forms of your Little Human Self in resistance - anger, frustration, sadness, grief, resentment, anxiety, fear - when you stand at the edge of your Next Evolution.

And that is okay.

You are *allowed* to experience difficult emotions and get swept up or lost in them from time to time, forgetting that you are an eternal soul, not just this human having this experience, that if you only zoomed out, you'd realise that the emotion itself is just an opportunity to return to the unconditional love that you *are*.

Because while you go on this journey in this (beautiful) form you decided to take, you are also incredibly fucking human.

You are taking your human (with all its emotions, and energetic imbalances, and preferences, and judgements, and beliefs, and fears) along for the ride with you.

So allow yourself to get lost in your humanness from time to time; to momentarily forget you're an all-loving Soul who signed up for the wild ride, who will be *just fine* no matter what happens. Feel the irrational fear you're feeling for no apparent reason whatsoever. Have a tantrum, stamp your feet, and shout at your spirit guides that they're *utterly useless* and that God has abandoned you in your time of need (believe me, I have).

Hurl axes at a wall, pluck out each of the hairs on your leg individually or punch a leather boxing bag until your knuckles bleed *if it makes you feel better* (although I certainly don't recommend taking your rage out on other living beings unless you wanna create a whole lot of karmic ripples for some alternate version of You to deal with).

Don't bypass yourself or your Little Self emotions, trying to be "above them" or thinking "If only I were more spiritually evolved, I wouldn't feel this way", because the emotion is already present, and *damn that part of you feeling that emotion took some courage to allow itself to be heard.*

Have compassion, allow the feelings to arise, and move them through you in whatever way you need to in order to enable that energy to be transmuted.

Feel and witness your feelings, but don't feel and witness them blindly.

Ask them what they're showing you, where they're coming from, and recognise what part of you is requiring something from you in order to feel safe in the moment (and is simply lashing out in an ego tantrum because you're ignoring it's "UNKNOWN THREAT" alarm, and launching yourself towards the thing that it *really doesn't want to do* because it equates to unsafety, and eventually its own demise).

Have the self-awareness to recognise where that Little Self is taking the wheel - where that fear of moving forward is creating resistance and preventing you from taking action.

Because once we have awareness, then we can gently steer that internal resistance, that fear, and that Little-Self-lashing-out-inside-us, back home to Love.

Go through what you need to go through and allow those emotions – the rage, the anger, the frustration, the grief, the sadness – to be the fuel that stokes the flames which bring about your own rebirth from the ashes of who you once were.

Just don't allow yourself to stagnate or go unconscious for too long, 'cause there's a whole other version of You awaiting...

Just on the other side of the Resistance.

THE MAYAN CONNECTION

It had been weeks since I had visited Ek Balam, and while there had been *some* bizarre and mystical things happening (like that light language I was making with my hands now becoming a spontaneous and constant thing that my hands would just randomly start doing, along with a vocal accompaniment in the form of a language I would later find out was Ancient Mayan), there wasn't any more clarity or insight into what my next step was in regards to the "sacred mission", or what it all meant.

I still was pretty in the dark about just how much of the Mayan grid-work mission was yet to unfold or the big cosmic reason why I was even in Mexico in the first place, other than the guidance saying I needed to be and for the upcoming conference.

In fact, at that point in time, I was planning on only spending a month or two in Mexico, then travelling onwards due to visa complications - thanks to transiting through the US on an ESTA, which automatically shortened my stay in Mexico on a silly bureaucratic technicality - before I returned months later to Mexico for the conference, and for my flight home.

I guess it shows how truly clueless and worked up our Little Selves can sometimes be over nothing, as I spent *considerable amounts of time* anxiously worrying about (and googling) the logistics of my travel, the visa run, where I needed to be for it, possible loopholes so I could get away with not doing a visa run at all, and being afraid of potentially having to go to Guatemala, which was the first place that pinged, where I had no desire to go as a solo female traveller.

(In the end, it would turn out I *would* have to go to Guatemala within the three month window anyway, and not even because of a "visa run" - it just happened to serve that convenient double purpose - so really, the issue was a non-issue and I was wasting my energy worrying for nothing.)

I was pouring all of my energy into planning events in the future with soul family in the States, as I had received downloads prior to leaving for Mexico that I'd soon be invited to co-create in-person events and conferences over there that would cause a big break for me in my career; which I can now see was my guides "dangling the carrot" for me, so I would go over that side of the world and continue my sacred mission. (For the record, I still see these potentials in my very near future; I just didn't realise that *this book* and all the initiations that came with it would come first.) I saw these first two months in Mexico as a kind of "holiday" or "bridge phase", so I'd be conveniently brought to that part of the world, where I'd maybe visit some pyramids and enjoy myself, before the "main event" which was the events I'd be doing in the States. I had *no* idea what was really about to unfold, how important my trip to Mexico actually was, or how it would ripple out and change not only *my* life, but many others.

Outside of constantly being on Zoom calls with new soul connections and friends I was making in the States, I was very much "in the void", feeling the intensity of the Tulum portal amplifying the codes that were dropping in, causing me to purge a *lot*. Being new to the area, I'd spend most days alone; migrating from my room to the gym, to the ice-bath, to poolside, to my favourite (ridiculously overpriced) cacao spot; day after day, without any exciting developments seeming to happen in my life in Mexico, or the sacred mission I was on out there. (Well, my bike chain *did* try to kill me once cycling the long mission down to the beach to meet a friend who was living in Tulum with her baby... but life was otherwise pretty uneventful.)

Little did I know, everything *was* being orchestrated for me behind the scenes, even if I couldn't see the way forward from my limited, present-moment perspective.

Looking back with the benefit of hindsight, I can see *all the pieces* were already starting to come together, some from even *before* the moment I actually landed in Mexico.

For instance, I landed in Mexico on the 4/8, and I had already set the wheels in motion for the larger sacred mystery mission a few days after arriving, during the 8/8 Lions Gate portal activation ceremony, I was guided to host online. I would later come to understand that *that* particular Lions Gate ceremony ("Lioness" was what I had called the event) called together the priestesses that would form the circle that supported the larger gridwork mission that would unfold in the coming months in Mexico and Guatemala.

And *during that ceremony,* we opened the portal for the entire gridwork mission and set the sequence of events into motion, unofficially "starting" the work, as it was only four days later that I visited the first site; Ek Balam.

I had also *already* been connected with the karmic soulmate I would then later go on to have a romantic relationship with - who I'd receive huge Mayan warrior codes and deep ancestral and past life healing with, who also would provide a vital connection for the next pyramid pilgrimage - within days of arriving in Mexico, via a Whatsapp group chat, I just hadn't met him in person yet. *(Yes, if you're following the story closely, the love I was told was waiting for me in Mexico.)*

Many seeds were already planted and beginning to slowly germinate, but being human, I was impatient and wondering *what's next?* I was frustrated, in resistance to *any* guidance and dealing with a lot of deep cellular shadow that was coming up to be purged.

My channel felt blocked, my guidance system felt blocked, my creativity felt blocked, and my business and finances certainly felt blocked. I was wondering *wtf* I was doing in Mexico at all when I could have been doing the same old stuff back "home" in Australia, where I'd finally started to enjoy being (something, I will add, that took me nearly three decades to accomplish).

I felt like I was simultaneously shut off from my inner guidance/channel and couldn't see the way forward while being overloaded with enormous amounts of energy that would wipe me out physically and render me in a psychedelic state; feeling the room warp all around me, unable to sleep at night, as I battled both metaphorical and *literal* demons inside of me.

Of course, looking back, I can see exactly what was happening to me in that time is what happens *any* time I'm in the process of channelling a new codex; the *initiation*, bringing up my resistance as I go through the death and rebirth process of *becoming* the woman who embodies the codex; integrating and creating space for the information to be received and understood.

It wasn't until I had a call with a priestess sister of mine to feel into what was going on with my business that was preventing sales from coming in that I realised the reason why I was feeling the way I was - I was going through a *huge* activation and integration process that started when I visited Ek Balam, weeks earlier.

I watched her try to describe the huge stream of codes that were coming into my crown and what they were doing to my field, and become overwhelmed by the energy of it. She is a very skilled and advanced priestess, so it was quite shocking (and equally validating, as no wonder I'd been wiped out for *weeks*) to watch her reaction to it.

I remember her just continually saying, "Wow, this is huge," as she tried to explain what was going on in my field, and then going on to share a few vague pieces that didn't land at the time that I was here to bring forth Mayan prophecy.

On the call, she also described my future lover to me by asking, "Have you recently met a man? There's a member of your soul family on the land where you are," and then describing his age range, his general vibe, and the mountains that surrounded his hometown. (Technically, I had met him; however, it was through a phone screen, so it didn't register for me at the time.) Not so important to the significance of what she shared about my mission, just highlighting her freakish accuracy as a channeller. I soon after met the soulmate she spoke of - whose family came from the mountains - and this book contains Mayan prophecy, does it not?

Until it was *seen* and *validated* by another gifted channeller I trusted, I didn't allow myself to fully grasp the enormousness of the work I was doing with those pyramids and how much energy I had actually processed and assimilated. On some level, I knew it was big, and my team had told me I had a strong connection to Ancient Maya... but it wasn't until this particular call that I realised and accepted I was a *custodian* of a part of the codex for this lineage.

It felt very "entitled-white-spiritual-woman" disrespectful of me to claim that I was the custodian of ancient wisdom that was not from my bloodline or heritage. (According to a DNA test my older sister did, we're 98% Greek, which is about as Greek as you can get; spare my father, who is apparently 100%.) This is why I shied away from admitting to myself what part of me already knew inside that first moment I touched Mexican soil in 2022. Terrified of being accused of cultural appropriation and cancelled, I just kept my Mayan connection to myself. (I already had the unpleasant experience of being accused of "cultural appropriation" once before, thanks to a photo of me holding a shamanic drum posted in a large online community group early on in my spiritual awakening... but I'll spare you the perspective of how my ancient soul has been around for far longer than some of the lineages I was blamed for "stealing it" from, and disrespecting.)

In fact, it took THREE separate priestesses that I trusted declaring that I was in some way a custodian of the Ancient Mayan grid AND a light-language expert confirming I was actually speaking Ancient Mayan (it's very rare, apparently, and she was very excited about the sample I provided for her library) to really be able to even claim this part of my mission, let alone write about it in a published book. Hence, all of the waffling about the "resistance" that would come up every time I'm asked to accept and claim a deeper layer of the codex I'm here to bring through. Three people (four counting the light-language expert) had to confirm it for me to finally accept that I wasn't just "making it up"; the first priestess who saw me sharing Mayan prophecy, the woman who would serve as my "Map Reader" for the Mayan mission (you'll be introduced to her soon), and the mentor/book doula who is supporting me in the process of birthing this book.

If you have ever experienced me talking about opening your channel and developing your intuition, you'll probably hear me say that we can't give our power away to others by relying too heavily on their guidance rather than accessing our own (I had to learn this uncomfortable lesson in the past by giving my power away to a teacher and *paying the price*, even if it was a super important initiation for me; hence why I am so discerning these days of who I allow to access my field or take on guidance from). However, there's a caveat here, in that sometimes we *require* ourselves and the fullness and bigness of our mission to be seen and witnessed because we're unable to accept it when we're told by our own guidance team. We think we're just being arrogant; or it's too big for us to do alone; or it's too good to be true; or, *"Oh, not me, surely not?"*; or *"I'm just making this up"* - and so we disregard it. (Some of us - *yours truly* - have had our heads cut off so many times by Kali Ma that we wouldn't *dare* claim something that made us seem big for our boots out of fear of being humbled again.)

<u>As Oracles here to leave our mark on and change the world for the good; to birth cutting-edge healing modalities and life-changing bodies of work, to write books and create art that activates an awakening and remembering in others; to channel warnings, prophecy and messages of hope - we need *another* to be able to reflect back the hugeness of our mission and *witness us in it*, for it to become real.</u> This enables us to make the transition point of stepping into and claiming our role as Oracle.

This is, essentially, what I do for others; I can see and put to words *exactly* what it is you're here to birth into the world and speak it into being; but I'd struggled to have someone do this for me, and felt too shy to speak the vision out loud that my guides have been preparing me for since the very beginning of this journey. This is what my mentor has been doing for me in the process of channelling this book: seeing the significance of this book, the impact it will make (even on the people who will *not* agree with it) and the process it is putting me through as I am birthing it.

This is what my Map Reader had been doing while I was travelling from sacred site to sacred site in Mexico and Guatemala; seeing the large network of Mayan sites, how they were connected, and how they were all lighting up again due to the work I was doing. This is what the priestess had done for me in this psychic business session; seeing what I was receiving energetically and how monumental it actually was. Having my downloads confirmed by others (that had not been primed with *any* information prior) around how big the mission I was here to fulfil certainly made it easier for me to accept it myself. Not to mention, it put my mind at ease that I wasn't developing a Messiah Complex, a spiritual ego, or that the kundalini had gotten to my head.

However, accepting the sacred calling of your Destiny Timeline and allowing for it to unfold without trying to *control it* or exert your will or timeline onto it... is another thing entirely.

After receiving the confirmation on the call that I was actually just integrating a motherload of downloads and codes, I allowed myself to soften and finally surrender; it was my permission slip to just *be*, because I was exactly where I needed to be. I allowed myself to be in trusting free-fall for a few days, perhaps a week, before I hit my next road bump.

I had been scheduled for an interview on another woman's show, and I had mentioned on the call that I was out in Mexico working with the Mayan ancestors and receiving a lot of information. As a natural curiosity, the woman interviewing me asked me what messages the Mayans had, and if I could share some of the downloads coming through. And that's when it happened; my *worst fear* as a channeller, realised.

I had always dreaded the moment that one day - on an interview, or during a live show, or a workshop, or some other place where I was asked a question and couldn't just stay silent and wait for the answer to drop in - I would open my channel up to receive guidance or share a message, and *nothing would come.*

No Earth-shattering messages of wisdom or guidance to share.

Complete and utter radio silence that would lead me to believe that in my time of need, God had abandoned me. *Oh, what a fucking fraud I would appear to be!*

And there it was, happening in real time, as I closed my eyes on the call, frantically searching my channel for any sign of life coming from the Mayan ancestors or my Mayan self. Being met with zero. Nothing. *Nada.* Suddenly finding myself in the awkward situation of facing my greatest fear; having to look like an utter *moron* on this woman's show; explaining that actually, at this point, nothing was coming through as it seemed the downloads were integrating still.

It was the truth, but one that I wasn't willing to accept because it wasn't convenient for my Little Human Self, who wanted to look like a gifted channeller on this woman's show, sharing all of this Mayan wisdom that nobody else was sharing.

"Oh, what a shame that is!" she had said, and then moved on to another topic while I was left to deal with the sinking feeling that was consuming my focus, finding it hard to process any of the other questions she was asking me.

Soon after, we ended the call, and I was left to process all that had happened. I had a huge emotional release, getting angry at God for "abandoning me" in my moment of need - one of my core soul wounds I've seen resurfacing time and time again - before praying and asking to be shown *why* this had happened.

After taking myself through one of the sacred activations I had recorded for my Soul Mission Accelerator around inner trust and knowing, I had a *huge* realisation that this had to happen so I could learn to *trust* my channel, trust the guidance, trust the timing, and trust that when the information was meant to come through, it *would*.

After releasing the expectation of needing to "know" what all of these codes I was receiving were - within the space of an hour or so - I experienced a gigantic unblocking, and suddenly, *all of the downloads* dropped in. Everything that I had been processing and integrating over weeks crystallised and started to make sense. I sat with it as my mind was blown and documented what I could before contacting the woman and explaining what had happened, asking if she would be keen to re-record that bit as now I had some messages to share. This time, when we connected, and I called in the Mayan ancestors, I *immediately* felt the connection. I had an awareness in that moment that there was a version of *myself* from another life - a dark-skinned, heavily tattooed Mayan man who was built like a warrior - channelling through me. After I shared the messages I needed to share, the interviewer (who was also a channeller) told me she had seen the same Mayan man I had step into me and speak through me.

After this experience, I learnt a *lot* about the mission that I was on, and just how important it was to *get out of my own way* in order to be a clear channel for what wanted to come through me. That actually, it absolutely was *not* about me and my ego (nor my dignity apparently) and when *I* thought it was the best time for things to happen.

There are a few teachable moments here, actually...

One is that in order to be a completely clear channel, we *can't force* or control when or how the messages come. *Allow me to repeat that.* **In order to be a clear channel, we cannot force or control when or how the messages come.** They come in *divine timing*, and sometimes being shown *just how much we're worried about looking like an idiot on a podcast interview* is exactly what is required for us to clear the resistance that is getting in the way of us being a clear enough channel to deliver the messages. So the messages *not* coming in for me at that moment was actually *divine timing*; the medicine I needed to be able to receive and transmit clearly, without making them about "me".

Another lesson is that if *any part of us* is fearing judgement - a.k.a. worried that we will come across like we're a crazy person or a fraud to others - or persecution - a.k.a. getting called out, cancelled, or challenged for the messages we are sharing - we will block the messages that are coming through, to keep ourselves safe out of subconscious self-preservation. Once again, I repeat: **if we are fearing judgement or trying to control the outcome of how people will receive the messages that want to come through us, we will subconsciously block them, and therefore, we are not a clear channel.** Many times, this links to the witch wound (a traumatic stain on our soul that is the result of persecution through many, many lifetimes where we showed up to share prophecy and were burnt at the stake, hung, excommunicated, ridiculed, and so many other brutalities), but often, it is also linked to our inner child who fears rejection and desperately desires to be loved and accepted.

As part of my initiation, I went through many experiences prior to this one and would go through many more following this one, where I was forced to question myself, question my faith, question my beliefs, and question whether I truly was just *"making it all up"*. These experiences would almost always only occur as a precursor (or sometimes, a symptom) of being asked to step beyond the realm of my comfort into a higher level of my gifts or of my sacred mission. Every time I was on the cusp of channelling some *far out* things that pushed me - or others - out of the comfort zone, I would go through a pretty rough period of my faith being tested beforehand. And every time I was being prepared to reach even more people with the messages that wanted to flow through me, I would be tested to make sure I could stand behind these messages without faltering, bending, or changing my mind because of a desire to be liked or accepted.

These experiences were forcing me to solidify and address any lapses in my faith, my trust in my channel, and my trust in the divine so that *no judgement or opinion* from outside of myself could take away from my conviction, my connection with God, or my own *gnosis*. Most of these experiences saw me feeling *completely disconnected* from the guidance, from the magic, from the connection I have to God, which I sometimes take for granted. In this absence, I would explore other paths and look down the barrel of a life *without* this connection - a life where I walked away from it all - to enable me to once again consciously choose it. It was only through finding my way through the darkness of feeling *separate and disconnected* - feeling that God, my guides, my higher self had abandoned me - that I was able to find my way back to my faith again. These crises of faith showed me that I *couldn't* actually do any of this on my own - separate and alone - and they taught me that I am *not supposed to* (nor are *any* of us).

Believe it or not, going through many crises of faith where you are led to question *everything you believe*, question your sanity, and wonder if you're just batshit crazy or "making it all up" are actually very important initiations and rites of passage for priestesses, channellers and oracles. They fortify your channel, they fortify your trust in your inner-knowing, they fortify your connection to the divine, and they strengthen you *beyond belief* so you can withstand *whatever* may happen to you as a result of fulfilling your Sacred Mission.

THE FINE LINE BETWEEN PSYCHIC & PSYCHOTIC

Multiple times today, I have had a song play in my head only seconds before it starts playing in the room I'm entering or on my device. Really random songs too - I'm not talking about top forty hits. In the moments after the song starts *actually* playing, I'm too tripped out to notice before back-tracking and realising, *"Wait a second, this was just in my head, and now it's not?"* wondering if I just disassociated, momentarily left my body and am just experiencing some weird sort of deja vu phenomena, or I really *am* just that psychic.

Wondering, *"Is this what it feels like to be crazy and think the TV is talking to me?"*

(I mean, sometimes God *is* talking to me through the TV and giving me the exact message I need to hear... but, you know...)

Life can be *really* psychedelic, and being this intuitive or tapped into that psychedelic nature can feel quite destabilising when you're just absentmindedly "humaning" and then suddenly feel like all the mushrooms kicked in all at once.

Is that tree waving at me?!

Suffice it to say, seriously questioning my sanity is an everyday staple of my existence; no matter how tapped in, tuned in, or connected I feel the majority of the time.

No matter how many times I'm actually thoroughly enjoying the psychedelic trip; the magical way that everything seems to be *speaking* to me, giving me signs, pointing me in the right direction; that the whole world and everyone I encounter is a benevolent Creator giving me a big, cheeky wink, as it leads me to miracles, magic and outcomes way better than I could ever dream up myself.

No matter how many times in my life my faith has manifested itself in some real, tangible, external "proof", I still question my sanity and worry that perhaps I'm just delusional and in dire need of checking myself into a mental institution...

Wondering if all the "downloads" I'm receiving on a daily basis are really just the product of a mental break, that the moments where I'm feeling God in some tangible way and having these "mystical experiences," some people search their whole lives for, are actually just a case of imbalanced mental chemistry.

Would a crazy person be wondering if they are crazy?

Would they be aware of themselves enough to realise that everything they were experiencing around them was simply a delusion, a fabrication?

From my postgraduate studies in psychology, I gleaned that perhaps that would not be the case. Someone delusional would probably not question whether they were delusional or not; their delusion would *become* their reality.

So, am I crazy? Are you - for reading this book? Are we all just sharing the same delusion? Does admitting that from time to time, I question my sanity undermine the legitimacy of what I channel?

I don't know the answer to those questions, but I could sit for days creating a reasonable argument comprising every single time something I channelled checked out; or I followed my intuition and it paid off; or where someone else tuned into the same cosmic radio station came forth with the exact same message I'd kept to myself, and told nobody.

And yet, frequently, I ask myself, am I psychic... or am I psychotic?

It seems it's a *very* fine line.

I can't help thinking about what would have happened if I was born somewhere else in the world, where this sort of thing was considered 'normal' - where there was a strong connection to, and understanding of, the Spirit world.

Where there were medicine men and women, shamans, or masters to take me under their wing at the start of this journey when I started exhibiting some of the symptoms (that looked a *lot* like a mental break-down, by the way).

Would I have to go through this mental battle all the time, wondering if I was just nuts?

Would this path have been a whole hell of a lot easier for me?

I guess I didn't need any of that, and I chose the parents I did for a reason; parents who I daresay are *exceptionally* supportive and under-standing, considering how challenging it would no doubt be to experi-ence the emotional rollercoaster of having *me* as a daughter. (I guess they chose me on a soul level, too - for that very reason.)

Yet, I still wonder what life would be like if I wasn't self-initiated (which I suppose is actually a direct-line initiation from the Great Spirit)...

I wonder what this journey would be like, had I been born somewhere where the gifts that I came into this world to share were acknowl-edged, encouraged, and catered for, along with the unique struggles that come with them.

Instead of being slapped with a diagnosis of Bipolar Type II at sixteen, which I fought tooth and nail; refusing to take any sort of medication until the age of 24, when I finally caved and took the SSRIs they prescribed me because I was suffering from intense suicidal thoughts daily. Only to stop them merely a year later because all they did was make me *numb*, and my inner guidance told me I actually *had* to feel my emotions if I was ever going to heal.

I wonder what our society would be like if we actually *encouraged* and advocated for people with these unique gifts - we understood them, we nurtured them, and we supported them... instead of just slapping a "mental health" diagnosis on everyone and leaving them to the mercy of the system. (For the record - I am aware that there *are* people with severe and crippling mental health conditions that *are* caused by an imbalance of chemicals or hereditary conditions. At the same time, I believe that with a better system - one that acknowledges the spiritual element of these conditions - they would have a much better chance at some semblance of a functional life. I also must add that despite what a clinical diagnosis might say, we possess miraculous abilities to heal and right *all imbalances*, given the right conditions and support.)

In most Indigenous tribes, the Shaman or Medicine Man/Woman singles out and takes under their wing those that are exhibiting these "psychotic" traits because they have an awareness that either they are being plagued by some sort of imbalance that more than likely has a spiritual solution, or the alternative - *perhaps this person is being initiated to become the next Shaman of the tribe.* They are taken away from the tribe and trained, given the adequate support and guidance, and *honoured for their unique perspective on the world* and their sensitivity; rather than being treated like a crazy person, told to go on medication, or excluded from society. Their experience is one of great care, inclusion, and even being *valued* for their unique predicament. Unfortunately for those of us walking the initiation path in the Western world - part of a society that has all but severed spirit from the equation - it's a completely different story, and many of us must walk it in isolation.

We are only *just* starting to create any real dialogue and awareness around mental health where we're actually addressing the root cause. We are only *just* starting to talk about holistic healing and trying different ways of approaching illness and disease. We are only *just* starting to talk about paranormal, spiritual or supernatural phenomena outside of the context of horror movies or taboos. Humanity is afraid of what we *don't understand* - issues that might be more intricate and complicated than we think and require us to open our minds beyond our limited understanding - and so we just slap convenient diagnoses onto everything. Putting things into neat little boxes and categories so as not to make anyone deal with the inevitable brain-melting conundrum of the *great unknown*.

I can't help but think of my yiayia (my dad's mum), who I grew up believing was schizophrenic - because that's what everyone told me - until one day after my gifts awakened, and she *came to me herself* in spirit to tell me I was carrying the same gifts she had, in my blood. Only after pressing my family about her did all the little details come to light about how she would do coffee cup oracle readings that were always accurate for the people in her village who would come to her and how she used to *"see things and speak to people that weren't there"*. (But I guess that's what warranted her "schizophrenic" diagnosis in the first place.)

Or how it was only when I started sharing that I had psychic gifts, did others in my family start to pipe up and share that they also have intuitive dreams and psychic phenomena happening for them... as if *everyone was so afraid* to speak up and admit it they're a little bit psychic because they didn't want to be seen as the "crazy one".

So am I the crazy one? Are *you*? Are we the crazy ones for actually admitting these things out loud?

I don't know the answer to that question, but I know that whether I am crazy or not, at least I am self-aware enough to wonder. To me, not even having the awareness to be able to *ask yourself that question* in the first place is the real insanity.

Pretending that you're not weird AF when the doors are closed, and nobody else is there is the real insanity. Allowing other people define you and put you into boxes; telling you what is 'normal' and what is 'crazy'; what is 'acceptable' and what 'isn't'; what is 'okay' and what is 'weird'; what you are 'allowed' to feel, and what you should feel 'guilty' about feeling; what you 'should' or 'shouldn't' talk about...

Giving a shit about what *anyone* really thinks about you to the point it inhibits your truth, or your natural, raw, honest expression...

At this point in my journey, *that* is the real insanity to me.

Insanity is watering myself down and pretending to be anything *but* the weirdest, most authentic, honest, truthful, raw, real, 'crazy' version of who I am; *even* if a part of myself frequently has shadow tantrums that stop it showing up and writing this book; questions whether I'm truly this Oracle, or just batshit insane; talks in third person about the different "parts" of myself all the time; and has questioned many times on this path whether I should just turn my back on everything I've been through over the past few years and light everything I've built on fire (at least twice so far while writing this very book, by the way).

All of that makes up who I am (although it may not be my "highest" soul truth), and so I'd be dishonest if I tried to hide it.

Because it doesn't matter how "tapped in" I am, or what ancient wisdom and knowledge I'm sharing, or what energies I'm connected to, or what codes I've held from what lifetimes and galactic incarnations I've had.

Right now, I am still (at least in part) human. I chose THIS human vessel to carry out this mission. I didn't choose to be a spirit guide, or a light being, or a dragon, or an angel, or something else.

I chose to enter a human avatar this time around (as did you) for a *very good reason*.

And from a 'human' perspective, what I do and who I am - what I'm tuning into on a daily basis - is kinda *nuts*. If any psychiatrist were to observe me for a week, I have no doubts about what their diagnosis might be. Hell, I don't blame them.

From a Little Human Self level, *it's all pretty fucking cray*.

And yet, as *human* as I am, I simultaneously need to come to balance this other part of me who is *so incredibly alien*; the part of me that seems to want to run the show and drag my Little Human Self along for the ride with her.

The part of me who *doesn't give a flying fuck* about how weird she appears; the part of me that is shameless about the fact that she's an ancient portal from outer space...

The part of me that couldn't even *fathom* why I'd be spinning myself out wondering if I was "crazy"...

The part of me who is *laughing at me right now,* going round and round in circles trying to justify that I'm *not really crazy, it's everyone else that's crazy...*

The part of me who is acutely aware that *she doesn't even really exist, so what am I even having this big old identity crisis about, 'cause none of it is real anyway...*

(Well, isn't THAT a trip...)

"You're an ancient oracle/alien, Bec... you're NOT human. Your guides are telling me that you need to stop pretending like you're normal 'cause you're NOT."

My mentor shared this insight with me (verbatim) when I started the process of birthing this book, and it kind of sums up the *entire mental battle* I've been going through for as long as I can remember.

Frankly, I've known for a long time *I'm a fucking alien;* even before I knew aliens were real.

I've had a sense I'm not "normal" and that I probably wouldn't be able to hold down a "normal" life or do the "normal" things that others do. My own guidance system has reiterated this to me many times.

I've known I'm not here to do things the way others do them, and that I very much need to pave my own way forward and blaze my own trail; that I simply can not and am not supposed to function or "do life" like others.

Sometimes, I would even pity myself because of it, wishing I was "normal" or just chose a "normal" life where it got to be "easy" and "simple". (I continually use inverted commas for "normal" because, truly, *what is normal* anyway? You will come to realise, as I have, my alien friend, that "normal" doesn't actually exist outside of a concept which has been weaponized against us; preventing us from expressing our soul's full, authentic, individual expression.)

My entire adolescence, I tried to dull and dumb myself down, conform and fall in line; pretending to be like everyone else just so I could *belong* - yearning to be loved and accepted by people who didn't truly love or accept themselves.

Forever feeling like I was on the outside, looking in.

Forever wishing I was *one of them* - not realising the greatest gift I could give people was my weird and wonderful alien self.

But as much as I knew on some level I was *really* not normal, I also struggled to accept and claim it in a healthy way instead of desperately trying to fit in. (The rage-filled, "middle finger to the world" rebellion of my teens and rock'n'roller early '20s does not count.)

As I started to cultivate self-awareness on my healing path, I often wondered whether I was just telling myself "I'm not normal" as an excuse to not do things; or in order to keep myself separate, or to put myself above others, as I've seen so many who have developed spiritual ego do (AKA - "*I'm a starseed from xyz star system, I'm therefore far superior to all these pathetic, unawakened humans... I wish I could just get back onto my spaceship and travel back to the planet from whence I came*").

I wondered if thinking I was "not normal" was just my wounded inner child trying to make herself feel special and important.

I wondered if thinking I was "not normal" was just a protection mechanism from experiencing rejection, my shadow self trying to justify hiding out in my cave and avoiding human interaction *because I didn't fit in anyway.*

I never allowed myself to just accept the blindingly obvious fact that *I'm really not fucking normal, and I'm really not like anyone else.*

And I don't mean that to negate the fact that *"everyone is unique and special and different"* because we *are...*

But I also just need to accept the glaringly obvious fact that in many ways, I really am just an ancient alien trying to squeeze into this skin suit and pretend to be 'one of the hoomans' and *it's awkward and uncomfortable as hell.*

(Can you relate? Or is that just the excess of "eccentric" Aquarius placements in my natal chart talking for me?)

I'm going to be honest and say *I don't know what purpose this outpouring is serving* other than to somehow verbalise the phenomenom of *'my brain melting in real time'* as all of the codes in this book start to really land and integrate...

With them, bringing upon some sort of identity crisis of *"am I really just fucking crazy, or am I actually this ancient alien oracle, even though I'm aware I'm simultaneously nothing at all"*...

But I'm getting to a point here, I promise.

My gift has always been feeling the thing that *everyone is feeling* but *nobody has the courage to say* because they're too afraid they'll *look like a freakin' weirdo.*

And then somehow putting words to that that make them LAND with flames of truth, full-body-fuck-yes-resonance, for whoever is receiving, listening to, or reading them.

And so, beautiful reader, as much as some future version of myself is probably going to *facepalm* this stream of consciousness, mental breakdown in real-time testimony to my insanity, they very well may use it as evidence when they're trying to lock me up...

(Goddamn it, Past Bec, did you really have to publish this and share your ENTIRE thought process with the whole damn world?)

I share this outpouring now because I *know how you feel.*

I know how it feels to feel like you're an outsider looking in.

To feel like an alien compared to those around you.

To feel like you're wearing a suit that is too tight and doesn't quite fit.

I know how it feels to *know in your bones* you are somehow different, but simultaneously be too afraid to claim it; because some part of you just wants to fit in.

I know how it feels to feel *so powerful* and so humanly fragile all at the same time.

I know what it is like to know deep inside of you that there is something BIG, something IMPORTANT, something POWERFUL you are here to birth... to feel the never-ending pressure of that weighing on you... but at the same time, being too afraid to admit it because you're worried you're just insane.

I know what it feels like to fight God every day since you were first shown your mission, saying, "It's too big, I don't want it"; begging for God to take it back or give it to someone else.e

I know what it feels like to constantly question, *'Who am I to do this?'* and *'What if I'm wrong?'* and *'What will people think?'* and *'What if I'm just crazy and making this all up?',* and *'nobody is going to believe me anyway.'*

I know what it feels like to relive the memories, to have the flashes of the moments and traumas and terrors of every time you have come here before and lived out some variation of this, and it didn't go so well.

This is why you're so afraid to claim and step into this now. This is why you are telling yourself you're just crazy. It's the imprint from every time they negated you, demonised you, persecuted you, silenced you, locked you up in the madhouse, labelled you a whore, a madwoman, a witch.

It is coming up now for you to reclaim this part of you. Your power.

I know what it feels like to have a frightened, bruised, battered Little Self part of you that is always running from - pushing against - your destiny.

And I also know that if you are resonating with *any* of this, then you're a Sacred Rebel just like me...

And because we're cut from the same cloth, I know that you're not going to give up or let any of that shit stop you (you ultimate badass, you).

So here is your permission slip to claim it.

Boldly claim what you are here for, what you came here to do, and who you came here to be.

Claim the knowledge and wisdom you came into this body with from faraway places and ancient times.

Claim what you don't know why or how you know; you just know it.

Claim that *sometimes* you're going to feel absolutely batshit, and that doesn't take away from the fact that you're *still* incredibly tapped in.

Claim that you're simultaneously human AF - you make mistakes, you doubt yourself, you fall behind - *and* you're a weird and wonderful alien from some other place far, far away.

The bottom line is; maybe you and I *are* just totally, absolutely, completely, 110% certifiably insane by most "normal" people's standards.

But I would prefer to be that. I would prefer to feel heart-breakingly, painfully ALIVE, with the colour and the volume turned up so intensely sometimes that it feels like my heart is going to explode; than to be so numb that I feel nothing at all.

I would rather be "crazy" and delusional... to live in a life that *gets* to be filled with imagination and magic; soul adventures and sacred pilgrimages; mythical creatures and past life memories from ancient civilisations... where *everything* is a cosmic sign that a God who *loves me and has my back* is speaking directly to me and guiding me every step of the way; where everything means *something* and nothing is a coincidence...

I would rather experience *that* than be living a meaningless, shallow existence where I am not allowed to dream outside of the parameters of what I'm told I'm allowed to; where I am shut off from feeling everything; where I despise and repress aspects of myself so as not to offend others... where *everything is devoid of life and meaning...*

Wouldn't you?

BECOMING A CLEAR CHANNEL IS A PROCESS OF UNBECOMING

In order to become something - to imprint - you need to first become *nothing*.

You cannot receive instruction from the field, or take on new codes of information if your channel is blocked. If it is too "full", there is no space for the download to be received.

You cannot take on a new identity as a higher version of yourself if you are attached to your old one.

You cannot be a pure vessel for divinity and love to flow through if there are human identities, judgements, attachments, stories or preferences in the way.

Think of the hard drive on your computer, for example.

You are not able to download a new operating program if there is no space left on the harddrive. You must first clear up space on the harddrive by deleting the old material.

This is where the saying *"you must become empty to become full"* that circles around spiritual schools of thought comes from.

You must become nobody and nothing to become everything and everybody.

You must pass the threshold of 'losing your mind' to let your mind step out of the way and allow something far greater to animate you.

You must be willing to let go of what is and what was to become what will be.

Yes, of course, there is still potential to embody in *part* a fractal or archetype - for instance, to bring through the frequency of a deity, a God/Goddess, or an aspect of the feminine or the masculine. However, it won't be a *pure* or clean imprint of that fractal or archetype.

It will not be able to reflect the totality or clarity of the frequency because it is hindered by your own distortions, trauma or programming. It will be like looking through a crystal that has a cloudy or scratched surface and trying to see the light refracted through it.

It will be the Dark Goddess, peppered with your own witch wound trauma, and so not harnessing the raw healing potential of her compassion.

It will be Aphrodite, addicted to validation and using her beauty and love to manipulate others.

Those who witness you channelling that frequency will see *you* channelling that frequency.

They will not be able to look completely through you - as you become a blank window, a vessel - to see God.

The priestess is one who has become a *hollow bone*; an empty chalice; a clear vessel, in order to let something far greater than her animate and flow through her.

She is an access point to the Divine for others because she has become One with the Divine.

This is essentially what we are doing in encoding ourselves with the frequency of the sun and enabling the sun to deconstruct and re-make our DNA in its image. We are quite literally *becoming* more like the Creator - we are becoming more light - as we enable the light of the Creator to enter us and affect our cellular structure. We are taking instructions from the light, on a cellular level, of how our body is to behave. As we become more light, we are able to transmit more divinity through our cells.

Light communicates information at a faster speed - the heavier the density, the slower the information travels. When something is dense or heavy, there is no space for movement, evolution or growth. If we do not let the old carbon cells pass through the threshold of *death* - which happens every time they take in this solar energy - they cannot create the space to receive the spark of Life and become Crystalline.

Each cell must first completely die and face the destruction of its current form, to then use its own body as the fertiliser for its rebirth.

We must face this death and destruction of these dense parts of *ourselves* in order to create the chrysalis for our own evolution.

Part of the prophecy imparted by the Mayans is that which is not willing to die - to *face and overcome its own death* - cannot rebirth and change form.

And those who cannot or are not willing to change form will be destroyed.

In order to move into a new cycle on Earth, we must face this destruction of all that has been in order to create space for the new which is wanting to be brought forward.

This is the "ending of a cycle" that the Mayan calendar alluded to.

A destruction of all that has been in order for a New Age to come.

It will be as dramatic as it needs to be to get us to accept the process if we do not heed the message and choose it for ourselves. But there is no denying or avoiding it - this destruction is coming, whether we face it willingly or unwillingly.

It is nature. It is Law. Destruction and creation are one and the same.

We mustn't resist our own destruction and transformation, as it is what enables us to shapeshift and continue to expand our limited experience.

Our own death and destruction are what we must be willing to face (over and over again) in order to become reanimated and fully alive. Winter must happen before Spring can come. Only in darkness can we see our light. And so the spiritual cliches continue.

The old material must be decomposed so the ground is fertile for the new seedlings to sprout.

It is nature. It is Law. Destruction and creation are one and the same.

Death and destruction are what we must face while walking the Diamond Light Path in order to rebirth, over and over again; in endless cycles and iterations of New Versions of ourselves, embodying the new frequency which we have been imprinted with.

This is the way of the divine feminine priestess and the Oracle.

Those of us who have gone through these initiations into the rebirth portal will already know; once we have descended into our own inner underworld, we are able to ascend to more monumental heights.

This process of evolutionary rebirth is what the priestess is here to master with her transition into Oracle; to create the template for all others to walk the path of light behind her.

Our process of ascension into a higher life form is actually one of *descension* first and foremost.

The path to our Greatest Becoming is actually one of Unbecoming.

We must descend into our bodies; we must descend into our lower chakras, we must descend into the densest parts of ourselves in order to alchemise them into light.

We must descend into the mycelium of the Earth and allow the heavy parts of ourselves to be *broken down and decomposed* so they can be used as fertiliser for our rebirth.

INITIATION 4: BREAKDOWN

You can access the recommended audio version of this initiation at this website: www.diamondlightoracle.com.

Welcome to the fourth initiation in this transmission.

The following is an activation to break down that which is no longer required, to become fertiliser for your growth.

In your mind and with your heart, set the intention that this is the work that will be done during our time together in this activation and that you are open to receive all that is in your highest good.

I now invite all the beings of the highest light who wish to support this activation taking place.

I welcome your Higher Self, your Soul Family and Oversoul Network, and invite them to support you in receiving what is of the highest for you at this time.

I declare that this is sacred space; only that which is resonating on the frequency of unconditional love is welcome in this space.

I ask that everything that takes place here today is for the *highest good of all* and in service to the Whole.

I ask that the work we do together here today ripples out and serves the collective.

And so it is, and so it is, and so it is.

We invite you to enter your Sacred Space - the safe and protected ceremony space in which you receive all calibrations, downloads, codes and activations throughout this transmission.

Acknowledging internally that *you have now entered Sacred Space.*

We are supporting you today to break down all density, all matter in your body and your energetic field which is to be used as fertiliser for your growth.

In the time since you received the last activation, a chrysalis-like structure has begun to form around you; a safe incubation container for you to be held in while this breakdown and decomposition takes place.

This chrysalis has been made of *your own energy*, it has already started to form from the matter in your body that is no longer required.

The evolutionary journey you are going through is much like the caterpillar transitioning into a butterfly. In a similar way that a caterpillar's body forms everything that is necessary for its chrysalis to be created, your own cells are behaving in the same way.

This chrysalis is a part of you.

Your body and your spirit knows what to do and what it is required to shed, for you to evolve.

Your chrysalis also contains information from your own soul codex; instructions encoded within your DNA around the Highest Form in which you are to embody here and now.

Take a moment to notice this chrysalis which is forming around your body now - what it looks like, and what it feels like.

Each person will receive this differently, depending on their own unique frequency.

Trust yourself and how you perceive this chrysalis, as it will be unique to *you* and *your* process.

You may see, sense, or perceive a shimmery, translucent, energetic sack or cocoon-like structure that has formed around your energetic and physical bodies.

You may see, sense, or perceive yourself in a type of birthing sack, surrounded by amniotic fluid, similar to a foetus in its mother's womb.

You may see, sense, or perceive your own skin or auric field is encased in a material, a colour, a shape, a pattern, or sacred geometry.

Notice how you feel inside this chrysalis and allow yourself the permission to just be held here.

For those who do not yet have a fully formed chrysalis, we are speeding up the process for you so that this container is forming now around your bodies.

This is a safe and natural process - we would like to remind you that it is one that you have gone through many times before!

Allow yourself to soften and be held even more deeply as this process unfolds - trusting your body, trusting your energy, trusting your support team, trusting your soul to create this structure for you.

As the casing of this chrysalis forms, now take note of the material inside of your incubator.

Notice yourself floating in this shimmery, crystalline, liquid-like material which surrounds your bodies. Notice its colour, its texture, its feel.

This crystalline liquid has incredible healing and regeneration properties - it can dissolve dense material just like acid, and transmute energy with ease and grace.

Allow this liquid to begin the process of breaking down all of the cells which are no longer in resonance with your Highest Versions of Self.

Trust and surrender to this process, there is no need to be afraid.

You are safe, you are loved, you are held.

Allow this liquid to break down and dissolve all calcifications, all density, all trapped emotions, all programming and all coding which is no longer required.

Allow this liquid to break down any and all trauma you are carrying - from this lifetime, from past or simultaneously occurring timelines across the multiverse - that is no longer required for your soul mission.

Allow this liquid to break down and dissolve anything which you have inherited from your ancestral line or taken on from anybody else - consciously or unconsciously, across all timelines and realities.

You may wish to pause here as this process takes place.

Notice that this chrysalis you are in has a large plug at one end of it, with a long tube-like structure feeding out of it.

Setting the intention now that this tube runs deep into the Earth, connected to Gaia.

This tube draws down and flushes all of the matter that is broken down, and it serves as fertiliser for Gaia.

See, sense, or perceive that you can send a pulse of this material down the tube now and watch how the Earth gladly takes it in.

Trust that this tube will continue to work in the background, flushing out the material as it is broken down, to be used as fertiliser for Gaia's ascension.

You do not have to focus on this process; it will be done automatically for you.

The process we have begun today will be an ongoing process that extends *past* this activation as your chrysalis continues to break down and dissolve density for you.

You will remain in this chrysalis for as long as it is necessary and appropriate for you to undergo the full transformation.

Please be gentle with yourself as you move through this process, and know that you may require more rest than usual.

The process for this activation is now complete.

Integrating and calibrating this now on the physical level.

Integrating and calibrating this now on the emotional level.

Integrating and calibrating this now on the mental level.

Integrating and calibrating this now through all levels and dimensions of your light body.

Integrating, calibrating and sharing this frequency now through all timelines and all versions of yourself across the multiverse.

We now shut down any and all open portals and gateways that are no longer required, and send back all energy that has come through any portals or gateways in the process of this work.

We now dissolve any bonds, chords or attachments that have been formed for the process of this activation and call you back into complete Soul Sovereignty.

We return all of your energy to you now as you call your Soul fully into your body.

Inviting in now Diamond Light to cleanse and close this space, bringing this sacred activation to a close and thanking all of the beings who have been here supporting in this process.

It is done, it is done, it is done, and so it is.

You may spend some time here in silent reflection, or receiving in your Sacred Space if it feels necessary.

If you feel complete, we invite you to gently bring yourself back into your body and into the room, wiggling your fingers and toes and opening your eyes when you are ready.

PART FIVE

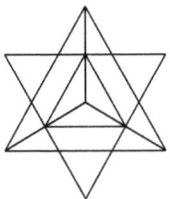

THE FEMININE

THE MISSION

After the Mayan codes finally began to stabilise and integrate into my field, things started to speed up, and the course became clearer. I was beginning to understand just how much I was receiving by being on that land and visiting the first pyramid, and was wondering where I would be called to go next.

I had been touching base frequently with another healer who I had a magical, kismet meeting with at a women's festival I'd facilitated at in Perth a year earlier, and she had been helping to support me since before I had even left for Mexico. She had seen in a healing session we had done that there was some cosmic work I was to do in Mexico, and so she felt like a safe place for me to land any time I was questioning my next step or what I was supposed to be doing. She was to become my "Map Reader" throughout the course of the gridwork mission; a pinnacle collaborator on the mission that helped me (and later the group of priestesses who would join us) to cross-reference the messages I was receiving, see clearly where I needed to be, and make sure I was crossing my T's, dotting my I's, and not missing anything.

The Map Reader and I had been going back and forth on calls a few times when I arrived in Mexico, where I had expressed my frustration of not knowing where I needed to "be" next. Relaying infuriatingly vague messages from my guides, I was not getting the clarity I desired, and she had been insisting that I just needed to wait for the next step to drop in because there was nowhere else for me to be yet. The only thing she had seen for me was several pyramids and me going on an epic adventure through the jungle to one of them (you best believe my Little Human Self didn't like that one iota). We hadn't yet pieced together where any of these pyramids were or if they were even in Mexico, although I had an inkling that one of them might be Chichén Itzá, which was relatively close by.

Numerous pings about different places to travel to next had dropped in for me, but none of them had been "clear" enough for me to want to leave the comfort and security of the familiar Tulum; a place where I had also *just* begun to make friends and connections.

Mazunte (a small "magic pueblo" near Puerto Escondido, on the coast of Oaxaca) had been one of them. While I was intrigued, I had a lot of resistance around going to Mazunte because it would mean I would have to get a flight and several buses, and despite how it might seem given my largely nomadic lifestyle, I *really* don't enjoy travelling (particularly not cross country in Mexico alone, as a woman). The housing situation in Mazunte also did not appeal to me at all after I did a quick search, nor did the thought of paying double what I was paying for comfort and luxury in Tulum for a run-down room with no AC in the middle of nowhere. However, not being clear and having no real guidance yet, I resigned to just enjoy Tulum and accept that maybe I wasn't meant to go anywhere just yet.

During this time, I met a soul sister at the gym on the property I lived on, who soon became my inseparable-two-peas-in-a-pod-joined-at-the-hip-borderline-codependent *bestie*. It was actually eerie how alike we were; I had never - and still to this day have never - met a soul sister who mirrored me so much. In fact, the reason we were connected was because another woman I met at the gym (who would later prove to be an important connection for me) introduced us, saying, "Wow, I have a friend here you remind me so much of, and I think you need to meet, do you mind if I give her your number?" It turns out that when my (soon-to-be) bestie messaged me, I saw her photo and instantly connected that *this was the girl* I had been crushing on at the gym, and she confided that she'd been feeling the same way about me. We'd been checking each other out and admiring each other from afar the whole time!

We were two tiny, little, tatted-up Pisces with serious sass, wild energy, curvy bodies, a love of twerking, and dark goddess vibes. We would spend every day together in the early days of our friendship; dancing like wild women and riling each other up into manic fits of hysteria by the pool; tanning; constantly amusing (or annoying, I'm not sure) the staff on my property with our shenanigans; riding around on our bicycles which were trying to kill us; going for lunch and endless over-priced cacaos; and causing entire groups of men to *act like rabid packs of wild dogs* when we'd walk past them on the beach. Being around each other was an instant vibe lift, even if we just sat in silence and said nothing, and to say our sisterhood was one of the greatest gifts I've received on my journey is an understatement. Of course, like any close friendship (especially of a transformative, soulmate nature where you're here to evolve together), we had our share of triggers to navigate, but we were able to do so with open hearts and clear communication, which only enabled us to go from strength to strength.

Around the time we met, there were a few other soul sisters I met who would bring in important pieces for the gridwork mission. The first sister who had introduced Bestie and I, who would later go on to introduce me to another key connection who would journey to Guatemala with me a couple of months later. Another new priestess sister, who the three of us met while sitting at the usual spot we'd go most days; who would join Bestie and me on our trip to Chichén Itzá. After sitting with Bestie and our new friend while drinking cacaos one afternoon, I expressed that I felt somewhat called to go to the pyramid. As neither of them had been yet, we decided to make plans to go together, the three of us. I started putting feelers out for tour guides to take us there, but nothing was aligning just yet.

A few days prior, I received a message out of the blue from a man I had connected with in the first few days of arriving in Mexico, who I had enquired about renting a scooter from. I remember when we first connected, sending some messages back and forth and laughing at his response to one of my messages. *"This isn't Bali, mami"*, he had said when I had mentioned that the price of scooters in Mexico was quadruple the price of what I was paying for a far superior scooter back when I lived in Bali. I don't know why, but even *without* knowing the guy; without seeing what he looked like (he had a photo of a scooter as his profile picture); and without even really having an exchange other than a few voice messages back and forth, I knew that I really liked this guy, and wanted to give him my business when I was eventually ready to rent a scooter. However, having just arrived and still getting the lay of the land, I had decided to opt for the push bike that was included with my apartment *(it hadn't tried to kill me just yet)*.

When he messaged me randomly that day in September on the Blue Moon (something that happens every thirty or so years, which is where the phrase "once in a blue moon" comes from), asking me how I was and wondering if I was still looking for a scooter, we wound up getting into a *long* back and forth exchange, that lasted well into the night and that verged far off the topic of scooter rental. Ordinarily, I wouldn't be one to indulge a random man striking up a conversation with me on WhatsApp - especially not in Mexico. Nor was I particularly interested in long texting exchanges with men I had no romantic interest in. But there was something unexplainable happening energetically that was making me feel that this person was somehow familiar to me, and I *enjoyed* messaging with him that evening. Despite being a complete stranger, without a photo, without really knowing anything about him other than his name, his age, and that he'd been born in Mexico but was raised in the States (hence the heavy American accent)...something about this man felt *comforting*.

When it was time for bed, he thanked me for the lovely conversation and told me that whenever I needed to borrow a scooter, I could just have it free of charge; that I could consider myself a friend now, and that he was at my service. I thought it was a lovely offer but had no intention of actually taking him up on it, partially because I felt kind of bad taking this man's livelihood off him and partially because I was still waiting for the 'catch'.

I didn't expect him to message me again and put the whole interaction out of my mind, but a few days later, he did, checking in and asking how I was. In the following days, messaging me here and there, he would find any excuse or reason to offer his help or assistance, like taking me to buy new flip-flops when mine broke, which I would politely decline (still on the cautious/paranoid side). At this point, I was curious as to his intentions; however, in my head, I had built this image of him that was *far* from someone I would potentially be into, so I put him firmly in the "friend" / "potential hook-up for a scooter" category, even though when it would come up in conversation, Bestie and I would joke *"wouldn't it be funny if it turns out he's actually the love of my life?"*

I mean, *what would the odds be of that?* I believe that it was one of those 'deep knowings that we disguise with humour because we're too afraid to feel the truth of it'.

Yep, a part of me knew *something*, alright.

For the sake of the linear progression of the sacred mission that was unfolding for me at the time, we're going to return to the sisters and our plan to go to Chichén Itzá - but you certainly haven't heard the last of this side plot. I received a ping to ask this new, helpful connection of mine (scooter bae) if he had any contacts, and the friend he suggested ended up being the *exact* perfect guy to take us - *of course*. He was a kind, open, fun and deeply spiritual man who was very excited to have a tour group that he'd be able to dive down wild esoteric rabbit holes with and share all his theories about the Mayans and the extraterrestrials that built the pyramids, which he didn't feel comfortable sharing with the "standard" tourists that were only really interested in the archeology. Far less so the hungover ones, who were not really interested in being on the tour at all.

The entire drive out to the sacred site, he was sharing his vast wisdom of Mayan astrology and was able to tell us what each of our "Mayan signs" were from the top of his head; which was very impressive of him and also surprisingly accurate. This was a man who was clearly passionate about what he did and was passionate about the Mayan culture; therefore the *perfect* person for me to springboard some of the downloads I'd been receiving. (The information I am channelling *always* has a habit of being confirmed with the information falling right into my lap at the exact right time.)

As my sisters chatted to each other in the back seat, and I chatted with our tour guide friend in the front - in Spanglish, as my Spanish was rapidly improving - it quickly became very apparent that we'd been led to the perfect guide for our journey, as many things he began to share started linking up all of these dots in my mind of the downloads I had started to receive, and finally begin to integrate and understand. Without sharing what I had channelled, I would ask him questions about his perception or understanding of certain things to do with the Ancient Mayan civilisation, and much of what he shared served as big, fat confirmations for me of what I already knew. So many things were landing in my body to highlight as "important" as he spoke, as connection points were being made mentally between things I'd energetically felt or understood but couldn't quite piece together conceptually yet.

We arrived at the sacred site well before the midday heat set in and before there were many other tourists around to disturb us. We were overjoyed about the fact that we had managed to show up on a relatively quiet day (of course, it's always *perfect* and divine) and that our tour guide was perfectly understanding around letting us 'flow' in our own way; to do our ceremonies and meditations before we walked around the site. I felt myself being guided across the site to a quieter part on the outskirts near the observatory, where the small crowd of tourists who had started to funnel in had not yet spread. I began my standing meditation, and I could feel the presence of my two sisters coming to join me. Our new priestess sister lit up her incense and began to make offerings to her various goddesses as she began her own ceremony while Bestie sat quietly in meditation, knowing that she would receive what she needed from whatever portals I was opening.

As with the previous pyramid, I allowed the energy to begin to channel through my body, moving my arms in whatever way they were guiding me; feeling my hands begin to make the same mudras and motions as they had been spontaneously making over the past weeks. The energy was intense and powerful, and I felt much more connected than I had at the first pyramid I visited. This time - unlike at Ek Balam - I was being shown a lot of images and receiving instructions about what to do while I was there.

I was directed to the central pyramid (*El Castillo*, or The Temple of Kukulkan - the feathered serpent) and shown to direct pulses through it to 'light it up' with my energy. Next, I was shown inside the main pyramid that there was an inner chamber, the chamber of the Red Jaguar. (The colour 'red' in ancient Maya was symbolic of giving life, but also for death and sacrifice, which they saw as synonymous with life.) I was shown to place my consciousness into that inner chamber to "activate it". I would later (many months later, once I had already left Mexico and started writing this book) come to understand in a shamanic journey that this inner chamber was one that very few people were permitted to enter - only the High Priest/ess - and that inside of it there was a crossing, a portal, a gateway into the underworld. Huge electrical pulses moved through me as I lit up the inside of the pyramid with my soul memory. Receiving, giving; giving, receiving.

As I was receiving these instructions to light up certain pyramids and "activate them", I caught myself in disbelief, wondering how and why I was being asked to do this; *'surely this is hubris, this is me just imagining that I'm doing this, or that I'm important enough to do this? Little Old Me, activate this big, ancient pyramid? Surely someone else more powerful and advanced than me had been guided to come here and activate it already? Is this disrespectful? Am I really meant to be doing this?'* But the guidance (and the Mayan ancestors I could feel speaking to me) didn't care about the Little Self identity crisis I was having... *I had a job to do.* It just kept directing me to different points on the pyramid to send pulses of energy from the Earth and from the Sky; through the open portal that was my body, and through the inner Jaguar chamber.

I felt a wave of orgasmic energy overwhelm me, and I began to let out hysterical laughter with the sheer intensity of it, as the coloured lights began to strobe behind my eyes.

I felt like I had jumped into a cold plunge, or had plugged myself into an electrical socket in the wall; a sudden surge of energy coming over me and uplifting me, as I felt like I could run nonstop for days on end.

I was shown this vast, spider-web-like network of lights turning on, one by one, as the energy pulsed out from the pyramid that I had just activated. I saw the points go all the way from this pyramid to Ek Balam to Tulum, linking up via the underground cenote network, the water of the cenotes acting as carriers and amplifiers for the energy. (It's important to note from an archaeological standpoint; El Castillo/The Temple of Kukulkan is built on top of a cenote, so it was connected to a larger underground network of cenotes. Many archaeologists did not know the reason for this, other than it being for religious reasons.)

I was shown the reason why I hadn't been given my "next step" was that my "next step" was actually to remain in Tulum for a little while longer, to tie up a few ends and make a few important connections. I just had to wait to visit *this* pyramid before I could receive the next step, as it opened the entire mission up and made it clear to me *what exactly I was doing* out there in Mexico. I had already visited the Tulum Ruins years earlier on my previous Mexico trip, but I was now told that I had to physically re-visit and activate that point next.

I was shown that the work I had been doing actually had started weeks prior in Ek Balam - well, technically, the foundational work had started two years prior, the last time I'd been to Mexico - before I was even aware I was doing it; and that there was a sacred circle of six other priestesses who were meant to support me on this mission somehow. I was told I wouldn't have to do it alone because it was far too big a task energetically for me to carry on my own. In fact, I hadn't actually been doing it alone from the beginning, as the Map Reader had already been playing an instrumental part and would go on to be one of the six women who formed the circle. If it wasn't for the visions that she shared, I would have missed the important nudge to visit Chichén Itzá, as at the time, I was not tapped into the fact that I was meant to visit sacred sites, other than the first pyramid I already attended.

(*Important aside* - this is why we must heal our sisterhood/brotherhood wound, as many of our highest and most sacred soul missions will be co-creations with others, particularly our sisters walking the priestess path. Yes, we must trust our own guidance and be sovereign enough to trust ourselves; *however*, we're not here to walk this path as lone wolves, even though you might feel like that in the beginning. Our sisters/brothers help us see the things we're missing; the blind spots we have for whatever reasons. None of this sacred mission would have been possible without the support, holding, guidance and co-creation of the twelve or so sisters who have contributed their magic or their connections somewhere along the way. This includes those who have held and supported me *after* the foundational "work" of this mission concluded; through the process of birthing this book. In the same way, I am initiating and holding you through the process of receiving this transmission, I have been held and sometimes initiated by others over the course of my sacred homecoming. You will go on to do the same for those you serve. This is the way it works; this is why mystery schools were held and initiates met in circles of five. We initiate and activate each other and guide *each other* home, each offering our vital piece of the puzzle, our special ingredient to add to the magic potion. Our magic and our potency amplify when we are together in co-creation with the same vision and intention.)

The guidance instructed me that the process had begun on the 8/8 Lionsgate portal (which happened to be four days prior to visiting Ek Balam) during the ceremony I had held then, and the women on *that* particular call had received an energetic invitation to continue the work. The five women who signed up when I ended up putting out a "call" for my mystery mission - along with the Map Reader - were *all* present at that first ceremony. However, not all the women in that first ceremony were to join us on the mission.

Spirit was *finally* showing me the reason I was called to Mexico; exactly what my sacred gridwork mission was, in a tangible way. I was to acti- vate this vast network of Mayan pyramids that spanned way down to Guatemala because there was nobody with the coding and knowledge actively maintaining or working that grid to the degree it needed to be - or perhaps who was capable of travelling the way I was - and it had crashed out of sync with the new waves of solar energy coming in. (Which is ironic, given that so much of the ancient Mayans legacy and codex is about synchronisation).

I was shown that each pyramid I was activating would "ping" the next one like a circuit board, turning the energy grid of the entire area back on and, with it, re-awakening the ancient wisdom and knowledge the Mayans had seeded into it. Any person to step on that land would now have an opportunity - if they were tuned into the correct frequency - to receive these codes from it. Not only that but by doing this work now and activating this grid, it was bringing *everything* back into "sync" with the new, extremely high frequencies that were hitting the planet.

It was on this trip that I solidified the concept in my mind of the Mayans being harmonisers or "synchronisers." In fact, this word "syn- chroniser" was our tour guide's main (yet important) contribution to my work. In my mind, I had a picture or a sense of how the Mayans would connect to the different elements, planets and such to bring everything into one unified frequency, and bring into balance any places where that coherence was disturbed.

The guide took this understanding further when he explained to us that he believed that the ancient Mayans were *"galactic engineers and interstellar travellers that would travel from planet to planet, synchronising different places back that were about to be out of sync"* (verbatim from a video recording I had of him talking about it).

When listening to him share this, I had a sudden visual of the Tree of Life and saw that it was this frequency of creation that they were bringing things back into "sync" with the vibration that is Source, that is harmony, that runs through All of Life. The Mayans were helping Gaia maintain and come back to balance in her pivotal transition and ascension process (and, by extension, all sentient and non-sentient beings who inhabit this planet and form the body of Gaia).

Unlike the tour guide, I don't necessarily believe the ancient Mayans themselves were interstellar travellers from another place, but rather that they brought with them into this incarnation memories of other civilisations and lifetimes on planets other than Earth; they were able to tap into their multidimensional soul memory. I also believe they were in close communication with galactic civilisations who supported them with the structures, wisdom and advanced spiritual technology they would teach the Mayans how to harness and utilise. *And* that they carried their alien DNA - which, if you recall me talking about the height of the royal family being much taller than the average Mayan due to their giant DNA, is also confirmed by the size of some of the features of their architecture.

Soon after this trip, the concept of the "Tree of Life" expanded into my awareness as a deeper understanding of the interconnectedness of Life; reiterating the importance of the tree and plant root system and mycelium network and how I was to co-create with this to support the gridwork I was doing, to be able to amplify the energy to affect even larger networks. Although not always a literal tree, the Tree of Life has come to me many times in visions as a symbol of this one resonant, unified frequency; the Oneness.

As I was switching these pyramids (or energetic pulse, or amplification points, you can also think of them as) "on" again, the frequency was flowing into the Earth, into the tree and plant root system, and into the mycelium, which was pushing those pulses out even further, to surrounding areas. Mama Gaia was receiving added support to bring herself back into balance and homeostasis via her root network; all the trees talking to each other, exchanging the gases which were necessary for them to come back to harmony.

All of it was making me understand *just how critical* maintaining a close connection to my body and to the Earth was, as a starseed who spent a lot of time early in my "spiritual awakening" doing everything I could to escape my body and go to those places in my astral travels that were not so dense and heavy. Places where there was no pain and suffering, only unconditional love; that were so difficult to will myself to return from.

But that was before I had well and truly come home to and experienced the *infinite* and *unconditional love* of the Great Mother, Earth - a journey that only unfolds ever more deeply and profoundly for me - and learned how to *truly* and willingly seed myself here.

HEALING THE MOTHER WOUND

In Aboriginal culture, the soul is believed to not be fully grounded and settled here on Earth until it returns to its Mother (Gaia), once it leaves the womb of its human mother and after the connection (the umbilical cord) has been severed. It is a rite of passage for babies to be "rebirthed" as children of Mother Earth; for her to watch, protect and have guardianship over. Until this "rebirthing" takes place, the soul is considered to be lost; possibly experiencing depression, anxiety, dissatisfaction, unrest, and unease as a result. I was privileged enough to take part in an Aboriginal Rebirthing ceremony on my home soil in Australia in 2023, the premise of which is symbolically returning your umbilical cord or placenta to the Earth, burying it deep into the Earth under a guardian tree, to "rebirth your soul here on Earth". I believe that *all* of us should have a similar ceremony, marking the re-connection to our Divine Earth Mother.

Our disconnection from Gaia - from Mother Earth - is the collective spiritual and planetary Mother Wound, which we all must heal in order to come into the fullness of our gifts and magic. Every single person in this modern age - regardless of their gender - experiences the imprint of this wound in some way as a result of being disconnected from our true mother, Earth. This is the level of the Mother Wound where the most work must be done as a lightworker to be able to seed yourself here and anchor heaven on Earth. However, full healing and integration on this level of the Mother Wound is only usually reached once you have dealt with the personal and cultural implications of the level of this wound related to your relationship with your human mother and "rebirthed" yourself as a Child of Gaia. These implications also affect every human, as not every human being *is* a mother, but every human being *has* a mother. (If you *are* a mother, I invite you to read this chapter from the perspective of a daughter).

The womb of our mother is our first point of entry into this physical world as a soul, and for many of us, that entry point is a traumatic and jarring one.

For women in particular, the Mother Wound we carry is connected to more than just our mothers but stems back ancestrally to our grandmothers and further. While it is known women carry inherited trauma in the womb space, there is a much simpler genetic fact that highlights how we are imprinted by the thoughts, feelings and even biology of our mothers (and their mothers before them). **A woman is born with all the eggs she will ever have already inside of her**. When your grandmother was pregnant with your mother, *you* were also inside of her, as you were already in your mother's womb. Reflect on what that means for a moment and how trauma in the feminine line can be passed down from mother to mother to *you* - simply in the process of your incubation.

From a biological point of view, our mother's mitochondria, microbiome and nervous system are what encode us when we are inside her womb despite our gender (all of which she has more than likely inherited from *her* mother). We come from bacteria, we are made of bacteria, and if the bacteria in our environment (the womb we inhabit) is not harmonious or healthy in nature - or sending electrical signals conducive for our optimal functioning - nor will we be. We attune energetically to the network of bacteria we are surrounded by - which carry information, like the other energetic networks we spoke about - and are imprinted by it. As well as receiving instructions from the nervous system of our mothers on how our own cellular structure should behave and regulate. Once we learn to re-harmonise our inner flora (bacteria), reconnect to the natural mycelium network of Gaia, and regulate our nervous system to Gaia's steady heartbeat, we can re-imprint ourselves into our highest functioning and harmonisation.

I must reiterate these are all the implications of the Mother Wound *before we've even technically crossed the passage between worlds as a soul.* Then come the events after our birth, which have a huge influence on our developmental process. In order to have a healthy developmental process as a baby - specifically, for our nervous system development, our sense of self, our attachment style and our overall emotional well-being - we *need* physical closeness and nurturing from our birth mothers in order to co-regulate ourselves; basic things like feeding, nursing and proximity to her heartbeat. If you think about how many of us in the Western world were birthed - in a clinical hospital setting, many of us taken from our mother's arms only moments after our birth, some of us taken into entire other rooms, and then others still, born via emergency C-section, with our mothers barely conscious for the process - you can begin to understand how those early traumatic moments of detachment from our birth mother affect our ability to form a healthy attachment style. This is *before* we even are taken home from the hospital, where many of our mothers are in some way unequipped to deal with motherhood or unable to meet our emotional needs.

We lean on our Little Human Mothers, as we are fully dependent on them in those formative years. Therefore, we learn what love and nurturing are from them, more than any other primary caregiver (although many of us carry our fair share of Daddy Issues, which we'll be addressing in a few chapters time, as it's an important part of healing our inner masculine). The blueprint of love and nurturing we receive from our human mothers is often far from what is required for us to reach our highest, fullest potential. And for many of us, it's not that our mothers *didn't try the best that they could* to nurture and hold us - after all, they were the ones who gave us life, which is the most uncon-ditionally loving thing you could do - but they were simply incapable of providing the level of unconditional love, nurturing and sustenance that our soul is used to. The kind of love, nurturing and sustenance we find in our Divine Mother, Earth.

Our mothers - dealing with their own Mother Wounds, passed down from generation to generation - unconsciously teach us that love is conditional; that we will only receive the nurturing and love that we require, and we will only have our emotional needs met when we behave a certain way. We learn that we need to perform to be loveable; we need to be on our best behaviour to be loveable; we need to achieve in order to be loveable.

Our mothers - dealing with their own disconnection from themselves and from Gaia - are not fully emotionally available for us or attuned to our emotional needs; able to hold and nurture us in the ways we require. As a result, we learn that we cannot trust love and nurturing to always be available when we need it. We learn that we cannot trust that we will not be abandoned or that our emotional needs will be met; eventuating in the development of anxious or avoidant attachment styles, anxiety, codependency, depression, and low self-esteem.

Our mothers - who could not fully love nor fully value themselves - pass to us a blueprint for how we value our own worth. As a result, we may grow up with our boundaries consistently being negated; learning that we need to people-please, overgive, and self-abandon, trading our self-worth and our personal power for love and accep-tance. Or perhaps they consistently cross *our* boundaries as infants or children, which we hold a lot of unconscious anger around as adults; the sacred rage welling up inside of us acting as a self-protection mechanism; teaching us the ability to say "no" we never had when we were young.

Our mothers unconsciously imprint us with *their* belief systems and biases; inherited from not only *their* mothers but greater societal conditioning towards women (and men). For instance, that a woman shouldn't shine too bright or attract too much attention; that a woman shouldn't be 'too much' (too emotional, too loud, too smart, too pretty, too interesting, too successful, too crazy, too wild, too opinionated, too strong, too aspirational, too whatever-the-hell-else); that a woman should be seen and not heard; that a woman can't be successful *and* be a good mother, so on and so forth.

Our mothers unconsciously imprint on us their relationship to the masculine via their relationship to our birth father or father-figure (or lack thereof). Any feelings of being unsupported, abandoned, judged as "too much" or "not enough", not getting enough attention, unsafety, anger, resentment, or bitterness will be inevitably passed onto us. Sometimes, our mothers even unconsciously project latent competition, scarcity, jealousy, and anger onto *us* as children for getting the attention from our father that they weren't. As a result, we learn that it's not safe for us to attract *any* attention from the masculine because it equates to rejection and abandonment by our mother.

As if *all of the above* wasn't enough, our mothers unconsciously imprint us with their projections, judgements, and sometimes even comparisons to us. Unconsciously (or consciously) belittling us to make themselves feel better; or manipulating us into feeling guilty, or somehow responsible for *their* lot in life; or living 'vicariously' through us, putting a lot of pressure on us to fulfil the dream they could not. We are made unconsciously responsible for our mothers' self-perceived 'failures' or shortcomings in life; for instance, that she sacrificed her dream of a career to have us, and therefore, it's our fault she didn't follow her dreams. As a result, we do not want to outshine her life with our own. Or perhaps our mothers have suffered in some way with a mental or physical illness as a result of birthing us; so we develop an unconscious belief that we cannot be happy if she is suffering because it's somehow our fault.

All of this combined manifests as low self-esteem, an unclear sense of self, lack of personal boundaries, a harsh inner critic, perfectionism (or under-achieving as a big "middle-fingers-up" rebellion response to the pressure to perform), people-pleasing, codependency, feelings of unworthiness, guilt, shame, depression, self-loathing, anxious or avoidant attachment style, and a dysregulated nervous system.

Healing the Mother Wound is *painful*; it means acknowledging and grieving all of the love and nurturing we required as infants and didn't receive. I found myself procrastinating for *weeks* to write this chapter because even though I've done *so much* healing around my mother, and our relationship over the years has come a *long way*, deeper layers of the grief and pain have surfaced as I deepen my connection to Gaia and return to the Earth Womb in the process of writing this book. The level of grief that has had me wailing, sobbing, curled up in a foetal position in my bed, as I am transported back into the heaviness of my mother's womb and experience all of the pain *she* was battling with as she grew me in her belly.

Grief and anger have welled up in me that I was so pure, so innocent, so full of love as a soul who had come onto this Earth. In that black, heavy space, I took on all of her pain as my own to try to clear it from her (out of unconditional love for her, not wanting her to endure her suffering anymore), and it imprinted me so deeply.

Grief that I somehow still feel responsible for her suffering and feel the need to punish myself as a result by suffering along with her. Grief for all the times the innocent little child in me felt she was not good enough to take mummy's pain away and make her happy. Grief because I *adore* my mother - I love her more than words can even begin to describe - and I wish I *could* take her pain away for her; but I cannot save her, nor am I responsible for her healing process.

Grief in realising that for my own highest good and evolution - in order to truly thrive - I must be willing to sever the parts of our connection which are co-dependent and unhealthy and let them die. In order to evolve, I must let go of the dependency a part of me has on my birth mother and replace it with coming home to my own Inner Mother archetype, fortifying my connection with Mother Earth.

To reconnect to the manifestation of the Mother who can give my cells instructions on how to be well, to function optimally and to reach my highest capacity as a human. The Mother who can *always* nourish and nurture me, and provide me with the sustenance I require to thrive. The Mother that always has space to hold, that can hold all of me and all of my emotions. The Mother that can love me unconditionally, no matter what I am going through. The Mother that can hold me as I birth my *own* creations in this world.

Until we have addressed our own Mother Wound and rebirthed ourselves as children of Gaia, we will have a distorted relationship to creation; of being the willing Mother of our creations. We will avoid it at all costs. We will run from any role requiring nurturing, selflessness, responsibility for another, and emotional maturity. We will avoid any situation requiring us to step into the role of Mother, Nurturer and Life-Giver in our own lives. Before I healed my Mother Wound, I would rather stick thumbtacks in my eyelids than become a mother myself. I would be terrified that I would traumatise my children and continue the cycle of inherited wounding that I've now realised must end with *me*. Now I eagerly await the day; knowing what a blessing it will be and what an amazing mother I will make.

As we heal our Mother Wound, we lay the foundations to embody the archetype of the Divine Mother within ourselves; the part of us that is here to birth sacred creations and offerings into the world. This birthing process is the threshold we must cross in order to receive and transmit prophecy into the world and go from Priestess to Oracle.

THE BIRTHING PROCESS

The priestess is the birthing canal for visions that have not yet materialised in the physical realm; the reflection of the archetype of the Divine Mother that births things into existence. Her womb space is the sacred incubation place, the chalice, which holds and gestates these creations prior to their physical manifestation (which is why it is so crucial to clear any trauma in the womb space and activate its magic, as this is just *one* of the many functions and gifts of the magical womb). The role of the priestess is to usher the soul - the living consciousness - of an offering (a work of art, a codex, a book, a piece of music, a sacred business, a healing modality, a transformational experience, or mystery school training, etc.) from the spirit realms, to this reality. Of course, women also do this with *human* souls; our wombs are the sacred crossing point of the soul space between lives and the physical incarnation.

Many of you who are walking the Diamond Light Path are here to birth offerings that are not just on an individual scale - a creative hobby, a source of joy, or an offering that you serve a small group of people such as those who choose to work with you. You are here to birth cutting-edge, paradigm-shifting sacred works that will impact and change the entire world. For instance, brand new healing modalities or training pathways that will revolutionise the space and help many; books that will become sacred texts; ideas and prophecies that will become a movement that mobilises large groups of people into positive action. The ripple effect of these offerings *reaches out and impacts the entire collective* in a profound way.

(For the record, I'm not necessarily talking about this equating to 'fame' or being well-known, as this is not a requirement for the offering to change the collective in some profound way. Your offering becomes exponential in its reach when you consider that one person you touch then goes on to touch another ten people, who touch ten people each - so on and so forth. Say, for instance; a healer that activates *other* healers, who then collectively go out and heal hundreds of thousands between them. Some of you will make offerings and contributions that impact the collective on a profound level that you will not get *any* recognition or acknowledgement for; much like the work I was doing with the Mayan grid. An Oracle does not birth the offering for fame, glory or recognition; nor does she have ownership of the consciousness itself. She is simply the sacred sherpa, the guide, the guardian, the vessel to ensure its safe crossing. She does it because she has been contracted, entrusted and chosen on a soul level by the living consciousness of that offering to bring it into the world and nurture it to its mature form; much like a human mother does for the soul she agrees to birth through her body. It is truly *unconditional*.)

As these offerings gestate within you - from the moment of their insemination in your womb space to the moment they are born through you and shared with the world - you will go through a sacred birthing process that you must honour. This birthing process is no different than the sequence of events that comes with the birthing of a physical baby.

First is the insemination; the penetration of *consciousness* (masculine) with an idea; or the *receiving* (feminine) of a "download" of information. The codex and the consciousness of the offering is received via the crown; the crown depicted as a many-petaled flower which opens up, much like a vulva. The idea then takes root; the implantation occurs in the womb space, where it gestates for several months (or however long it takes, depending on the offering). It is at this time that the vessel (the priestess transitioning into oracle) goes through the transformation necessary on a physical, emotional, spiritual and energetic level to be the embodiment and custodian of that offering. In this process, she moves from Maiden to Mother; from Priestess to Oracle.

The actual *birthing* process is the one I wish to focus on as most important, as it is quite the same as the process of giving birth to a human baby. Despite how adamant we are that *we want this damn baby out of us now* (or so I've been told by recounts, having not yet birthed a human baby myself), we don't really get a say in how and when the baby wants to make its appearance into the world. All we know is that when those contractions hit, we best be pushin'.

The process for me of writing this book is a perfect example of this entire birthing sequence. From the moment of implantation to the moment of its crowning. The first few months, *I didn't even know I was pregnant,* even if I had that moment before leaving for Guatemala I was told I was to birth a book about my experiences. (To go with the analogy, I'd equate this to having an intimate encounter while you're ovulating, having the thought of "I might get pregnant", and conveniently forgetting about it until you realise your period is a month late.) The codes were growing within my womb-space and preparing me without my conscious awareness.

Then came the second nudge that I was *meant to be writing this book.* With it came the awareness that my whole life was about to change, and I experienced the identity crisis and grieving process some women do when they first discover they're pregnant (for some this happens in the post-partum period) where they realise that *nothing will be the same after this;* while the codex of the book was gestating in me and transforming me from the inside out. (Of course, I would like to acknowledge that when it comes to human birth, this "shock" can manifest instead as "excitement" for those who are prepared for the transition into motherhood or have planned pregnancy for a long time.)

Next was the water breaking; the *"we're really in this bitch now"* moment, when I first began writing and *the floodgates opened;* the first round of downloads rushed out of me and onto the page. This started the "passage" into the material realm, which solidified the moment it wasn't just a faceless Seamonkey growing in my belly; it was really happening. Finally, the contractions started, and it was time to push. First, they were spaced out with a larger duration of waiting between; I would write a section and then go through a period of nonaction for days as I integrated the codes and purged whatever resistance I had to share them. Often becoming impatient and frustrated because I wanted to continue writing, but I couldn't. Through the painful contractions, I would be purging shadow left, right and centre, to be witnessed by my family and doula - much like the woman in the process of giving birth who is yelling at her husband that she hates him for doing this to her (or so went *my* dramatic and fiery entry point into this world, according to my mother).

Then the next contraction would come, I'd push through the pain which seemed to be *even worse than the last*, and more and more of the book would reveal itself; each contraction getting closer and closer together, where it would soon be mere *hours* between channelling something, and moving through the entire initiation and integration of it. Towards the end of this process, the contractions were coming *so quickly* that I was jumping in my word count by sometimes 10,000 words in a day. It was coming whether I liked it or not, and I had no choice but to sit at my desk for hours a day while it did; barely able to pause for a toilet break or a cup of tea. Then came the final push; revisiting all of those difficult or challenging parts of the book I'd saved for last and the things I was avoiding claiming through writing them. With that, the baby (my first draft) was born.

Once born, the offering must be protected and kept close to your heart at first while it gains strength and you recover from the birthing process, having just crossed the threshold. To continue the metaphor, I would equate this with the point where you introduce the baby to close friends and family, and you spend most of your time at home adjusting to being a new mother. For me, this would be handing my first draft over to select trusted people for second opinions.

Then, finally comes the day the offering is ready to be revealed to the world. The idea is to take this analogy of birthing a baby and apply it to the varying stages of your own sacred creation, whether that's a healing modality, an experience, a work of art, a podcast, or even a book like mine. The content of the stages might look different, but the journey is the same.

Another important piece that I feel to share is that we must learn to love our creations like they are our own children we have birthed; to stare at them with such awe, wonder, and adoration that our heart overpours with love towards them. It is almost a rite of passage for every person birthing a creative idea or project to want to burn it to the ground at some point; to judge it as "bad"; think they have wasted their time, that nobody is going to "get it", or that they're just terrible at their craft. Early in the process of writing this book, I would read back over chapters I'd written and have a meltdown as I'd tell myself, *"What the fuck am I even writing?! This is just so dull, and I sound like a raving lunatic... nobody is going to want to read this pretentious crap...who do I think I am?"* If I had believed my rather compelling Little Self tantrum (afraid of judgement, rejection and various other things; attempting to railroad my attempts and keep me safe from sharing this vulnerable piece of work) and stopped writing, then I would never have published this book.

As I got closer to finishing the manuscript, I began growing more fond of this transmission. It started with a moment when I read back over some of my writing, and I saw it with completely new eyes; I was actually in awe of the things that were coming through me and onto the page (that's how you know you're truly channelling something - if what you're learning as you write is a surprise to even you). I stopped seeing myself in the creation, and I started seeing the consciousness of the offering - in all of its perfection - instead. I started seeing how this transmission would serve to activate and support others. My guides have told me many times that, *technically*, I would be able to write the most poorly written piece of crap ever (in fact, *perhaps I have*), and those who are meant to receive this transmission through me would *still* receive what they are meant to because it's a frequency and a codex, more than it is words on a page. Yet, we judge ourselves and our art so harshly, even if, a lot of the time, *it's not even about us* (silly little humans). The truth is our creative work is inspired by something much larger than us, which animates our work and brings it to life through us.

Mothers are created to embrace and adore their children unconditionally; much like Mama Gaia unconditionally loves us. In order to do so, we must heal the unhealed aspects of the Mother within us - *becoming* the embodiment of the Divine Mother, birthing our *immaculate conception*. We must be like the unconditionally loving Mother as we birth our offerings; allowing our sacred children to take their own form, according to their own highest soul path. We mustn't judge them, force them to be something they are not or rush them in their process. We must stand by and defend them with the fierceness of a lioness protecting her cubs. We must be there lovingly through the process of their birth; nurturing them with our lifeblood, holding them as they evolve into what they are here to be, and allowing ourselves to evolve right along with them. It is a symbiotic relationship, much like the one *we* have with Gaia as she takes her evolutionary leap along with us.

Ultimately, we will find that Gaia - our Divine Mother - is doing the same with *us*. She is here to hold and nurture us through the birthing of our own sacred children and creations to enable their safe crossing as well as ours. However, we must first learn to rewild ourselves and reclaim our connection to her in order to allow this sacred holding to happen.

RETURNING TO OUR SACRED MOTHER AND SEEDING OURSELVES HERE

Prior to my spiritual awakening, I was a self-proclaimed "big city girl". I yearned to be in and amongst the bustling city, full of life; overlooking a skyline of lit-up buildings. I always loved the beach and the ocean, but I would take staying in a fancy hotel in the centre of a city, over camping in nature any day. In fact, growing up in Australia where we're taught that virtually everything outside will kill you (deadly spiders, snakes, dingoes, angry boxing kangaroos, the harsh landscape of the outback itself), I had an underlying fear of nature that took me *years* to repair. Being alone out in nature was my biggest fear, second only to my fear of the dark. I couldn't even fathom doing something like a vision quest alone in the wilderness, which would encompass *both* of those things; even the mere thought of it would send chills down my spine, probably because it was exactly the thing I knew I needed to do.

Even if I loved nature from the moment I started to "wake up", I wouldn't really want to be "in and amongst it". I would prefer to be observing it from a nice view, in a cosy Airbnb, rather than hiking through it on a bush walk or sleeping in it in a tent. When I would go on bush walks or shorter hikes, I would find myself on high alert; paranoid that I would be attacked by a snake or bitten by a spider; startled at every single sound.

Nowadays, I marvel at walking through the trees as I look up at their leaves, gently breathing and communicating with me; feeling the pleasant tingling sensation in my feet as I walk barefoot, relieving the ache of their desire to touch the Earth.

However, the journey of my rewilding was not an overnight process. It was layers upon layers of stubborn conditioning which I would uncover and heal, from not just my own consciousness but the collective consciousness; each layer bringing me closer to acceptance of my true, wild woman nature.

Over time, I slowly began to let go of all of the things that represented my domestication; I stopped straightening my hair and let my natural, curly hair go wild. I stopped punishing myself with gruelling workouts when my body said no and took up gentle walks and movement practices instead. I stopped wearing a bra or spending hours every month in beauty appointments for false eyelashes. I spent more time barefoot, in nature, letting myself get *dirty* - more days covered in salt from the ocean, dirt from the Earth, and sand from the beach. I released my 'high-maintenance princess codes' and became more natural, slow, relaxed, and laid back. My outer transformation into this bronzed, natural goddess was a reflection of the inner work I was doing of coming home to my connection with the Earth and learning to love and accept my own body.

When I finally began to connect to the Earth - or rather re-connect - I could feel the magic, the power, the potency of it... and I believe that was a large part of the fear holding me back from connection for so many years; resistance to what I always knew deep down was going to be unlocked inside of me. In connection with Mother Earth, I was reclaiming my full power, something I have tended to avoid at all costs. Her sheer beauty, her power, her chaos, her unpredictability frightened me because I could not bear to face those parts of myself. I could not control her, nor could I control the wild, chaotic feminine within me which was deeply activated in her presence, and so she terrified me, and I avoided her at all costs. I would make excuses as to why I didn't want to be in nature; I would be disproportionately triggered when my 'nature-loving' friends would insist I go hiking with them; I would avoid camping trips like the plague; I would make up stories about why I wasn't spending time at the parklands by my parents' house because *"I didn't like the type of trees that were down there"* (I mean, come on). Any and every force of resistance my subconscious could muster to avoid me actually grounding deeply into my body and spending the time in nature that I knew was the catalyst for my next highest evolution.

The more I began to rewild myself - the more I began to heal the relationship to my own body and being seeded *here*, rather than escaping my body or spiritually bypassing my human experience through my travels in trance elsewhere - the deeper my reverence and love of nature became. The deeper my yearning to retreat from the city and be *out* in nature, in and amongst it. I began to find myself in an emotional resonance with the Earth; feeling the land in my heart, feeling the trauma that She had endured; randomly bursting into tears as I'd drive through particular points on the freeway because I could feel the damage that had been done to her root system at the hands of man-made infrastructure. I could feel the inconceivable damage we'd done to her through our greed as a humanity: pollution, abusing her resources, taxing her delicate ecosystem with our selfish lack of gratitude or reverence for all the ways in which she nurtures and sustains us.

Perhaps that connection - the trauma and pain that our Great Mother had endured at the hands of mankind - was all too much for my heart to bear, and so I shut it down so I wouldn't have to feel it. My desire to escape my body and my connection to this physical realm - to really seed and ground myself here - was my desire to escape the pain that inevitably came with it. It's much nicer to travel up and out of my body to places where that pain doesn't exist than to have to be present with the experience of density; of the pain and suffering that is so present in this human experience.

Like so many starseeds, I was still in the phase of spiritual immaturity, which included bypassing the suffering rather than actually facing and making peace with the darkness that exists or standing up against the injustice and trying to actually change things instead of perpetually living in avoidance, with my head in the clouds. Like so many starseeds, I was so hell-bent on focusing on the "light" that I didn't want to come to terms with or accept the parts of myself that were the dark, raw, wild, chaotic, primal nature of the feminine who could not be controlled. Like so many starseeds, I was still under the illusion that the goal of ascension was *escaping this body entirely* - not realising that my true power was in being fully anchored, seeded, *here*; recognising that the keys to ascension were *within* the body.

I've tended to notice on this journey that whenever I have strong resistance towards something, it usually points at the *exact thing I need to do for my highest evolution.* Yoga and Qi Gong were two things that I disproportionately judged earlier in my journey - because they were "boring", they "weren't real workouts", and they were a cliched "waste of my time" - and now I see that they were *exactly* what was going to take me to my next stage; mastery over my physical vessel. The masculine element of the grounded, strong container for all the feminine life force that wanted to move through me. As I began to incorporate intuitive movement practices that took from and borrowed from these disciplines, along with dance and primal movement practices - my own unique blend of different practices - I noticed I was slowly able to hold and move more and more energy through my body. Not only that, but I was becoming less wiped out by it.

At the early stages of my journey, I would be virtually incapacitated by the high-voltage flow of kundalini moving upwards through my body. I would be unable to do anything for days, weeks, months on end; spending most of my time in bed or lying by a pool, basically passed out because I was so physically drained. The more I began to come home to and clear the channels within my *body* (and the trauma stored in my fascia, muscles and organs) through bodywork and somatic practices; the more I learnt to focus the flow of energy through my body through movement practices which connected me to my body like yoga, dance and Qi Gong, the more gracefully the energy would flow through my body, and the more energy I could hold as a result.

Previously, my energy channels were like a hose that was kinked; the life force would have to come up against all sorts of stuck trauma, density and gunk in the pipe, which did not allow it to flow easily. And so, every time my stream of kundalini would be activated, it would be building immense pressure, having to burst through these blockages and calcifications, releasing them all at once and wiping me out in the process. Or, the energy would be building and building with nowhere to go because I was not directing or channelling it out of my physical body; either sending the excess energy back into the Earth via a grounding practice or directing it and sending it out towards my creations.

However, I was not only dealing with the kundalini rising through my body from below, which was wiping me out and rendering me incapacitated but a never-ending stream of energy from above - Light codes, Soul codes, Galactic codes, Solar codes, Source codes - that was wanting to come down through my body, to be anchored into the Earth. Nor was I using discernment as to whether *everything that I could channel* was actually *for* my highest good or completely necessary for my soul mission. (Just because you *can* access and channel it, doesn't mean you should - this is another pivotal point in transition from being a priestess or 'channeller' to an Oracle who has extreme discernment over what they are channelling and who maintains full integrity and sovereignty whilst receiving the downloads.)

The energy wanted to flow both ways, but I had no grounding point to be able to anchor that downward flow of energy into the Earth. I was often able to tap into these incredible higher potentials, energies, timelines and light codes, which would have me in awe and elation feeling them; but I was not actually *anchoring* them properly here on Earth (bringing Heaven to Earth), enabling them to actually manifest in the physical. My body was too dense to hold them, and their frequency was far too high for me to hold alone.

I came to learn that it wasn't actually fully my job to hold a lot of them in my body all on my own, as it was far too much for my poor little human body; I needed to learn to let the *Earth* help me hold them. I have not actually known anyone who channels or feels energy in the same volume or visceral way as I do. Nor have I met any human mentors or guides (until recently) who have been able to support me with my unique skill set, making it very isolating at times, as I have never really known anyone who has gone through what I have in this specific way, to be able to understand or help me. Much of my journey has been a self-initiation process; a process of trial and error, putting together puzzle pieces as to what this energy is for and how I am to move it, retrieving pieces of the past along the way. The process of being self-initiated in this way has been a *long* and *relentless journey,* and it has not been something that I "figured out" overnight. In many ways, I'm *still* learning, growing and evolving, as the amounts of energy that channel through me exponentially seem to expand, as my heart opens more and more and the 'locks' on my power are lifted, one by one.

Even to this day - as I am being initiated into holding higher and higher volumes of energy - I have moments where I feel "wiped" and "physically incapacitated" for a few days, as my body has to upgrade to be able to hold the volume that wants to move through me and into the Earth. The more energy that wants to flow through me, the larger the underground network that is required to hold it; oftentimes, the higher the volume of energy, the bigger area of land I am being asked to "light up". If I forget for a few days to do my grounding process (connecting myself up to the mycelium network with bare feet on the ground and sending excess energy out through the network) I feel overloaded, and my electrical circuits get fried; leaving me anxious, exhausted and with intense aches and cramping feelings in every part of my body, as my cells struggle to hold the volume of energy moving through them. If you can imagine the tenderness and the muscle fatigue that you feel the day after a huge workout, it's kind of like that, particularly in my hands and my legs. To ensure I am doing my job properly as an activator and gridworker requires a lot of somatic work, clearing out my energy channels and my connection points to the Earth.

My interest in Chinese medicine and specifically the meridian system has been something which has been marinating in the background since the early days of my awakening when I would see a kinesiologist, and it has deepened more and more as I learn the significance and importance of the meridian system as it pertains to both our connection to Gaia, and our ability to do gridwork with the Earth. After receiving the downloads about the Mycelium network in Mexico, I began to draw the parallels between this intricate network under the Earth and the network of the energy channels within our own bodies. It was my most recent mentor/book doula who took me through the extended process of connecting up each of my meridians to Gaia's meridians (and as a result, she has co-created the energetic facilitation of the next activation in the book, as this is her realm of expertise). As she began this process for me, I felt the sensation of finally being able to *spread out*; like my energy had been cramped up in a space that couldn't contain it and was wanting to explode out of my body. And this was true! I was unable to expand my own energetic field or bring down the sheer volume of energy that I require to do my sacred work, with only the single 'grounding cord into the centre of the Earth' that I had been taught would suffice. The feeble little grounding chord could barely hold a fraction of the energy that wanted to flood through me!

As I deepened my connection to Gaia even more than I'd ever been before by linking all of my channels to hers, I noticed the sensation of finally being *held* - all of me - that I had never experienced before. I felt an ease, a softness, an expansion; a shimmery, pleasurable tingle run through my body, as I could feel the energetic pulses of the mycelium network running through my meridians; or the same feeling trickling down through my feet, as stagnant energy is flushed through my system and pulsing into the Earth.

Utilising the mycelium network and connecting all of my meridians up with Gaia's enables me to push the incredible, high-frequency energy I'm here to bring through my channels as far out as it needs to go to be fully *anchored here* (often spanning acres and acres, being transported via the root system). In the following process, you will be connected to this network in order to deepen your relationship to Gaia and to be able to fully anchor your Sacred Mission here on Earth.

Please know that while we commence the process for this connection to Gaia's meridians in the following initiation, it may take some time for this connection to be fully established. This process is usually one that is usually carried out over a number of weeks to allow the body to safely and smoothly integrate the connection in each meridian.

INITIATION 5:
RETURN TO GAIA

You can access the recommended audio version of this initiation at this website: www.diamondlightoracle.com.

Welcome to the fifth initiation in this transmission.

The following is an activation to reconnect you to the Earth Womb of the Great Mother, the Mycelium Network, and begin the process of connecting each of your meridians with Gaia's.

In your mind and with your heart, set the intention that this is the work that will be done during our time together in this activation and that you are open to receive all that is in your highest good.

I now invite all the beings of the highest light who wish to support this activation taking place.

I welcome your Higher Self, your Soul Family and Oversoul Network; and invite them to support you in receiving what is of the highest for you at this time.

I declare that this is sacred space, only that which is resonating on the frequency of unconditional love is welcome in this space.

I ask that everything that takes place here today is for the *highest good of all* and in service to the Whole.

I ask that the work we do together here today ripples out and serves the collective.

And so it is, and so it is, and so it is.

We invite you to enter your Sacred Space - the safe and protected ceremony space in which you receive all calibrations, downloads, codes and activations throughout this transmission.

Acknowledging internally that *you have now entered Sacred Space.*

Imagine yourself floating in the chrysalis you have been in now for some time - this safe container acting like an embryonic sack to facilitate and protect your evolutionary process.

Notice how you are feeling, what the energy in this place feels like, and what feels different from the last time you brought your awareness here.

You may see, perceive, or feel yourself transported back to the sensation of being a baby in your mother's womb as you float here, submersed in the crystalline liquid that surrounds you.

Now imagine yourself - while still in this chrysalis - in a vast and expansive magical forest, at the foot of a large, ancient looking tree with wild, expansive and twisting roots.

As you are placed at the base of this tree, the roots begin to grow over you, but it is a comforting sensation, like receiving a loving and tender hug from your grandmother.

Allow these roots to continue to grow over you until your entire chrysalis is covered by these ancient, wise and loving roots which give life.

These roots now begin to draw you down into the Earth, as you start to be gently pulled through the layers of the Earth; first the soft yet dense soil, then the layers of the mycelium and the root network.

Allow yourself to be drawn down, down, down, deeper down into the Earth; as far down as is required for you to be rooted and anchored Here and Now.

In the depths of the Earth, you find yourself now transported into - returned to - the Womb of the Great Mother.

See what you see, hear what you hear, feel what you feel as you return to this place of ultimate nourishment and unconditional love.

Receive all that you required but were unable to receive as a human baby in your mother's womb.

Stay here for as long as you feel is necessary.

In this place, we are now re-routing the tube that has been emptying the density from your chrysalis, as it becomes your umbilical cord connecting you to Gaia.

Through this cord you will not only release what is no longer required, but you will receive further sustenance, nutrients and nourishment from the Earth as you move through this process.

This cord brings you into harmonic resonance with Gaia's heartbeat and the steady but gentle pattern of her breath; the same pattern breathed by the trees, the leaves, the roots, the plants, the entire greater network of Life.

It soothes your nervous system and sends a pulse through your entire body to bring it back into right balance.

Allow your heart to slow down to meet Gaia's heartbeat.

Allow your breath to slow down to meet Gaia's breath.

Allow yourself to sync up with the electrical pulse of the network of mycelium around you; to receive, to give, to receive, to give, harmonising with its frequency.

You may see, sense, perceive, or feel the visual of a larger network around you of tiny electrical pulses and sparks as this happens, like neurons firing in a brain.

Stay here for as long as you feel is necessary.

We are now beginning the process of connecting up each of your energy channels (meridians) to Gaia's.

This process will commence today but will gently unfold over time *within your highest alignment* and soul's timing.

You may feel slight tingling in your feet, a warm sensation, a rush of energy.

You may feel the need to release stagnant emotions, to be drawn out of your body and into the Earth to use as fertiliser for her.

Knowing that this density does not harm Her, it supports her, as she is able to transmute it into the fuel she requires.

This is the ultimate gift of the Great Mother.

We will now connect your elemental meridians to Gaia's meridians.

We are now connecting your Fire meridians - your heart, small intestine, pericardium and triple burner meridians - to Gaia's meridians.

We are now connecting your Water meridians - your bladder and kidney meridians - to Gaia's meridians.

We are now connecting your Wood meridians - your gallbladder and liver meridians - to Gaia's meridians.

We are now connecting up your Metal meridians - your lung and large intestine meridians - to Gaia's meridians.

We are now connecting up your Earth meridians - your stomach and spleen meridians - to Gaia's meridians.

We will now connect the 8 extraordinary vessels within your body to Gaia's meridians.

We are now connecting your Governing Vessel to Gaia.

We are now connecting your Conception Vessel to Gaia.

We are now connecting your Thoroughfare Vessel to Gaia.

We are now connecting your Belt Vessel to Gaia.

We are now connecting your Yang Linking Vessel to Gaia.

We are now connecting your Yin Linking Vessel to Gaia.

We are now connecting your Yang Heel Vessel to Gaia.

We are now connecting your Yin Heel Vessel to Gaia.

Trust the process however it is unfolding for you, knowing that this work will continue to unfold over the coming days, weeks, and months; however long is required for this process to complete in a graceful way.

This activation is now complete, although the process we began today will continue unfolding until its completion.

You may wish to stay here in Gaia's warm embrace, recycling and receiving revitalised energy, sustenance, and fuel.

Knowing you can never truly leave this place; you are always held in the safety of her Womb; protected, nourished and nurtured by her.

If you feel ready, you can let the roots pull your consciousness back up through the layers of the Earth, returning to the base of the Tree of Life you first found yourself in front of.

Ask this ancient tree you travelled beneath, to watch over your Soul as guardian of your time here, and a representation of your connection to All of Life.

You are now rebirthed as a child of Gaia.

It is done, it is done, it is done.

And so it is.

Integrating and calibrating this now on the physical level.

Integrating and calibrating this now on the emotional level.

Integrating and calibrating this now on the mental level.

Integrating and calibrating this now through all levels and dimensions of your light body.

Integrating, calibrating and sharing this frequency now through all timelines and all versions of yourself across the multiverse.

We now shut down any and all open portals and gateways that are no longer required and send back all energy that has come through any portals or gateways in the process of this work.

We now dissolve any bonds, chords or attachments that have been formed for the process of this activation and call you back into complete Soul Sovereignty.

We return all of your energy to you now as you call your Soul fully into your body.

Inviting in now Diamond Light to cleanse and close this space, bringing this sacred activation to a close and thanking all of the beings who have been here supporting in this process.

It is done, it is done, it is done, and so it is.

You may spend some time here in silent reflection or receiving in your Sacred Space if it feels necessary.

If you feel complete, we invite you to gently bring yourself back into your body and into the room, wiggling your fingers and toes and opening your eyes when you are ready.

PART SIX

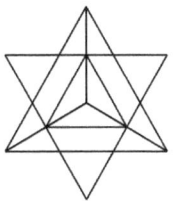

THE BRIDGE

THE OLED SCREEN

It's about a month into the process of writing this book and well into the process of having my meridians connected into Gaia.

My doula/mentor has just sent me a text message to let me know she's about to get to work in my field again. It only takes moments before I can feel it like someone has turned a tap on. I close my eyes and allow myself to fully drop in.

I can feel the shimmery, translucent and warming energy moving spontaneously through my body. The subtle electrical pulses as they begin to make their way down into my feet.

My calves, my feet, feeling this rush of frequency, this tingling sensation, as I feel each of my meridians sinking down, down, down, further into the mycelium network, to be deeply earthed.

I can feel my field finally get the space to expand out; all of the energy that has been wanting to flow through me to suddenly have the spaciousness it needed, to spread into this intricate network beneath me; feeling the spark of electrical pulses like neurons firing in a brain as connection points are made.

My whole body is overcome with calming waves of tingling energy; every cell and fibre of my being releases a deep exhale as this pleasant and pleasurable feeling floods me. The only things I could possibly compare this sensation to is a gentle caress of a lover, sliding into a hot bath on a cold winter's day, or the exact moment when the morphine drip kicks in, and even these do not do it justice...

I see myself as the Tree of Life; an ancient, magnificent tree with intricate interweaving roots like a Banyan that span down into the Earth beyond where the eye can see; pulses being sent down each of the roots and connecting to the mycelium which carry these pulses further, further, further still...

I feel the shimmery energy continue to run down the back of my spine; bringing a heating yet comforting pressure in my tailbone and my perineum as if someone was gently pressing down on them with their healing hands.

The sense of peace overcomes me like I could rest here in this moment forever.

The sensations of a comfortable weightiness in my feet anchor me down, but it feels good to stay and be still.

I allow myself to sink further into the softness of my bed, which now feels like nestling into a cloud and let out a deep, long exhale.

A few hours later, I walk into an electrical goods store to help my mother choose a new TV, and there it is - *not even trying to be subtle...*

The cosmic wink at me, the synchronicity-so-blindingly-obvious-that-it's-laughable, the *"yes, this is really what is happening"* confirmation, my private inside joke with God; right there for all the unsuspecting shoppers to see (and take no notice of).

I stop dead in the middle of my sentence as I am speaking to the salesman and laugh out loud. *Are you fucking kidding me?!*

On the incredibly clear, high-definition OLED screen my mum is considering buying - in the exact moment we happen to approach it -

there is the scene of a clearing in the middle of a mystical and magical forest at night.

Tens of ancient looking trees with these twisting and winding roots, sitting and waiting patiently in near darkness.

Suddenly, shimmering golden and colourful sparkles float down from the sky like magic, to be taken in and swallowed by the tops of the trees reaching branches...

As they make their way down the tree, into their ancient roots, deep into the earth, these coloured sparkles are carried further and further out, lighting up the ground and the entire root network surrounding the tree...

The mycelium network in the Earth is being lit up as the TV screen depicts the marvellous spectacle of this energy breathing, moving through the Earth and spreading, far, far, out...

Every plant, every flower, every leaf in the vicinity is illuminated with this sparkling, brilliant colour as the colours multiply out and become the rainbow...

A magical symphony of colour and frequency, dancing and bringing the forest to life with the swirling, animated energy...

Indeed, I'm being shown an external visual depiction of *exactly* what I've been visualising in my mind's eye every time I've been down at the park doing my daily devotional practice, working on the modality I'm birthing; connecting each of my channels into Gaia and bringing down the energies that are for this network.

I'm standing there, staring at the screen for a good moment or so, smiling my ass off.

You best believe we're buying that TV.

THE MAP

After returning from the trip to Chichén Itzá, I had clear instructions for my next steps, and finally the mission was beginning to take form. I knew that I had to put a call out for the women who would be joining me, and I knew there would be about five who would hear the call.

I created a vague video about a mystery offer, encoded with the frequency of the sacred mission, and within a few days the women who were called had already taken their places, and the first call was scheduled. It was at this point I confirmed what I had channelled around the connection to the initial Lionsgate ceremony (which commenced the work as I observed all the women who joined were also present for that ceremony.

On our first call, I led the women through a Solar Attunement, and each of them received their own special messages and unique sets of codes as they stepped into the centre of the altar, one by one. I was understanding the specific codex and soul lineage of each woman and why she was an important part of the mission. What I was being shown was that each of these women was located at a specific point on the Earth where they would anchor this grid and that they each had connections to particular ancient civilisations and galactic races in their soul codexes as well. They were opening portals where *they* were situated to receive the frequency and anchor the work that I was doing with the Mayan codex in Central America. That, in turn, was rippling out into the Earth via the mycelium network, spreading the work we were doing, so it was spanning out to a more global reach. I was scheduling the meetings when spirit was guiding me to every fortnight, but looking back now, they all fell on particular numbered dates; there was some significance or pattern numerologically that was present. Between our calls, we would keep in contact via a group chat, sharing anything that was coming through for us individually as we were in the vortex of energy together.

I knew that my "next stop on the map" was the trip back to the Tulum ruins/archeological zone, but I managed to distract myself with work and the budding romance that was unfolding for me at the time for the entire week after our trip to Chichén Itzá.

That Saturday morning, we had a power-out (which would happen quite frequently in Tulum, and it seemed to conveniently correspond with the intense solar storms occurring that weekend), and I had a sudden urge to go to the beach, so I messaged Bestie to see if she wanted to join me. She had asked if we could go somewhere quiet because she felt she needed to meditate, and I remembered the nudge I kept getting that morning to go out by the ruins again (which is right on the shoreline). My lover lent me his scooter for the day, and off we went. After forty-five gruelling minutes, which should have been a twenty-minute drive - thanks to the road that used to go to the ruins being re-built, and me not realising we had to divert to go all the way around - we arrived very delirious, sweaty and sunburnt at the entry of the archeological site.

I knew that I didn't actually have to go inside the site this time, that I just had to find a spot in that surrounding area that was thick with jungle, as whatever work I would do would be carried throughout the tree root system and mycelium network.

We subtly slipped off the main path where the construction workers were digging out the road, a few metres into the bush, hiding behind one tree I felt particularly drawn to, with ancient-looking twisted roots extending wildly out of it. Popping an awkward squat, trying to hide in the thin trunks of trees from tourists passing by and the construction workers who were still in sight; I closed my eyes and opened my channel; clinging to the tree so I wouldn't topple forward with the energy that started to surge through me.

For a short session - not to mention one that seemed so ridiculously hilarious, hiding behind the bush not metres from tourists and construction workers going about their business, none the wiser - it was still incredibly potent. My hands began to move with their usual mudras, and light language formed in what felt like perfect sentences from my lips; whispered in a low chanting under my breath so as not to draw attention to us hiding in the bushes.

I was guided to share the frequency from the previous two pyramids and connect up the points; flushing the energetic portal at that point with the energy that was streaming through me. I could also feel a lot of heavy energy lifting - much heavier than was present at the two previous sites. We were only sitting there for about ten minutes tops before it was time to get up; noticing my exposed bottom - thanks to the booty shorts I would exclusively wear in my time living there, as it was too hot for anything else - was covered in insect bites.

Once complete, we headed off to the beach where we - both exhausted from the day, overstimulated by the energy and taking our crankiness out on each other - had our first tiff, which lasted all of twenty minutes, before we both apologised, spoke our truth and owned our end of the conflict. If only all relationships could be navigated with such ease and transparency!

After laying on the beach for a couple of hours, I had the sudden, *very strong* taste of a particular drink I loved to get from a cafe downtown (spirit occasionally appeals to the part of me who is incredibly food motivated; guiding me to places I need to be with strong, random food cravings from specific places, or tastes in my mouth). Bestie and I decided to take a detour on the way home to give the electricity at my apartment complex some more time to come back on and to stop at the cafe for a late afternoon snack so I could fulfil my craving. Alas, the craving was not just a craving; it was me following the breadcrumb trail of messages that would redirect me somewhere I was required to be that evening.

While sitting at the cafe enjoying our beverages, we were talking about what I would do with myself that evening if the power was still not on at my place. Staying at my apartment without electricity, as I had the night before, was extremely uncomfortable as it was a hot box without the fan or AC running, so it would mean another very unpleasant sleep for me, and I was exhausted after our big day. The water was hooked up to the electrical grid, so I also wouldn't be able to shower after our day at the beach or brush my teeth. My friend suggested I could stay with her, and we threw around other options I had of places I could stay, including my new man I was spending most of my time with (which didn't appeal to me in the slightest, as he was staying at his workshop at the time), or other girlfriends.

While we sat discussing my options, I got a strong and sudden flash of the Airbnb I had stayed at the first time I was in Tulum two years prior (the room where I had entered into a sacred vortex, purging all of that trauma from the grid with the help of my past-life-lover). I had a vision of myself lying in the big, ludicrously soft and comfortable bed, tucked into the clean, crisp, white sheets; watching a movie on the enormous TV and enjoying takeaway. But it wasn't just a vision; it was visceral, and I felt it in my whole body, almost like I had transported myself into the timeline where I was already there.

I felt my muscles sink and relax into the cloud-like fluffiness of the bed beneath me; the coolness of the powerful AC unit gently blowing on my face as I was tucked under the pleasantly weighted blankets; the reaction of my tastebuds to the yummy flavours of the food I was eating; the warm feeling of comfort, relaxation, and just delicious, juicy, satisfied, '*yessss this is exactly where I want to be right now*' washing over me, bringing with it orgasmic tingles of pleasure. It was such a strong and clear feeling in my body that I couldn't shake it. The more I sat with it, the stronger the feeling felt, and I knew that I was being given this strong impulse, this desire for a reason. (Hot tip in case you haven't figured it out yet - the tingling, juicy, orgasmic sensations or 'turned on feeling' in your sacral or yoni when exploring potentials is *usually* your body telling you "YES, THIS". Follow these sensations, and watch what happens.)

As I was sitting with all the other potentials of the other places I could be - including the potential that my electricity would be on when we arrived back, and I could just stay at my own place - this option had a gravitational pull; the visual was bright, and I could *see, taste, feel* it.

"I think I'm meant to stay at the Airbnb I stayed at the last time I was here for some reason", I shared with my friend, "and actually, the last time I was staying there, I also went to the ruins and was purging *a lot of crap*."

We searched my Airbnb history on my phone, and I found it; the only room on the property available that night was the exact one that I had stayed in, and the price for one night was $111 (*of course*). But *just in case* it wasn't obvious enough for me - because you know, sometimes you need a 'sign-ier' sign - my friend suggested I ask for another sign, as it seemed indulgent to book a room for a night when I had places to go for free, and I was on a tight budget with my upcoming travel. So I declared, "Okay, spirit, if I'm meant to stay there tonight for whatever reason, I want a loud and clear sign."

About five minutes later, I accidentally knocked my helmet off the bench we were sitting at, and it hit the floor with a loud CRASH, causing everyone else in the cafe to turn around and look at us, as I awkwardly laughed and picked it up. *Oops.*

A few minutes later, we were getting up to pay, and once again, my helmet flung out of my hand, hitting the floor once again with another loud CRASH (I mean, I'm a little clumsy at times, but I'm not *that* clumsy). A girl sitting on a table nearby working on a laptop lifted her head from her screen and said (and I quote), "Jeeze, that must be a sign for someone, hey?"

We all laughed, but it wasn't until we were on the scooter about two minutes from my apartment that I joined the dots, and it actually landed.

"Wait a second," I asked my bestie, "do you think that was the 'loud and clear' sign I asked for?" and we both burst into laughter because the words that had come out of the woman's mouth were quite *literally* "that must be a sign", and neither of us had clocked it until ten minutes later. At that point, I had decided to go to the Airbnb *regardless* of whether my power was on again at my apartment or not - partially as there was clearly a reason I felt guided to it, and partially because it just felt damn good to.

I arrived home, and the power was still off, but I could see that there were workers on site fixing something, so it would probably be on soon. I booked the room, quickly threw some things into a bag for the night, and jumped back on the scooter to head there. As I rode the scooter there, the downloads began to come through as to why I was guided to stay there that evening. As I'd taken the aligned action, the 'why' could now be revealed - which is often the case with my intuitive nudges. I often don't know the "why" until I've already trusted and said yes to the initial impulse. The reason I was being guided there was because I had opened a portal the last time I had gone to the Tulum ruins for the day and then returned to that room to process the energies, and it needed to be closed.

I'll be honest with you; it's never a boost to your confidence as a priestess, nor a pleasant experience to have to backtrack and clean up your own mess years later when playing in the quantum realms - one of the reasons I was so hesitant to jump into any of this gridwork or portal work in the first place. The fear of *'what if I open something I'm not supposed to and all hell breaks loose?'*

I will say that this has only happened twice (that I forgot to close a portal I'd opened, and things started to leak out of that portal that weren't supposed to), and both times that I rectified the situation, it hadn't ended up being that big of a deal. But there was a time before I really knew what I was doing in the non-physical realms, where I didn't even realise the work I was doing was opening portals in the first place and that I was accidentally leaving them open, which was a big no-no. It wasn't until my mentors (who were helping me clear my field of intrusions at the time, after enduring horrendous energetic attacks for upwards of six months) brought up the concept of "open portals" in early 2022 that I learnt I had to *intentionally* ask to close all open portals and send all energy back which is not required at the end of every session. They had seen in my field that I had open/active portals and were guided to show me how to close them. Since then, I have made this a *non-negotiable* after every session and haven't had any further problems or needed to backtrack to close portals I accidentally opened and didn't shut. So there's your lesson for anyone who needs to read this - if you're opening portals for whatever reason as a part of your sacred work, make *damn sure* you're closing them when they're no longer required!

Alas, back in 2021, I had opened a portal to assist me in clearing all of the ancestral trauma that was stuck in that part of the grid when I had last visited the ruins, and I had not properly closed it. I was shown all of this heavy, black, gunk-like energy that was leaking out of this portal, clogging up the grid with residual trauma and lower frequencies that were flooding through it. That's the best way I can explain it visually, but it was more complex than that. It was more like an "open time loop in the quantum which then reverberated out, attaching to all these other lower, simultaneously occurring resonant timelines of trauma". Actually, an even more specific explanation would be to say that *I* (as in, my body) was acting as the portal the energy was coming through, and once I left the location physically without properly "closing" the connection point, which was flushing the trauma, I left a gaping void in the space that some not nice stuff was able to come through. In summary: *no bueno.*

I flushed the portal with diamond light, cleared the energy out of the grid and plugged the hole. I was then guided to re-calibrate it to the larger grid I had already lit up with the frequency of the two pyramids I'd visited; noticing that as I did this, an even *larger* network of lights switched on, as the underground waterways of the cenotes and the mycelium network transmitted the frequency.

A week earlier, the Map Reader had located a map online of all of the Mayan pyramids, which showed that the network of Mayan pyramids spanned up to the border of Yucatan and Quintana Roo - Chichén Itzá being very close to the "top" most point - all the way down past Guatemala City; with some spilling out to the right of the Guatemalan border, into Belize and El Salvador, and to the left in Chiapas, Mexico. (This crucial discovery is what warranted her nickname, "The Map Reader".) There were a few pyramids at the northmost point of Guatemala - around the centre point of the map - which we felt may be important for me to visit at some point, as there was a large expanse of protected jungle that covered the border between Calakmul in Mexico, and El Mirador in Guatemala (a jungle I'd later find myself hiking in, but I didn't know that yet).

In my mind, I could see that with this manoeuvre, the entire area down to about the centre of the map had been lit up, and it solidified for me that what I was essentially doing was travelling down the centre line, lighting up the sites along the way.

Not only that, but I realised it meant that without a doubt, the Map Reader was right, and Guatemala was my next destination... *much to my Little Human Self's dismay.*

The Map Reader had been suggesting since prior to Chichén Itzá that I might have to go to Guatemala as part of this mission as it kept coming up for her (especially after locating the map of pyramids), and I had always had huge resistance to it. I felt very overwhelmed by the prospect of having to travel there alone and make the travel arrangements, which did not seem straightforward after some initial research. I was looking at multiple plane trips, overnight airport hotel stays, and most likely having to find a tour group to go with; all as a solo female traveller with multiple suitcases, on a tight budget. It was a terribly unappealing journey to me at the time.

I think it's important to reiterate that while in hindsight the trip was fairly smooth, and the thought of travelling like this doesn't bother me so much now - as I've already done it, and while quite exhausting, it was a lot smoother than I thought it'd be - I am not and probably never will be a "back-packing", "long-haul overnight bus and plane trips in foreign countries", "off the beaten path", "adventure-tour", "travel-loving" kinda girl; even if I *did* enjoy a brief stint of a fortnight or so of van life with one of my former boyfriends. (Or maybe the "not enjoying travelling in this way" is just a story I'm telling myself, but at this moment, as I write, it stands.) I like my morning routine, my comfortable bed and my personal hygiene *way* too much. If that makes me a diva, fine, I accept that; although I do believe I have come into this lifetime with certain codes that have made me accustomed to a certain standard that I'm not really willing to sacrifice unless I absolutely *must*. According to my parents, I came into this life with expensive tastes, high standards of cleanliness and a desire to be comfortable. They continually like to share a story about when I was three, and I walked into a motel we were due to stay at on holiday, saw a cockroach on the wall and declared, "I'm not staying here; take me to a hotel". *True story: I was a diva even at three years old.* So, while I have certainly rewilded and relaxed my high standards a *lot*, I can't say that I'll ever get rid of the diva/goddess inside of me who would *much rather* my personal space, my privacy, my pleasant surroundings, my comfort, or a good night's sleep, than what is required of travelling in this "adventure off the beaten path" kinda way.

In fact, there was a time only a few years ago when even spending a night away from home was something I'd actively avoid because I liked my comfortable, harmonious, aesthetically pleasing, familiar surroundings so much. I am so sensitive to subtle frequency that I am affected in a *visceral* way by disharmonious surroundings, such as loud or disruptive noise, poor aesthetic/design/lines/shapes, or a lack of natural light. It hurts my nervous system in a way that's hard to explain, even if I have been training myself to have mastery over this and not react. I travel for the necessity of my soul mission because I am required to. However, lugging my entire life - jammed into a suitcase and a duffel bag - with me to new places on unfamiliar travel paths does not appeal to me on a Little Self-level in the slightest. Part of me deeply yearns to be grounded and comfortable; to set down roots somewhere safe and familiar. Part of me is exhausted from living out of a suitcase, having no place to call my 'home', and not being able to tell people where I plan to be even two weeks in the future. Part of me would *love* to get all in my Pisces vibes, decorating a place to my refined yet quirky artistic tastes; a beautiful, quiet and warm property surrounded by nature where I can raise my children, build my own temple and music studio, and grow my own vegetables. However, my soul path has always seen me pushing the boundaries of what my uptight Little Self desires, to let go of resistance and break down my walls, one by one.

I won't bitch and moan, pretending like spirit had me going from "living in an inner city apartment in Melbourne" to "travelling Central America by myself, hiking in the middle of the Guatemalan jungle" overnight. I can see how, prior to this initiation, I was prepared little by little to let go of my familiar surroundings and my "safe home" to find comfort in the instability and uncertainty of constant travel and living nomadically, following the mystery of my intuitive pings.

The first initiation (which was a major one, the catalyst for my entire soul mission) was to let go of my apartment of six years, leaving Melbourne and my entire "adult" life behind - as I grew up in Sydney, so Melbourne was my "chosen" home - when I heard the call to go to Bali, back in 2019.

Then, once again, I was stripped of my security blanket when I was guided to leave my long-term apartment in Canggu (Bali), which I adored, as it was a stunningly designed, feminine, safe cocoon for me during the initial stages of my spontaneous kundalini awakening - in 2021, to move to a different part of the island, away from all my friends and familiar surroundings. I might add that this happened to reroute me to a part of the island, which was still fairly lax and 'open' in the same week that the whole of Canggu began enforcing vaccine mandates and a stricter lockdown, so it was certainly to my benefit.

Then, in the latter part of 2021, I faced the hugeness of the initiation that was travelling to Costa Rica alone in the middle of the pandemic to meet a near stranger, which basically obliterated any kind of fear I'd had around travelling. (Although, not without my Little Self trying to seriously sabotage me going at all by having such a huge panic attack that I nearly didn't get to the airport on time, then again by manifesting complications with my documents that took a *miracle* to resolve, just in time for me to board the plane.)

I share this all so you can imagine why - even after so many initiations and preparations to get me to that point - I still didn't take delight in the thought of having to travel to Guatemala alone. It was yet another leap off a cliff into the Unknown for my Little Self, and frankly, it felt like a logistical headache.

Even less appealing than the thought of travelling to Guatemala alone was the vision the Map Reader had shared of me hiking deep through the jungle to a particular pyramid that was important for me to go to. The first time she had told me of this vision, I had brushed it off, thinking, "Well, maybe it's metaphorical," or "Maybe it's in the future", to deny the very real possibility of having to go as part of the mission.

As the mission became clearer and clearer - and now grasping the understanding of what I was doing, travelling down this Mayan map, activating pyramids as I went - I was realising that my loud resistance to the hike meant it was *exactly* what I needed to be doing. There was some piece in the journey itself that was going to be a HUGE initiation and death of a former level of identity for me - which was probably why I was dreading it so much. In fact, it seemed like the most "out of my comfort zone" thing I could possibly think of doing; so, therefore, the thing that was probably going to catapult me into a whole new level of being.

Sure, I loved nature and enjoyed a day hike, as long as I had somewhere comfortable to return to, a nice shower and a hot meal on the other side. However, the thought of trekking for several days through the unrelenting jungle seemed like my own personal hell on Earth (and for the first few days it *was*, as you already read). Far less something I'd have to *pay* money I didn't have at the time to do. I still hadn't dealt with my fear of nature or the dark at this point, so just imagining myself in the middle of the night wandering out in the pitch black jungle, needing to relieve myself, with my weak bladder that has me up at all hours of the night... it was a little too much for my mind to fathom.

For some reason, my Little Human Self had concocted a worst-case-scenario horror story that I'd be hiking *au natural* style in the thick of the jungle with maybe one or two others; basically sleeping amidst the trees and cooking my meals on a portable gas burner; having to carry all my belongings on my back for days on end. It didn't really occur to me that there were people who arranged tours with multiple guides, specially laid out base camps with amenities (such as "toilets"), and mules that would take our gear for us. (On the other side of this initiation, the former scenario actually doesn't sound so unbearable to me now.)

So - as I do whenever I come up against something I *really* don't want to do but know is for my highest good - I prayed. I prayed that if I was really required to do this as part of my mission, God would make my path clear and as easy as possible.

A few days later, I stumbled across the website of a hostel in Guatemala, which intuitively pinged for me, as it had the same name as the property I was staying at in Tulum, which ran several tours to the two main pyramids near Flores, Guatemala; Tikal and El Mirador. The former was a day trip, and the latter was a five-day hike that began at the town of Carmelita, a couple hours away from Flores. Something in me told me, *'Goddammit, this is it, this is the hike I'm meant to do.'* I contacted the hostel, and they informed me I needed a minimum of two people to secure a spot on the tour and make a booking.

It felt like a closed door as I was needing to make plans to go within a fortnight - to coincide with my visa situation - and I didn't know any of my friends in Tulum who wanted to go with me (frankly, I didn't blame them one iota).

Once again, I prayed. *'God, if you want me to do this, sort it out. Make it easy. And please, please, please don't make me do this alone.'*

The guidance told me to wait, that I wasn't going to have to go alone, and that there was someone I had not connected with yet who would be journeying with me. So, as wild as it was at the time for me to trust to this level - to just go about my life getting closer to the impending date I had to leave my apartment without sturdy onward plans of any sort - I did. Surprisingly, it was the most freeing, liberating and exhilarating feeling I had ever had (for most of the time, anyway, when my Little Human Self wasn't thinking about it). I had unlocked a whole new level of trust within myself; of being completely calm, surrendered and internally secure regardless of the fact *I had no fucking idea* where I'd be in less than a fortnight's time.

About ten days out from the date I knew I had to leave Mexico, I had a moment of panic. I hadn't booked the hike because I couldn't guarantee the tour would run without a second person, nor had I arranged any of my travel, my hiking equipment, or my onward plans. There was basically the hypothetical "Guatemala hike for five days", followed by a big gaping void of a month and a half until it was time to go to Mexico City for my conference, which I'd not yet been guided to fill. I was also starting to dwindle in funds, fast, as the energetics of everything I was facilitating, the heaviness of eclipse season, *and* the karmic relationship I was navigating were collectively beginning to take their toll on me, once again putting a halt on my ability to generate income. But the guidance kept telling me to wait, to not panic; that I was going to meet someone to go with. Even though I felt low-key delusional by this point, I trusted and surrendered once again; after all, my channel had been right about pretty much *everything else* on this trip.

A few days after my momentary panic attack, a sister of mine from the gym (the one who had introduced Bestie and me) introduced me to *her* best friend at our local coffee spot. We didn't talk for long - probably five minutes or so - but we hit it off immediately as we vibed over astrology. Shortly after, my friend told me that her bestie would love to get to know me more and invited me to join them on a day trip to Playa del Carmen that weekend. Always down for adventures and new friends, I said yes, and we were off. It was about twenty minutes into the car ride that I shared with them how I was being guided to go on this hike in Guatemala and all the resistance that was coming up for me as a result. I shared how I was being told the right person was coming in and jokingly asked if either of them wanted to come with me.

After a brief pause, my new friend gasped from behind the steering wheel, "Bec, I've been intuitively guided to prep and be ready to go on a hike for *months*, and I don't know why, but I think it's me that you've been waiting for." All three of us erupted into excited exclamations and commented on feeling immediate full-body chills. The energy in the car was palpable, and I had a sudden surge of kundalini in my body, screaming, "YES, it's her!" As we began to talk through the larger spiritual purpose of this trip, I could feel - it would be transformative for her to join this journey as well, as she was being called on her own medicine path - and the logistics of how we could make it work (my new hiking buddy had several dogs that needed looking after), everything seemingly fell into place and sorted itself out. By the end of our day trip, it was almost *certain* that she was coming with me, and I didn't have to go alone.

You cannot even begin to imagine the relief and gratitude that washed over me as it dawned on me that God had come through with a miracle yet again; not only would I have company on my trip, but I was going with an awesome new friend who collected hunting knives for fun. This was an exciting adventure for her, the kind of thing that she genuinely enjoyed doing!

That was the *exact* sort of energy and person which would support me to feel a whole lot less terrified going into the experience.

About a week out from leaving, we caught up to book everything, and planning the trip just seemed convoluted and hard. It was not flowing, or easy, or exciting, and just felt like a big pain in the butt... I began dreading it once again. By this point - with all the magic that had unfolded already on my Indiana-Jones-like mystery adventure - I had learnt that if things aren't flowing, it's because there's often an easier way. As we looked at the map once again to try to figure out which would be the easiest route, mere moments away from booking our flight, my friend exclaimed, "Wait a minute, Bec, why don't we just drive?" Once again, the whole thing opened up. It was like a weight had been lifted off us, and suddenly, everything seemed *so much more effortless.*

My friend loved driving and actually felt more comfortable driving than flying; she didn't even mind driving the full twelve-hour trip on her own (she did it all the time, she told me). For me - with my multiple suitcases containing my whole life and my guitar - it was solving a lot of baggage issues, and it also felt like it opened me up more for future plans moving on from Guatemala, as I could always just come back to Tulum with her in the car and go from there. Not only that, but she had always desired and felt called to travel to Lake Atitlan (towards the bottom of the Mayan map), but we didn't know how we would get there from Flores, where our hiking tour began, with our original plan of flying (little did we know there's actually entire travel agencies dedicated to helping people travel this route, which is affectionately known as the "Gringo Trail"). I had previously felt drawn to go to Lake Atitlan - before finding out about the map or any other details around the mission, when I was first researching places I could go for my visa run - but the logistics of organising it felt very convoluted and unappealing to me, so I had decided not to on this trip.

Now that we were driving and I had a friend who was keen to go, we could do the entire thing as one big road trip together. Both of us felt relieved and excited, as all we had to do was book the hostel for the nights on either side of the tour and then allow ourselves to play it by ear from there onwards, flowing with what felt right in the moment. For me, having a friend with me who was happy to just follow the intuitive pings and soul bread crumbs felt like we were starting off on an exciting adventure I was now keen to go on; rather than flying blind all by myself, in a foreign country, in survival mode.

I spent the week or so leading up to our departure in a bittersweet energy, saying goodbye to the soul family I had met in Tulum (not believing at the time I was returning, as I'd travel onwards from Guatemala) and to the safe and comfortable home I'd created for myself in the three months since I first arrived. Tulum had been the stage for so much magic and evolution for me, and leaving it - along with the few very instrumental soulmates I was also leaving behind - to leap into the unknown certainly made me feel tender.

Amidst my bittersweet *"it's not goodbye, it's I'll see you later"s* and my Little Human Self moments of frantically googling *"do jaguars attack humans?"*, I was being prepared - mentally, spiritually and emotionally - for the sacred vision quest I was about to embark on.

BI LOCATION,
INTERDIMENSIONAL TRAVEL &
SOUL JOURNEYING

In preparation for my jungle mission, I experienced many spiritual initiations and was taken through training in the quantum with my soul team; which I was sharing with the mystery school of women supporting the mission and also sharing to a less advanced capacity with the other group I was leading through my psychic development accelerator at the time, 'Psychic AF'. In one particular initiation, I was approached by the spirit of Grandmother Ayahuasca, whose presence induced a full-blown medicine journey where I was transported deep into the jungle.

For context, I frequently drop into trance and enter into altered states of consciousness, psychedelic states and soul journeys without the need to consume any sort of plant or mind-altering substance. Quite often I commune with different plants in spirit form and experience their effects without needing to "consume" them physically. I have never sat with Ayahuasca in a physical ceremony as I have not yet felt the call, although I have sat with Grandfather Medicine (Huachu-ma/San Pedro/cactus medicine once, and Psilocybin (mushrooms many times earlier on my journey, including once taking a heroic dose, which to me basically felt like *I might as well have taken Ayahuasca*. There was also a time recently when I would use rapé (burnt tobacco -

also known as "mapacho" - mixed with the ashes of other sacred plants that are blown into the nostril) often to ground me. In fact, it became an unhealthy dependency/addiction, and the plant would often tell me off for abusing it (these days I use it *very* sparingly and am always amazed at its power, now that I use it the way it was *meant* to be used; with respect and reverence). However, the more sensitive I become, the less it feels good for me to consume any sort of plant medicine. I believe that these master plants are only here to help us tap into states which we can access purely from our own energy, and anyone who has experienced a full-blown kundalini awakening can attest to how psychedelic and "trippy" life can feel without even needing to take anything. In my "pre-awakening" former life, I used to use psychedelic or semi-psychedelic substances like mushrooms, LSD, MDMA and ketamine semi-frequently, so I know what these substance-assisted altered states of consciousness feel like and am able to emulate their pleasant side effects (feelings of euphoria, heightened connection to everything, even sometimes psychedelic visuals) without any come down or negative side effects. In many ways, I believe my attraction to these substances back in the day was actually my gateway back to God; the feelings, sensations and moments of divine love I experience in altered/heightened states of consciousness that I could only then touch through these substances. I also believe that these master plans are *here* for people who cannot yet reach these states on their own, to guide them back to that gnosis. I have deep reverence for them being used in the correct set and setting, as long as people understand that they do not 'need' anything outside of them to reach these states of being or develop an unhealthy dependency on the plants; sitting with Ayahuasca 59 times a year without actually integrating anything they journey (*shots fired*). But I digress...

In this journey, Grandmother Aya transported me deep into the jungle and showed me how nurturing, how safe, how held I can feel there; that there was no need to be afraid. She took me into the dark, black void of night and showed me how still, how beautiful, how peaceful it was, that it could feel like being held in my mother's womb rather than suffocating. She helped me connect to a part of my soul who lived in the jungle; a strong Mayan warrior who would commune with the plants and the trees, who had no fear and would travel miles each day barefoot, using only the stars and the sun to navigate. She told me I would meet the frequency of the divine masculine - of a man who embodied Christ Consciousness - in the jungle. (At the time, I had interpreted this as if it was someone who was 'outside of me' - and it is true to say that both of the tour guides were beautiful, loving men - but in hindsight, I understand it was my own inner divine masculine I was meeting.) I was instructed that I was to channel a book from the experiences of this sacred mission and that I would be receiving many of those transmissions whilst hiking in the jungle (*and here we are*).

She showed me how to bi-locate and connect with the version of myself already on my jungle trek and to anchor myself deep into the Earth to receive the codes from the mycelium network from my past lifetimes in which I'd imprinted into the ground.

She then showed me that I was to jump "forward" - even though technically, in the quantum, there is no 'back' or 'forward'; everything is happening simultaneously - in time to take the frequency I was receiving while I held my ceremony on the top of the main pyramid in El Mirador (I had not yet travelled to), and share it with every past version of myself that had already visited a pyramid to activate them, one at a time. She explained that when I was visiting these pyramids at any given time, I was receiving data and energy from past/future/simultaneous versions of myself from all different incarnations and dimensions, as it had been whenever I was doing some sort of portal, grid or activation work, back when I didn't "know" what I was really doing. The energy that I was transmitting and receiving when I had had these huge experiences (at Chichén Itzá, at Ek Balam, at the Ruins) was, in a huge part, my own; coming from *this* version of myself, and the version of myself who was already in the jungle; along with past/simultaneous Mayan incarnations of myself, and past/future/simultaneous versions of myself in other ancient civilisations and non-human life-forms.

I was shown I did not need to physically travel to every single pyramid on the map during this trip - much to my lazy Little Self's relief - that I could bi-locate my consciousness into versions of myself who *had* travelled to these points on other timelines (as each potential exists the moment I conceive of it), and use the multidimensional network to activate a connection point to each of them. Then, at the crucial ceremony, I was yet to do in the middle of the jungle, all I had to do was list each of the names of the pyramids on the map to activate them, along with the main pyramid at El Mirador.

She gave me visions of the future and told me there would be a time coming when I would be called to 'sit' with her in the physical sense because, with the medicine running through my body, I would be even more in tune with the plant kingdom. She showed me the energy of the divine masculine partner I was destined to meet and ceremonies we would hold together; where we would be travelling to various sacred sites across the world, extending the work I had begun here, and taking others with us.

But above all, in this quantum training, I was beginning to understand on a much more embodied level the concept of 'imprinting' I had already begun to understand previously (and have already touched on earlier in this book). However, rather than 'imprinting' to affect and change physical matter (like my explanation in the section around alchemy), I was imprinting and sharing data with different versions of my multidimensional *self*; essentially enabling me to bi-locate and hop through time.

I am going to be perfectly honest: some of the scientific concepts (like interdimensional travel or bi-location, for instance) I am trying to explain adequately using human language in this book are probably not going to do justice. Firstly, because I'm not a quantum physicist and my 'scientific' vocabulary and understanding is limited, and secondly, because using 'human language' to explain things that are *far beyond our human realm of understanding* is virtually impossible. I am trying to explain things in a way that my human brain understands them and simplify very advanced concepts in terms that *your* logical mind might be able to grasp. Whenever my soul team has tried to explain things *scientifically* to me, my brain blurs all the words together into one, long, incomprehensible drone, as despite what my Aquarius rising and moon signs would lead one to believe, I am not scientifically nor logically wired. I am driven by creativity, emotion, feeling, sensation, sound and art; I derive more meaning from hearing music, from seeing visuals, from being shown something than being explained how it works. A lot of the time, I don't know or understand the mechanics of what I am capable of doing in the spiritual realms; however, I have an innate understanding of how to do it (I just put my 'mind' to sleep and let the part of me who knows, do the work for me, as I've already said). So please forgive me if my manner of explaining these concepts is simplistic or unsophisticated, but know that you are receiving an instruction within the frequency of this book on how to actually *do* this yourself. Much of what is happening on a cellular level is activating you *beyond* the logical mind, initiating you into using (or rather stimulating an awakening/remembering of) this quantum technology *within* you.

The repercussions and applications for bi-location, imprinting and tapping into our multidimensional nature have already been touched on in this book in terms of being able to receive and share information from versions of yourself across time and space who have already attained certain knowledge, codes, or states of being; enabling you to 'quantum leap'. Even just the act of being able to bring online dormant soul memory and gifts like the ability to heal or intuit the future this way is an amazing discovery, as are the applications that I've shared of being able to share frequencies with different versions of myself to transmit information and frequency. However, in this chapter, there's a far more magical application I want to highlight, one which our star brothers and sisters have already mastered: an ability that *we have encoded in our DNA.*

I believe that a large part of the reason we are being taken through this ascension process of becoming crystalline is that one day in our near future, we will be able to not only bi-locate through multidimensional versions of self in the astral realm via our 'light body', but we will be able to *take our physical bodies with us. Yes,* meaning that we will be able to move through space and time; to "teleport" like I so often joke that I wish I could. In fact, the spaceships of our galactic sisters and brothers are already using this technology, appearing both physical and non-physical at the same time, enabling them to move in a 'jumping' pattern from one place to another. I would like you to consider that there are *already* versions of you out there in the multiverse who are initiated with the skill of hopping from one place to another like it's nobody's business. And that in this next activation, all you need to do is connect to them in order to bring this technology online. While I cannot promise that you'll be able to suddenly teleport yourself to lying on a beach in Hawaii and back after receiving this initiation - as at the time of writing this, our dimension is still confined by certain universal rules and constructs pertaining to space and time which limit our ability to do so - I *can* tell you that you will create the foundation, to begin to awaken cellular memory on how to do so, perhaps someday in the future. Whether it is something humans are able to achieve within *this* lifetime or not, I am not sure. But it is certainly on the horizon as a part of this evolutionary leap we are making.

INITIATION 6:
TRAVELLING ACROSS THE
MULTIDIMENSIONAL NETWORK

You can access the recommended audio version of this initiation at this website: www.diamondlightoracle.com.

Welcome to the sixth initiation in this transmission.

The following is an activation to bring your awareness to the multidimensional network, to enable you to begin the process of shifting your consciousness into different versions of self across time and space, and ultimately, to prepare you for the ability to bi-locate completely.

In your mind and with your heart, set the intention that this is the work that will be done during our time together in this activation and that you are open to receive all that is in your highest good today.

We will take you through the process of visiting three time points together today, but this process will be the same if there are more than three time points that have been highlighted in this journey for you to visit.

You can either choose to journey to these points by yourself upon conclusion of this activation - as you have received the initiation to do this yourself - or you can simply go through this entire journey from the beginning again.

At any time you desire, you may pause this process to remain in any time point longer.

If at any point during this process, your soul desires to take you into a different journey to show you more information about this timeline, allow yourself to follow that impulse.

I now invite all the beings of the highest light who wish to support this activation taking place.

I welcome your Higher Self, your Soul Family and Oversoul Network, and invite them to support you in receiving what is of the highest for you at this time.

I declare that this is a sacred space, only that which is resonating on the frequency of unconditional love is welcome in this space.

I ask that everything that takes place here today is for the *highest good of all* and in service to the Whole.

I ask that the work we do together here today ripples out and serves the collective.

And so it is, and so it is, and so it is.

We invite you to enter your Sacred Space - the safe and protected ceremony space in which you receive all calibrations, downloads, codes and activation throughout this transmission.

Acknowledging internally that *you have now entered Sacred Space.*

Setting the intention internally today and requesting that the versions of Self you are connecting to during this process are only the highest, most resonant timelines and versions of self that will support you to bring forth your sacred mission in this lifetime.

We now request your soul-contracted team and your higher self to assist and oversee this process.

And so it is, and so it is, and so it is.

See, sense, or imagine yourself in the centre of a large disc-like mechanism.

This disc mechanism exists outside of time and space and is used as a jumping-off point to access *all* timelines and versions of yourself across the multiverse.

Standing in the centre of this disc, we are now beginning to activate this mechanism so you are able to see a visual representing every single version of you existing in the multiverse, expanding out beyond this disc all around you.

Every timeline, every decision, every version of self.

See what you see, feel what you feel, hear what you hear.

You are now connected to your Multidimensional Network.

You may see these as threads coming out of this main disc - flowing out of the version of Self in the centre of this mechanism - creating an intricate web of overlapping timelines all around you.

You may see these as thousands and thousands of sparkling lights in space, spanning as far as you can see.

You may not see anything and simply have a sense of this connection taking place.

Set the intention now that you are going to be refining and honing in on the specific versions of self that you are accessing, to only access those which have the **highest priority and strongest resonance** for you in *this* specific mission you came to carry out in *this* incarnation.

Setting the intention now that **we are calibrating this mechanism to those timelines in which there are latent gifts, codes, information, memories or experiences for you to access now** or which desire to support you in some way today.

These may be other incarnations and lifetimes in ancient civilisations where you hold important pieces of wisdom for yourself or the collective.

These may be other timelines or versions of yourself in *this* incarnation - perhaps at different time points or locations.

These may be lifetimes in non-human lifeforms, with galactic codes, technologies or higher frequencies for you to access and integrate.

You may feel called in this session to do your own planetary grid work to support the collective - setting an additional intention to connect to the specific versions of you at sacred sites or pyramids across space and time, to receive and share the information streaming from this version of You, currently undergoing this initiation.

Trust yourself and whatever feels right for you at this moment, knowing that wherever you are called to connect, it will be for your highest good. There are no mistakes and no 'right' or 'wrong' way to do or experience this activation.

As you stand in the centre of this mechanism with the vibration of this intention to connect to those timelines which are of the highest priority and resonance to you now, it now begins to spin as the timelines are configured and moved around you so that those non-resonant timelines fall away, or become more dull.

Allowing for this technology to work now.

As the technology slowly ceases its spinning or reconfiguring motion; seeing, sensing, or perceiving the rainbow bridges which are appearing, connecting you to a certain number of time points.

Notice now how many points or timelines are in resonance with this intention.

These are the time points your Higher Self wishes for you to connect to today.

Once again, we are reminding you that you will be taken to *three* of these places today in this guided journey together, but you may return to these time points and journey more if you are shown more than three places.

Allow the timeline with the strongest resonance to pull you first.

You may feel this timeline is somehow stronger, brighter, or more magnetic.

You may see this timeline highlighted for you in some way by a symbol or a colour.

You may just sense or know.

Trust what you feel and how this is being made apparent to you now.

Connecting you to this time point now, allowing your consciousness to step out onto the dimensional bridge to this time point and be transported along the bridge now.

Allowing your consciousness to travel into this time point now.

You are completely in this version of Self now, seeing through their eyes.

See what you see, feel what you feel, hear what you hear.

Notice how the surroundings feel, and look around.

Look down and notice your body, if you have one.

Notice how it feels to be in this body.

See if you can make out who you are, where you are, and *when* you are, or if there are any insights of why your soul has chosen to take you here into this moment.

You may not see, sense or feel anything, and that is also perfect; trust yourself and whatever is taking place here.

Now setting the intention to receive from this version of Self what you came here to receive, if anything.

You may feel a rush of energy, of information, or sensation at this time.

You may receive flashes of insights or downloads.

You may pause here if you need to receive what you need to receive.

Now, setting the intention to share with this version of Self anything you came here to share, if anything.

You may feel a rush of energy, of information, or sensation at this time.

You may receive flashes of insights or downloads.

You may pause here if you need to share what you need to share.

Taking a few more moments to share and receive any more information or frequency with this version of Self.

It is now time to travel back up the rainbow bridge.

Allow yourself to step out of this timeline and be transported back down the dimensional bridge, to come back to the larger part of your consciousness waiting for you on the disc mechanism.

We will now reconfigure this mechanism.

Allowing this mechanism to reconfigure now, to come back to equilibrium, and close any open portals or gateways which are not required.

Once again, setting the intention to connect to those timelines which are of the highest priority and resonance to you now.

Allowing the mechanism to spin as the timelines are reconfigured and moved around you so that once again, those non-resonant timelines fall away or become more dull.

Noticing which timelines are being highlighted for you.

Repeating the same process as before, allow yourself to be pulled towards the next timeline of highest priority and resonance.

Connecting you to this time point now, allowing your consciousness to step out onto the dimensional bridge to this time point, and be transported along the bridge now.

Allowing your consciousness to travel into this time point now.

You are completely in this version of Self now, seeing through their eyes.

See what you see, feel what you feel, hear what you hear.

Notice how the surroundings feel, and look around.

Look down and notice your body, if you have one.

Notice how it feels to be in this body.

See if you can make out who you are, where you are, and *when* you are, or if there are any insights of why your soul has chosen to take you here into this moment.

You may not see, sense or feel anything, and that is also perfect - trust yourself and whatever is taking place here.

Now setting the intention to receive from this version of Self what you came here to receive - if anything.

You may feel a rush of energy, of information, or sensation at this time.

You may receive flashes of insights or downloads.

You may pause here if you need to receive what you need to receive.

Now setting the intention to share with this version of Self anything you came here to share - if anything.

You may feel a rush of energy, of information, or sensation at this time.

You may receive flashes of insights or downloads.

You may pause here if you need to share what you need to share.

Taking a few more moments to share and receive any more information or frequency with this version of Self.

Once again, it is time to travel back up the rainbow bridge.

Allow yourself to step out of this timeline and be transported back down the dimensional bridge, to come back to the larger part of your consciousness waiting for you on the disc mechanism.

Please wait a moment while we reconfigure this mechanism.

Allowing this mechanism to reconfigure now, to come back to equilibrium, and close any open portals or gateways which are not required.

This is the last time we will repeat this process together.

Once again, setting the intention to connect to those timelines which are of the highest priority and resonance to you now.

Allowing the mechanism to spin as the timelines are configured and moved around you so that once again, those non-resonant timelines fall away, or become more dull.

Noticing which timelines are being highlighted for you.

Allow yourself to be pulled towards the next timeline of highest priority and resonance.

Connecting you to this time point now, allowing your consciousness to step out onto the dimensional bridge to this time point, and be transported along the bridge now.

Allowing your consciousness to travel into this time point now.

You are completely in this version of Self now, seeing through their eyes.

Notice how this timeline is different to other timelines.

Notice how it is similar.

See what you see, feel what you feel, hear what you hear.

Notice how the surroundings feel, and look around.

Look down and notice your body - if you have one.

Notice how it feels to be in this body.

See if you can make out who you are, where you are, and *when* you are, or if there are any insights of why your soul has chosen to take you here, into this moment.

Now setting the intention to receive from this version of Self what you came here to receive - if anything.

You may feel a rush of energy, of information, or sensation at this time.

You may receive flashes of insights or downloads.

You may pause here if you need to receive what you need to receive.

Now setting the intention to share with this version of Self anything you came here to share - if anything.

You may feel a rush of energy, of information, or sensation at this time.

You may receive flashes of insights or downloads.

You may pause here if you need to share what you need to share.

Taking a few more moments to share and receive any more information or frequency with this version of Self.

It is time to travel back up the rainbow bridge.

Allow yourself to step out of this timeline and be transported back down the dimensional bridge, to come back to the larger part of your consciousness waiting for you on the disc mechanism.

Please wait a moment while we reconfigure this mechanism one last time - coming back to equilibrium, and closing any open portals or gateways which are not required.

Setting the intention now to share *all* the frequency and information that you have received from today's journey, deep into the mycelium network and into the Earth.

Take a moment to send and share all of the frequency and information you have received today to be anchored into the Earth and seeded here, now, in physicality.

As this process comes to completion, know that you may now use this mechanism at *any* time to explore, journey into and receive from versions of yourself across the multiverse.

Integrating and calibrating this now on the physical level.

Integrating and calibrating this now on the emotional level.

Integrating and calibrating this now on the mental level.

Integrating and calibrating this now through all levels and dimensions of your light body.

Integrating, calibrating and sharing this frequency now through all timelines and all versions of yourself across the multiverse.

We now shut down any and all open portals and gateways that are no longer required and send back all energy that has come through any portals or gateways in the process of this work.

We now dissolve any bonds, chords or attachments that have been formed for the process of this activation and call you back into complete Soul Sovereignty.

We return all of your energy to you now as you call your Soul fully into your body.

Inviting in now Diamond Light to cleanse and close this space, and bringing this sacred activation to a close, thanking all of the beings who have been here supporting in this process.

It is done, it is done, it is done, and so it is.

You may spend some time here in silent reflection, or receiving in your Sacred Space if it feels necessary.

If you feel complete, we invite you to gently bring yourself back into your body and into the room, wiggling your fingers and toes, and opening your eyes when you are ready.

PART SEVEN

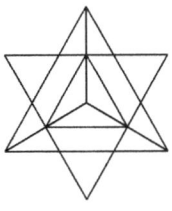

THE MASCULINE

TO BE OF SERVICE

I'm smack bang in the middle of the highly charged Eclipse portal, and the process of writing this book and the ensuing energetic initiations are starting to grate on me. The pressure of the energetic current building up inside of me is pushing me to my absolute upper limit; I feel I am getting closer each moment to breaking point. I don't know whether I need to drive out to the middle of nowhere and let out a primal scream, or I need to start throwing axes... either way, I'm a volcano of emotion about to erupt at any minute, and I pray for those in my path when I finally explode.

I have spent the past two days either in the foetal position, curled up in a ball on my bed sobbing, or flailing madly on the floor of my bedroom, trying everything I can to *move this goddamn energy out of me*:

Dancing, sprinting, shaking, jumping up and down, bodywork, yoga, qi gong, full blown exorcisms on myself, self-pleasure... nothing seems to shift it or release the pressure building up in me, no matter what I do.

It doesn't seem to dissipate; it just seems to intensify.

Every night, lying in my bed, sweating profusely from the heat of the electricity surging through me that makes me feel like I am plugged into a wall socket. Waking up every morning *exhausted*; feeling like I've been hit by a bus, with barely any will to see through another day.

Staring at this screen, unable to focus on the words as they warp from the energy-brain I've got going on.

The energy is filling, filling, filling up inside me... much more than my nervous system, my circuits, or my poor body can take.

Despite my best efforts, it has nowhere else to go.

I feel my tailbone, my hips and my spine swaying involuntarily left to right like a metronome as I sit here typing, I feel the soles of my feet supercharged with the warm static of the energy that flows out of them.

I keep asking, "What do I do with all this energy? What is it for? Where do I channel it? How do I get rid of it?" but my guidance team doesn't respond because I already know the answer...

The only thing that gives me *any* sense of relief is going down to the parklands by my house daily, practising the modality I've been working on - something I have to muster up every bit of willpower and discipline inside of me to do.

Truth be told, most days, I find it quite tedious, time-consuming and boring.

Not to mention, there are only so many hours in a day that I can spend down at the park, pushing the energy into the mycelium network and dispersing it through the grid.

Visualising a huge amplification pyramid, I build around myself in the quantum; sending the corners as far, far, far out as I can to give the energy as much space as it needs for it to spread out so it doesn't continue building up inside of my body with nowhere to go...

Standing there like a *nutjob* in the middle of a park, in trendy inner-city Sydney, swaying back and forward like a metronome; chanting and making all of these mudras with my hands, which kind of look like I'm just throwing up gang signs, or speaking sign language to an invisible person standing with me...

Wondering what people innocently passing by walking their dogs are possibly thinking about this *raving lunatic* and their *loco spiritual practice.*

Chuckling to myself under my breath when the thought crosses my mind at how bizarre I would look; noticing this amusement is a pleasant change from the fear of judgement I used to feel.

Searching, searching, searching for a single fuck to give, not seeming to find one...

Some days, after mustering every ounce of discipline I can to go down there and begrudgingly practise, I feel surprisingly connected throughout the process and amazing when it's finished. A wave of peace descends on me as my nervous system can finally wind down, and my body can have a moment of reprieve, and I remind myself, *'This is why we do this every day, Bec, it makes you feel better'.*

But only a mere hour after going down and expelling the energy, the pressure builds up and becomes overwhelming again.

So, what... am I meant to live down there?

All of this energy is streaming *through* me right now, but it's not actually *for* me.

Some of it is the energy I am remembering how to cultivate in order to bring the technologies of ancient civilizations back online and birth the modality I am being asked to bring forth. (The same energy that we used to charge our sacred artefacts and energy-transmitting tools with to create all sorts of miraculous effects.)

A lot of it is the new, high-frequency energies that are hitting our planet, desiring to be anchored into the Earth.

It is my job right now to bring this energy down through the portal that is my body and into the network...

And part of me is fucking *bitter about it.*

The hard lump of energy that has formed just under my rib cage - between my heart and my solar plexus - is so dense that it is causing me *actual* physical pain; throbbing with an intensity so loud I can't help but feel compelled to be pulled into its emotional story, opening with it pandora's box; a can of worms containing *all the anger and frustration I have been bottling up for lifetimes...*

Why should I serve in this way? Why should I show up for this assignment? What's in it for me? This whole path has only led to suffering for me. This mission has only ever brought me pain. This energy is rendering me incapacitated most days, so I can't even work to pay my bills right now, and yet I'm still having to show up and serve? I don't think so...

Everything I've asked for has been denied... yet when I ask for support, when I ask for guidance, when I ask for ease, grace and sustenance, I get radio silence... what more does God want from me?

My hands and my legs are aching with all the energy that wants to flow through them. I feel like my mother, who I watch every day, suffering from rheumatoid arthritis. Scarcely able to make my hands work the way I want them to because the energy moving through them is causing them to cramp up. I can barely type, I can't play my guitar, I can't write in a journal; my thumbs are cramping up so badly that I can barely form a message on my phone to my mentor/book doula to bitch and moan about all the physical pain I'm in and ask if I'm going to be going through this forever (then feeling a pang of guilt afterwards, because I don't want to subject anyone to this heinous shadow explosion - *even if* she's told me many times she's here to hold me through all that is bound to arise in the process of my purification)...

My salty Little Human Self is on the warpath...

Fuck this mission. Fuck this path. Fuck this book.

Fuck my guides. Fuck my higher self. Fuck God. Fuck everyone. Fuck it all to hell.

I keep going round and round in my mind, wondering if it is truly serving me to be going through it in this way or if there's an easier road (and if there is, *how do I get on it, like yesterday*).

Asking my spirit team, *"How can I make this process more graceful? How can I stop this suffering - surely I do not need to suffer this intensely for this mission? How am I supposed to support and activate others with this power I'm here to wield when I can't even use it to help myself?"* Over and over again, begging and praying for any sort of guidance or assistance to end the hell I'm in.

They respond in vague circles and spiritual cliches, which just infuriate me even more. *My damn spirit team, always sitting back and honouring my 3-line desire to let me figure shit out for myself this lifetime...*

I'm oscillating wildly every day from being *"so unbelievably identified with and in the trenches of all my Little Self-suffering"*, to taking the higher perspective, understanding all of these angry, bitter, frustrated, self-serving, shadowy parts of me - the oh-so-compelling story of my suffering, my martyrdom and victimhood - are being unearthed so I can love them back to wholeness as part of this process.

I'm realising I'm being asked to reach an entirely new level of discipline, commitment and service to my mission; mastery over my thoughts, my emotions, my energy, my body and my practice.

I'm realising I'm journeying *exactly through the process of what I've been saying over and over again in this book...* and oh lord, it ain't enjoyable to be squeezed this tight.

I'm being shown *all* the places where I say I'm in service, but I'm actually just serving myself; to *actually* come to a place where I am *truly* of service, with no self-serving agenda.

Obtaining through direct experience and initiation, the mastery that is required to birth the energy modality that wants to come through me.

All of this is to help others who will go through this process because I've paved the path before them by anchoring it myself.

I'm going from *'begging for the suffering to be taken away'* one moment... to understanding that *'what I'm going through is the divine medicine I require'*, the next; realising there's no point resisting it or asking for the suffering to stop. Having moments of complete clarity, peace and acceptance of *what is;* even if to my Little Human Self, *what is* right now, *sucks some serious balls.*

Realising I need to lean all the way into it; the discomfort, the anger, the frustration building up inside me, and use it as fuel for my rebirth...

I call on the part of me who is already on the other side of this transformation; the part of me that genuinely takes joy in serving her sacred mission.

I try to zoom out and detach from the emotions or the physical pain I'm in.

I call on the parts of myself who can see the humour and hilarity in the situation and how *damn seriously* my Little Human Self is taking all of this.

I connect to the translucent, shimmery, moth-like wings I have felt growing out my shoulder blades in the process of this rebirth - one of the symbols of my Diamond Light Body, which has begun to take form - and allow them to lift me to a higher perspective.

The truth is, dear reader, that in order to wield the power of the Creator, one must have the purest of intentions. To *truly* be of service to the Greater Good rather than the Self.

One of the questions that might arise as a reflection for you - as it has been for me over the years of my initiation process - is *who and what are you really in service to?*

To answer that *honestly* and *truthfully* will require you to get REAL with yourself and see the parts of you that you don't really want to look at and *certainly* don't want others to see.

A large part of this initiation for me has been being shown *all the places* in which I say I'm in "service" to love, but really, I'm just in service to myself.

The places in which I say it's about fulfilling my soul mission, but really it's about the money.

The places in which I say it's about reaching the people who need to hear the messages channelling through me, but really, it's about the validation my Little Human Self gets from the views, follows, comments and likes.

It's been a process of having all of those things stripped back to see whether I'd still show up and serve without all of the gratification our human selves get so attached to (the very Little Self tantrum I'm experiencing as I write this).

The ultimate test of: *what are you doing and who are you being when nobody's watching? How intently will you serve when there is no fame, no glory, no riches, no acclaim, and no credit in store for you?*

Frankly, the result has proven to be quite eye-opening.

It has shown me where I have yet to come into full spiritual maturation and mastery where I still have a *lot* of work to do.

It has shown me the parts within that *say* I'm committed to this path but aren't willing to do what is required to attain mastery or who want to bail or have a tantrum when shit gets hard.

It's not at all comfortable to look at or admit, but I must be willing, as do you, if you're on this journey.

Some of us have learnt from the 'manifestation guru' rhetoric that we are here to 'receive, receive, receive' unconditionally from the Universe, but we have not yet learnt to *give* unconditionally. Ironically, when we *give* unconditionally, we also *receive* unconditionally (often much more than what we require). When we *truly* are of service, giving unconditionally from our hearts, we will naturally attract everything that we require.

However, in order to *truly be of divine service and committed* to our mission - to embody the traits of divine masculine energy in servitude of the divine feminine (the Earth) - we must do so without an agenda, without expectations, without demands, and without requiring something back. We must do so with a pure heart because it is our unconditional, genuine desire to serve. We must uplevel our inner masculine so we are truly of *service* to the greatest good of all and to our divine mission; rather than using *it* to serve *our* Little Self agendas.

In the process of doing this (and regardless of our gender), we must address all of those places within where we're holding onto wounding and distortions around the masculine so our Inner Warrior can rise to meet the Oracle within.

THE 'LOVE WAITING IN MEXICO'

It feels appropriate that the side plot of the *"love waiting for me in Mexico"* I had felt (and was told was coming is an entirely separate chapter from the retellings of the "mission" and everything else that was unfolding. While the duration of our connection actually spanned the entirety of my time in Mexico and even followed me on my journey home - so chronologically, our love story should be peppered throughout most of the book - we would come apart and then come back together many times. Trying to present our relationship chronologically amidst the other parts would, I feel, take away from the fluidity of the retelling of the mission; much like it took *me* off course and distracted me from the mission itself, at times.

And so, as you read this, keep in mind that while I have compartmentalised this piece of my journey (much like I've tried to compartmentalise my heart's yearning for sacred union and the desire to fully *merge* with another, that has been a constant source of pain for me since I was young, it was a frequent, consistent thread underneath everything else. I have chosen to place it into its own little insulated narrative, separate from everything else that happened, in order to do our story - and the outpouring of my heart - justice.

I had hesitated to what depth and detail to share our story, and to what degree it was relevant to my mission, this book or the codes it would hold...

Is it too personal? Does it invalidate me and my authority as a divine feminine leader for not being as "embodied" as I think I am, for falling so far backwards when I thought I had already 'healed' and 'dealt' with the wounds that had me self abandoning the way I did?

Does it take away from the potency of the ancient wisdom I am sharing, to share my story so personally? Does it make me an unclear vessel?

What if I'm just in the drama of my feelings, and when I look back on this some-time in the future, when I've healed and grown, I can't imagine that I ever felt this way?

The last one I daresay is true, as months after first writing this, the majority of the pain in my heart has all but disappeared, as crucial pieces of our karmic imprint on each other have been uncovered and healed, and necessary soul fragments have been retrieved. I no longer feel the strong magnetic pull to him I once did, compelling me to continue to go around and around in circles. I find the level of grief I was moving through hard to believe now having come out the other side of the grief portal, and I can say I have well and truly retired any fantasies of a potential future life together. I have moved on, as have my romantic interests. However, I have chosen to leave these words as they first were written to do honour to the version of myself who wrote them and to support anyone reading out there who may be journeying something similar.

It terrified me to have to put everything I felt and thought on paper permanently, perhaps for someone else to see someday. Like those feelings and emotions - my moment of vulnerability and heartbreak - would forever be solidified and *real;* I would actually have to do the weight of my grief justice (which I had always brushed off because how could I grieve this much from a connection that was so brief and fleeting in *this* human lifetime?)

My doula/mentor insisted that anything that happened on my journey was relevant to the mission - and therefore this book - and that a large part of this transmission was the sheer vulnerability in sharing my heart's truth.

As it stands, I could not really do this journey or myself justice if I left him out of it.

So, dear reader, I hope that sharing this piece of my outpouring heart serves, and that in our story you can see yourself. I believe - and have experienced many times - that part of walking the path of a priestess is experiencing soul connections that defy all logic and understanding. These soul connections shape us, encode us, activate and awaken us; they crack our hearts open so we are able to be the pure vessel of divine love that can fulfil our mission.

I believe that through these soul connections - these great past life loves from ancient times and across galaxies - and the memories that are awakened in us every time one resurfaces, we remember *who* and what we are; we awaken our multidimensionality and our capacity to love far beyond the spectrum of Little Human Love.

And I believe that ultimately, those of us holding this blueprint of hieros gamos - *sacred marriage* - are destined to experience many deep (and often heartbreaking) soul connections to prepare us for a Love that surpasses all of these Little Human Loves. The template of both inner *and* outer sacred union that manifests as an unexplainable yearning for a love that is so deep, so wild, so divine, so mystical, so magical that it defies all else. A pure, all-encompassing, selfless, unconditional, and ego-obliterating kind of love. A love that will ripple out from the container of the sacred union or the love between the two beings and be an offering to the world. A kind of love that can only be shared by two people who are already so whole within that - rather than needing to fill each other up - their love can ripple outwards and heal the world. *That's the kind of love I'm here for - how about you?*

This love I am about to share, this connection, is the closest I have come to touching that place of deep, unconditional, soul love with another I have been yearning for my entire life and have only ever found in God, even if I was acutely aware that it wasn't *it*. He was not the first *"soulmate love from a past life coming back to clean up some karmic baggage"* that I had encountered, but he was the first who was willing to truly, openly claim me and pour all of his love into me. He was the first one I welcomed and experienced with a fully open heart; willing to allow myself to love all the way through, even if it meant I would experience the grief of losing him.

Coming closer than I'd ever come to something I had been searching for my entire life and then choosing to walk away and not settle because I knew I yearned for (and had to believe I could have) *more* was one of the greatest initiations I'd ever have to go through.

Somehow, it was even bigger than all the Mayan codes I was receiving or the great mystery I was asked to lean into throughout my mission. It was a test I did not pass with flying colours the first, second, third or even fourth time - and often I asked myself *how* I could let things happen the way they did. It required me to develop superhuman levels of self-compassion, patience and understanding. And ultimately, it required me to heal, awaken and reclaim parts of myself that had been separating me from the Wholeness I am; the wholeness that doesn't need a man (or any person outside of me) to feel full.

As I walked out of the lobby of my apartment complex, I was in disbelief and a little shocked when I saw the man who had come to deliver my scooter. In my mind, I had somehow pictured him *completely different*. He was younger than my usual "type" and not exactly tall, but he was still dark and *very* handsome. He gave off laid-back, surfer/skater vibes with his board shorts and t-shirt, messy, dark hair flipped over in this way that made him seem effortlessly cool, his huge dimpled smile which would extend all the way up to the lines framing his enormous brown eyes that you could drown in, and the tattoos on his hands and legs.

"*Well, you're not at all what I imagined*", I remember myself thinking as he showed me the bike, whilst simultaneously thinking "*Uh oh, I'm in trouble.*"

As I leaned in to get a hug from him, it didn't at all help my cause that he smelled *amazing;* his natural musk combined with an aftershave that was sweet and masculine all at the same time.

I could sense that he was somewhat guarded and perhaps self-conscious as he was trying to play it "cool", even though I could also sense that he was interested in me. After standing there for a few minutes, we agreed we'd hang out properly soon, as he had to head off to the next appointment. As he walked off, I remember thinking, "Well, that was unexpected", and resolving to just brush it off as a happy surprise that the kind stranger I'd been messaging all this time was actually *kinda hot.*

It didn't take long for him to message me again - maybe twenty minutes after he left - and one thing that I have come to learn about Latino men (well, at least the ones I have encountered) is that they have basically *zero* chill. The *caliente*, spicy, Latin-lover stereotype exists for a reason; when they're interested in you, it's borderline love-bombing from the very first moment they meet you; they certainly don't hold their interest back, which generally to me screams "red flag, run". True to form, he had messaged me checking in, saying in Spanish how cool I was and that he needs a girlfriend like me. I panicked momentarily and thought I had probably just mistranslated due to my poor Spanish skills and that he was actually just talking about his girl-friend, so I asked him what her name was. Granted, we were both confused as heck for a few moments before I realised that he was, in fact, just blatantly hitting on me, and there was no girlfriend to speak of. After jokingly brushing it off and insisting that he get to know me better before making assumptions about what kind of girlfriend I'd be, he took it down a notch, and we chatted on into the evening.

Only a couple of days after meeting him for the first time in person, I was already dealing with some triggers that were arising for me because he was being flakey and communicating poorly around plans when we were meant to catch up. It was something that was a non-negotiable for me at that point in my relating journey, but I had chosen to give him the benefit of the doubt and another chance because he really did seem to have a good heart. I first learnt that not everybody shares the same respect and love I do of "showing up on time" and "making solid plans" in Bali while noticing how everyone seemed to be perpetually operating on "island time", which drove me *nuts* at first. In Indonesian, there's a word *"besok"*, which means "tomorrow", but it also loosely means "any day in the future". *Kind of sums it right up.* The same principle seemed to apply in Costa Rica when I was there and certainly in Mexico. I understood that timeliness and time management might be an area where there would be cultural differences, and I needed to perhaps lessen some of my expectations and rigidity, particularly when I had just met the guy, and he didn't really owe me anything. (I also came to realise that the flakiness I so despised in the men I'd constantly attract was the flakiness I had yet to address within my own masculine - *oof, yep, bet I punched you right in the ovaries with that one.*)

After expressing to him that I *really* desired solid plans and better communication if we were going to hang out, we made plans to go to the beach together the next day. He rolled up to my apartment complex on his scooter and picked me up - apologising for keeping me waiting for ten minutes because "I should never be made to wait for him" when, ironically, that ended up being a consistent theme of our relationship that eventually led to its downfall. There was a little awkwardness in the air as we sat at the local restaurant where he ate lunch (I had already eaten, so I just took a green juice) and I noticed the conversation wasn't really flowing. In hindsight, I believe he was just nervous, or perhaps he was trying to calculate in his man-brain *what the hell witchcraft* I had done to him to cause him to have such a strong, energetic attraction to me. However, something seemed to shift in the energy when we got back on the bike and started heading towards the beach, and the speedbumps on the road were forcing me to slide up closer to him on the seat. As we became physically closer when I stopped fighting the road and allowed myself to wrap my arms around him (instead of inch-ing to the back of the seat as I had been doing previously), the tension eased, and he placed his hand on my leg. My whole body melted and softened as I felt my chest press against his back, feeling his heart beating through his rib cage and into mine, a warmth spreading into my entire torso. My whole body relaxed, and there was a relief of tension as if I was finally taking an exhale I had been waiting for my entire life.

As we rode through the streets of Tulum and the long stretch of road, which slowly became less and less gentrified and more swallowed by jungle, I allowed myself to sink into the feeling of comfort and security of being driven by this man who I immediately felt so comfortable with. After months of feeling exhausted from being on high alert all the time in a foreign and unforgiving country, having to take care of myself and keep my eyes open, it felt incredible to finally just be able to surrender and allow myself to be led. I didn't have to think about the road, where we were going, or any of the logistics along the way, like speaking to the park rangers or avoiding being ripped off. He took care of everything.

After sharing that I wanted to go somewhere quiet, he drove us to a stretch of beach beyond the hotel zone, where there was nobody around. It was just him and I in paradise; this breathtaking view of the pristine, crystalline, turquoise Caribbean ocean, surrounded by jungle and palm trees, with no obnoxious beach clubs blasting music, nobody trying to rip us off, or people trying to sell us things. We were alone. For a moment, the thought slipped into my mind that perhaps this wasn't the best idea for my first date with a near stranger in Mexico, but everything in my being told me I'd be okay, and my intuition had not led me astray yet.

We found a spot on a hilly part of the shore, and I found myself impressed (and a little enamoured) as I watched him create a shelter for us by positioning palms and branches to create a little hut and flat-tening the sand out so we had a comfortable place to lie. He was bringing some seriously sexy, masculine, "hunter-gatherer" energy, which I had been deeply craving, and it immediately spoke to some primal instinct within my body. As we lay there on the sand, our conversation became more organic, and I felt much more ease coming from him as he opened up to me and told me about himself and his life. In fact, after I got him talking to me on that first day, he wouldn't stop - even if he had confided in me that he didn't open up to people or say much, he seemed to feel instantly safe with me. There were also many moments where it felt natural for us to just lie there and not say anything at all; a rare experience to be able to sit in comfortable silence with someone you technically "just met".

I had promised myself that I would try my best to keep my distance when it came to any sort of physical intimacy so I could take things slow, but I was finding it very difficult as he kept encouraging me to come closer to him and everything in my body was desiring the same. Not to mention, as he took his shirt off, I realised with surprise, for a fairly slender guy, *damn... the dude was ripped.* I was trying with all my willpower to avert my eyes from his hard, dark body and fighting my animal-body urge to run my fingers along his unassuming yet surprisingly defined six-pack. When we would go down into the ocean, he would lure me playfully out deeper so I would be forced to hold onto him (I was still holding onto a little anxiety around being in the ocean due to a rather terrifying surfing incident I'd had a few years earlier in Bali) and he could pull me into his body, wrapping me around him like a life jacket. As we bobbed in the water together, I told myself, "Avoid his face... don't kiss him, don't kiss him, don't kiss him", but there was this magnetic energy running through my veins, almost compelling me that I could feel myself trying to fight.

I had done enough work on myself in the realms of relating and had navigated more than enough "trauma-bond" situationships by that point to know that generally, a magnetic, electric feeling and a sense of being "activated" is not a good sign (even though the whole of Hollywood would have you believe that true love feels like fireworks). I had trepidation because I wanted to trust my body; I wanted to trust that this man - while there was indescribable *magnetic* energy and obvious sexual chemistry between us - didn't make my nervous system feel "activated" in any way, which was a positive thing. Perhaps it *wouldn't*

DIAMOND LIGHT ORACLE

be yet another painful karmic relationship here to bring up all my childhood and past life trauma after all (*ha ha ha*). At that point, it was kind of like "take a number and get in line" every time I met a man who I had to clean up some past life baggage with or who had come into my life to help me learn to finally love myself.

To the contrary, he made me feel very grounded, anchored and safe - like my whole nervous system could just relax in his presence. However, I was also aware that if your nervous system is so dysregulated that "unsafety" actually feels like "safety", someone who is a trauma bond *might* actually feel like safety to you. So, by that point, still not fully trusting myself and what I was feeling, I desired to keep a healthy physical distance before I could get to know him a bit more and understand where this magnetic feeling was coming from.

Despite my best intentions, trying to fight the urge in my whole body to not be physically close to him was like a heroin addict trying to fight the urge to shoot up. *Basically impossible.* It was like there was an invisible force pulling us together that I had no control over. No matter what I had told myself about holding boundaries around any sort of physical intimacy on that first date, it just felt so right. And while I managed to hold myself back for most of the day, by the time we returned to my apartment later that afternoon, we had found ourselves in the hot tub at the spa, my legs and arms once again wrapped around his torso like a koala bear on a gumtree. Before I knew it, something had taken me over as I found myself - without thought - hurling my lips towards his almost involuntarily. *Oops.* However, I wasn't going to beat myself up or launch into a spiral of self-loathing and guilt for not holding the boundaries I had just chosen to cross (been there, done that, bought the T-shirt one too many times as I let my spicy, passionate and impulsive "Venus in Aries" get the better of me). I checked in with my body and my inner child to see how she was feeling and noted that Little Bec felt completely fine. Following my internal green light, one thing led to another, and, well, this isn't that kind of book, so I'll spare you the juicy details, but suffice it to say, it certainly didn't feel like we were meeting for the first time.

Being physically intimate with this man pretty early on did not feel wrong to me, and I have no regrets. While I can see in hindsight that physical intimacy so early on definitely added to the emotional intensity of the whole situation, I know that absolutely everything unfolded exactly as it needed to for us both to receive the soul lessons we had come together to learn. And so if you were to ask me if I would do it all over the exact same way again with him, I would. However, perhaps next time I meet a man I have a magnetic connection to, I would take a little more time getting to know them before launching into a relationship that was so heavily physical. (I think, maybe... *let's see...*)

In saying that, though, I think it truly is a case-by-case, moment-to-moment basis, and if my body is giving me the green light, who am I to say no to something that feels organic and beautiful at the moment? Who are we to shame ourselves for desiring the basic human need of physical touch and affection and allowing ourselves to have what we so deeply crave? Unlike many on the "spiritual path", I do not believe that we need to suppress all our human, primal urges in order to live a truly divine and spiritually masterful life. In fact, I believe these urges (particularly our sexual ones) are divinely guided if we act on them *consciously* and with *intention*, from a place of self-awareness and respect, but I digress...

From that first moment we "reconnected", we launched into a rather intense relationship that was characterised by a strong physical pull and magnetic attraction that didn't dim the whole time we were together, it only intensified. From that first "date", we would spend most days together; he would get up in the very early hours to go for a run - usually waking me up in the process as I'm a light sleeper and not particularly a morning person - then returning to wake me up again just as I'd finally fall back asleep, to shower and head off to work for the day. I would reluctantly (after my interrupted sleep made me sluggish and grumpy) pull myself out of bed and start my own morning routine. Later in the afternoon or evening, he would return, and we would share dinner and spend some time together before retiring to bed, where he'd often pass out from exhaustion mid-conversation, with his jeans and socks still on, as I'd be stroking his hair. On weekends or days, he didn't have to work, we'd go on adventures or spend days at the beach clubs or even just do basic everyday errands like grocery shopping or going to the gym, which felt somehow nicer with him around.

When it was good between us it was *magical* – I'm talking melding-into-one whilst making cosmic love, sun-kissed days at the beach, rolling around like lovesick teenagers together on the sand, riding around Tulum on the back of his scooter laughing my ass off, feeling seen, safe and loved through rather intense emotions, tender "I love you"s, stormy afternoons in bed, date nights, sneaking photos of him sleeping cause he was so damn *adorable*.

But in the moments in between – the evenings when he'd get home from work exhausted and commandeer the TV without really acknowledging my presence, making me feel *even more alone than I was when I was by myself*; or proceed to do that thing that I told him *really* gave me anxiety, flicking through instagram reels with the sound on full blast when I was trying to have quiet time; or talk non-stop about what was going on for him, but never ask me about my life or how I felt; or when he'd smoke joints in my bathroom and ash in the sink when I'd ask him not to, or leave T-shirts, bottle-caps or crisp packets lying around my apartment, so I would be left to pick up after him like his mother; or worse than any of the above, when he'd ignore my very basic needs of communication I had expressed *over and over* again by changing plans last minute and not thinking to update me, leaving me hanging for hours at home waiting for him (sometimes with his dinner already on the table) – I spent a lot of time feeling *utterly unmet*.

On those days, I would find myself staring blankly at him as he would talk at me, thinking, *"What the hell am I doing? This is barely scratching the surface of my capacity for connection compared to what I've already experienced with other men far more evolved than him... why am I settling?",* and then spiralling into frustration, guilt, shame, and self-judgement for feeling incapable of ending it. A lot of the time, it would cause me to withdraw into myself completely, or I would tell him that I felt unmet, which only just drew a bigger wedge between us because then he'd feel inadequate and become defensive or childish as a result.

Although he did not meet me in *so* many other ways, this man was able to meet some of my core needs that were not previously being met, which made it so difficult to walk away; affection, physical touch, holding, feeling desired, and being claimed. The way he looked at me, spoke to me and made love to me (when he was fully present and dropped in with me, not when he was just following a sexual impulse) made me feel *so* desired and loved; like there was no other woman in the world; like I was loved unconditionally for who I was. He touched a place inside of me that was longing to feel seen and accepted, flaws and all. The way he so fervently declared from early on that he wanted to make me his, that he desired to claim me, to get a place with me, to have his baby, that he had no problem fiercely - *often stubbornly, relentlessly and infuriatingly* - pursuing something serious with me, when all men before him had made themselves perpetually unavailable for commitment. No matter how dark, stormy, emotional or moody I would be, he never stopped desiring me. No matter how much I tested, tried to push him away or say "no" when he'd relentlessly pursue something serious with me, he kept coming back. No matter how many reasons I'd come up with for why we'd never work, he kept trying. And eventually, he won me over with his sheer persistence. (I can never say the man wasn't committed, and he *continued to be,* even well after I had checked out completely and left the country.) I never *once* doubted how he felt about me, even if by all rights I should have, given the issues we had arising.

Most of the time, he would not even need to say anything because it was something that was so deep and unspoken; I could *feel* his love for me reverberating through his heart and filling mine when I would place my hand on his chest.

The way he would just hold me and pull me into his arms as I sobbed some days, completely unphased by the intensity of my emotions - in fact, telling me he felt even *closer* to me because of them. The way he was on board with all the wildness of me in my full tantrika mode; speaking in other languages, channelling things, tapping him all over his body as I moved energy through him. Even though he had no idea what was happening, nor had he done any sort of work in that space, he just fell into it with me naturally and held the space without needing to be told. The way he would just stand and stare at me with adoration in his eyes, even when I was doing *seriously unsexy things* like sitting on the toilet seat trying to wee (which would almost be impossible with him standing there admiring the curves of my seated silhouette).

I knew he loved me from the very first moment he met me, and I felt the same because, on a soul level, we were very much just picking up where we left off. Despite the fact that there were so many ways we were hopelessly incompatible - culturally, emotionally, intellectually, maturity levels, communication styles, life goals and paths - there was a warmth, an easefulness, a familiarity and a connection between us that surpassed all words or human understanding; like we had known each other our entire lives.

While he was not on the path of mysticism to the degree I was, he was a spiritually open man and would surprise me from time to time with unexpected wisdom that would come from someplace inside of him well beyond his years. He accepted (and agreed) that we had known each other over many past lifetimes - in fact, it was him that jokingly had suggested it before we even got together. This was not the first past life love that I'd re-encountered, so it didn't rattle or surprise me to be going through this all over again; particularly not as I had received the message there was love for me in Mexico, and this man aligned with all of the features of the soulmate that my priestess sister had seen already when she'd read my energy for me and asked if I'd met a man there.

It was only the second or third time we were intimate when I found myself suddenly breaking down in tears, finding myself saying (once again, without knowing where it was coming from or why I was saying it), *"I need to love you enough to let you go"* over and over again, as if it was some other part of me saying it, breaking some sort of spell I had cast in another lifetime. He just held me and said nothing as I went on for at least an hour, processing the emotion that was coming from some former event that had transpired between us. After tuning into it, I recognised some of the karma we were coming together to clear. In a previous lifetime, I'd held him back from his mission because I couldn't let him go, and in this life, the roles were reversed. He had come into my life to redirect me to focus on my soul mission and had to love me enough to let me go (which we would both seriously struggle to do).

To add a further layer of validation that I desperately required after the second attempt to break up with him had rendered me in a crippling grief I was unable to shake and wondering why it was so painful and hard considering we'd not been together that long, the Map Reader would later confirm all the downloads I'd had about our connection after seeing a photo I'd posted of us, telling me this is the man she'd seen in a vision with me in Mayan times. She insisted that there was a higher purpose we had come together for and that the whole way it was playing out - including my inability to walk away - was by design. It put me at ease and made me carry a lot less shame about feeling unable to "love myself enough" to fully cut ties, to know that there was something compelling me to play out our karma and calling me back to him.

Even though he was *terrible* at understanding some of my core needs (like communication, feeling *heard*, reliability, and consistency), he was one of the most genuinely thoughtful, kind-hearted, service-focused men I'd met, considering the trauma he'd endured throughout his life. I'd see him frequently commit random acts of kindness for strangers and do thoughtful things for myself and others. I'd see him consistently give people the benefit of the doubt, forgive, and be generous even though he had little. Not to mention he was constantly going out of his way to do things for me to please me when he could, as his love language was acts of service. Taking my washing to the laundry, lending me his scooter, running errands, buying my groceries for me and taking me out for nice meals (even though he probably couldn't afford it). It was hard to stay mad at him - even when he consistently let me down - because not only would he melt my barrier within five seconds of being around him because he was so adorable with those big, brown doe eyes and that Naughty Little Boy grin (god damn it), he was also not a bad person. He wasn't *trying* to let me down or upset me - I could see his anxious little boy surfacing every time he'd come, trying to repair the situation because he could see I was hurt. He was just on a completely different planet to me a lot of the time, and couldn't understand what I could possibly need more than his adoration, occasional material provision and desire to sire my child.

I am not making excuses for him when I say I *knew* he was truly as in love with me as he would say and was not just 'love-bombing' or 'manipulating' or any of the other words people would associate with a narcissist (everyone's favourite buzz word to throw around these days). He was just not able to consistently show it to me in a language I understood or required to feel he cared. I *knew* he loved me; he just was at a completely different level of emotional maturity than me, from a completely different cultural background where the dynamics between women and men were borderline misogynistic and had done basically *no* work on intimacy or relating. On the other hand, I had spent nearly a decade working on myself, my inner child wounds and my anxious attachment style, cracking my heart open through heartbreak and rejection, overcoming the discomfort of claiming and vulnerably expressing my truth and needs to men. I wanted to work things out; to communicate and lay it all on the table so he could understand me and we could improve our situation together. He was hell-bent on bypassing all the issues by telling me to "relax" or "stop being dramatic" and sweeping shit under the rug.

I *knew* he loved me; he was just here to mirror the exact same dynamic of the love that my parents have, so I could forgive my father and all the resentment I inherited towards him from my mother, uplevel and step into my own masculine warrior; desire more for myself and heal and release the repeating cycle of 'feeling let down by men'. (I feel it's important to add that my father loves my mother and vice versa; I know this deep in my bones. They have stood by each other through some *shit* where by all rights, they should have gotten divorced a long time ago. He just isn't able to show her that in the way she *needs* to feel truly loved. And although he has a tendency to be stubborn, to gaslight, to negate and to shut down when emotional needs are expressed - like a lot of men in the Baby Boomer generation who are basically emotional invalids - it doesn't mean he's a bad person, or that he doesn't *love her deeply*. Considering his upbringing and background, my dear old Cancerian dad can be surprisingly sensitive and compassionate at times, just not consistently enough to meet my sensitive mother's emotional needs.)

I *knew* he loved me - just as I did him - but he was looking for a doting housewife and a woman to carry his seed; I was looking for my spiritual, emotional and intellectual equal.

I *knew* he loved me - just as I did him - but he wanted simple, easy and uncomplicated; I wanted a man who could penetrate my deepest depths and unravel the mysteries of the universe within me.

I *knew* he loved me - just as I did him - but he was content to walk our different paths and come together in the between spaces; I knew in my heart I was always destined to walk this path beside someone else.

I *knew* he loved me - just as I did him - but he believed love was enough and was content to settle with a simple life; and love or not, I simply wasn't prepared to settle for anything short of pure magic.

I *knew* he loved me - just as I did him - but sometimes, loving and choosing someone else comes at the cost of fully loving and choosing yourself.

WARRIOR CODING & PURIFYING THE DISTORTED IMPRINT OF MASCULINE POWER

This soulmate had come into my life for more reasons than one, but one of the primary reasons we were brought together was for a *lot* of healing around the masculine. He was forcing me to deal with my soul gripe with Sky Daddy (aka God), my Daddy Issues, and to forgive my inner wounded masculine who did not protect my little girl or my divine feminine by holding strong boundaries but instead consistently allowed me to self abandon for validation, affection and love.

There were other soul wounds I recently uncovered with the help of my mentor, around some *"Danaerys and Jon Snow in the final season of Game of Thrones"* type shit, where he was my soldier, and I was his queen, and he was forced to kill me because I had become corrupt. This had come up for me to revisit this fear of stepping into my full power again and becoming corrupt and to clear the grief of the ULTI-MATE betrayal of having the man who was supposed to "protect me at all costs" being the one to take me out (if that's not gonna cause some karmic "masculine protector" wounds, then I don't know what would). It's also kind of wild because Danaerys (who became corrupt and mad with power) was the Mother of Dragons, and "becoming the dragon" has been something that has been an undercurrent metaphor for me on this journey of stepping into my full power.

I now understand that until this particular soul fragment (this part of my power) had been retrieved, I was unable to 'let him go' and continued to grieve the way I did. He was one of the many initiations I had to go through in order to reclaim my power and step into my role as an Oracle. Since releasing this, all the unexplainable grief has lifted, along with the magnetic connection pulling me back to him. It turns out it was just a part of my soul I was grieving that he was holding onto.

Perhaps even more pivotal to my divine mission, he provided the foundation to help me to fully understand, awaken and bring online my own divine masculine warrior coding, which would later deepen in the initiation I received in the Guatemalan jungle. In hindsight, I laugh at how obvious this piece is - God does have a sense of humour - as that word "warrior" was in his screen name when we first met, and he continually would tell me he's "at my service" from the very first moment we met, also commonly referring to himself as a "soldier of life", and to me as his "Queen". I believe this was a source of primal attraction for me in the way this warrior energy manifested itself positively through him in some ways (and also no doubt brought up the steamy memories of when he *actually* was my warrior lover in another timeline). I was attracted to the personal will and masculine power radiating from his solar plexus that I was lacking in my own. So much so that even having his solar plexus anywhere near my lower chakras brought on energetic orgasms (even if he was lying in a completely non-sexual way, with his head resting on my stomach while I'd gently stroke his hair as he so adored, to send him off to sleep).

He filled the void; the part of me desperately yearning for that strong masculine warrior who could claim, protect, devour and ravage me in all my wild feminine emotion and chaos - the part of me who was never actually outside of me to begin with.

One day, as we were lying in bed together, I went on a journey and was shown his blood lineage from his father's side and was given many downloads about this man and the codex he was carrying through his bloodline. I was also shown the intense trauma he and his family had endured. He had told me many times that he was here to be the "best in his bloodline" and I could see and understand that; inside his DNA, there was a magic encoded into it from his mother's side (in his words, she was a 'witch' and the medicine carried through into his blood), and a warrior essence encoded into it from his father's side, that he was here to purify and return to its divine form. While his father's side was from up north - so historically and geographically speaking, they probably would have been more Aztec than Mayan - it was warrior coding that had lost its pure essence, becoming wounded and twisted through years of abuse and violence. This manifested down the line as much of his family being involved with some dodgy circles, taken out by the cartel, or incarcerated. His father was in prison while he was growing up, something he had told me he had only learnt as a young adult when he finally returned to Mexico. I could feel the heaviness in his heart and the baggage he was carrying as he told me with a silent tear rolling down his eye (and I cried with him) of his many family members who were murdered in his hometown before he decided enough was enough and he had to go somewhere far away from it all, as the cycle needed to end with him. The man had some *demons* to battle, that was for sure.

Seeing and feeling his story - encoded in his blood - made me understand the culture of trauma that I was beginning to uncover within the Mayan bloodline, which began with having their culture decimated by colonisation from the *"conquistadoras"* (some of which, I have had to relive, experience and heal myself over the years through brutal flashbacks and memories) and also the trauma many of us collectively carry around the masculine.

When it becomes distorted, imbalanced, or is not channelled in a healthy way, warrior coding - which is a form of pure, divine masculine POWER - turns into violence, aggression, the need to "conquer" at the cost of others (and the Earth), substance or porn abuse, callousness or coldness, little regard for human life, and brutality. If violence, brutality and callousness are all you know and have experienced from the masculine, that is the imprint of toxic masculinity you will continue to impart on future generations.

Without even going too far back into our *early* history - I'm talking about the times of mass genocide, colonisation of Indigenous peoples, and brutal conquering that has been going on since men first removed the Goddess from her rightful place out of fear of her power, and uplifted themselves into positions of leadership - we need only look back over the past hundred years or so, to see this trauma perpetuating itself in the masculine line.

This trauma has stemmed from generation after generation of men who went off to war, *just following orders* - leaving their women and children behind, creating abandonment wounds; to only return as empty, traumatised husks of who they once were. Men who - because they were part of a culture who told them to just "toughen up and be a man" - would be unable to deal with or unpack the horrors they endured; so then their trauma would be made manifest through the abuse of substances, or taken out on the ones they loved. How can a man who is plagued by inner demons be present for his family or provide a good example of healthy masculinity for future generations? And how can you trust masculine energy or embody divine masculine energy within yourself if you have never had a healthy example of what this actually looks like?

We're finally seeing some beautiful divine masculine leaders stepping up, but this has taken a *really long time* to happen, and the main example we've seen of masculine leadership for hundreds (if not thousands) of years is barbaric, cruel, power-hungry, greedy, corrupt, egotistical and arrogant, to the detriment of the highest symbol of the feminine; Mother Earth.

This is difficult for me to share, as it is a *very tender* topic that requires grace and understanding to properly unpack and navigate - while I am not of Mayan descent in this lifetime and carry no "blood" ancestry, I feel I do not fully have the right to claim I am an authority on the subject, nor am I desiring to ride up on horseback as the White Saviour. However, the ancestors who speak to me and support me with writing this book - and the part of me who *is* Mayan in many incarnations, and still is, in my heart - insist I share it. It shows us just *one* of the many repercussions that have happened at the hands of the wounded masculine - the trauma of which is still echoing through our collective unconscious, perpetuating in unresolved loops of victimhood, and humanity who is hesitant to rise up into their full power and sovereignty. The greed, violence, cruelty and excess of wounded masculine conquerors wiped out many of the Mayan bloodline; it decimated their rituals and their practices; it forced them to practise their culture underground, and as a result, much of the ancient wisdom and *sheer power* of their lineage was lost. (For the record, we see this in *most* Indigenous cultures, not just the Mayans - we see this in Australia, my country of birth, with the atrocities done to the Aboriginal people; however much of the Aboriginal culture has endured.)

To sidetrack for a moment, I was shown that the reason why many gridworkers (including myself) have been called to Mexico since 2021 was because there simply are not enough gridworkers from that lineage with a knowledge or understanding of maintaining or working the grid, particularly not where I was. (It is not the case for other places where there are Mayan descendents, like in parts of Guatemala where I ended up, where Mayan culture is protected.) Of course, I am not saying that there are none of Mayan lineage practising rituals, ceremonies, and carrying on the culture in many other ways. But this particular piece - the "harmonisation" piece - has been neglected, or perhaps forgotten about altogether (I'm not entirely sure which). And of course - to call out my own privilege - perhaps those who may still carry this knowledge, do not have the luxury of being able to travel around Mexico doing gridwork. The reason *why* it is not being upheld, I cannot say with certainty; all I know is that when I began my mission there, it came with a weight of responsibility of knowing that if I didn't do what I was instructed to do to activate this grid, it wouldn't be done.

In contrast, it is not the case in Australia where - despite facing the traumatic repercussions of colonisation - the Elders are *very much* still holding onto their traditions, their practices, and working this grid; the "songlines" or "dreaming tracks", as they are called here. In fact, I have felt and been told by the ancestors in spirit here not to do gridwork in certain places I've been; that it is not required, as those holding down the line know what they are doing and have "got it covered". There have been some places I've been called to where I was allowed to support, but there were also a few times where that was certainly not the case. The first time I was "warned off" by an Elder spirit was quite a confronting and humbling experience; a few years ago, wandering off the walking path in the Blue Mountains, I went to close my eyes and start doing my thing, and I felt a strong, unwelcoming sensation warning me to 'back off'. At the time, it perplexed and frightened me quite a bit, as this had *never* happened in any other place I'd been. Where the ancestors of Bali, Costa Rica and Mexico had welcomed me with open arms, the ancestors in my country of birth seemed to push me away with almost hostility. (A strange thing indeed, but I certainly don't blame them for wanting to defend their powerful, pristine, magical land and culture at all costs.)

The majority of those with Mayan blood who lived on from the colonisation of the Spanish were stripped of their culture, punished for practising their rituals - as they went against the Catholic religion, which saw these rituals as "devil worship" - and were so severely repressed that they fell into an ancestral, karmic cycle of poverty and suffering they have not been able to break out of (as in order to end a karmic cycle of victimhood and slavery to the system, one must liberate themselves from oppression and reclaim their power - until they learn this lesson, they will continue this pattern on a karmic level). It *breaks* my heart to see my people struggling (I say "my" as the Mayan part of myself writes this), and sadness would be stirred up within me every time I would encounter somebody speaking Mayan while in Mexico (it only happened twice, but it broke me down both times). However, not from a place of pity, but from a place of regret that they have not yet realised or woken up to the power of the sheer *magic* that is encoded in their blood. If only they could *remember* who they truly were as a people - who they truly *are* - and the contribution their lineage has made to humanity. If only those in suffering at the hands of the wounded masculine patriarchy could realise that the only way out of the cycle of victimhood is *through*; to reach out and take your power back by rising up and saving yourself.

Of course, I feel it *incredibly* important to mention and not negate the systemic imbalance of power, violence, greed and corruption that is present in many parts of Mexico, making it an uphill and almost *impos-*

sible battle to fight. Coupled with the exploitation, gentrification and enormous imbalance of wealth and resources happening in many areas (particularly Tulum, which I felt *much guilt* around contributing to while I was there), which have been overrun by tourists and developers, causing the locals to be unable to afford to sustain themselves on their own land. However, not having been there for enough time to properly unpack and understand the intricacies of everything going on, I cannot really offer any solutions or say much else that others haven't been able to say much more eloquently and thoughtfully on this matter.

This warrior coding - this ability to *rise up* against the injustices of the patriarchal system that has birthed us; out of collective victimhood, into our sovereignty as a humanity - is desiring to wake up in the world. It *needs* to wake up in the world if we are to make it through this transition period. The divine feminine has weathered enough of this birthing process on her own. The collective divine masculine *is* rising, but it has a ways to go, and like any part of the healing journey, it starts on an individual level first; as we each forgive the wounded masculine, address our own masculine distortions, and begin to reclaim our warrior power.

Through my ability to read my partner's energy, receive messages around his lineage, and support him to clear and bring online warrior codes from his own bloodline through our intimacy - or as he would often joke, "doing witchcraft on him" - I was bringing forth a deeper understanding of this masculine warrior coding which I had been traumatised by in its wounded form, and starting the process of awakening it within myself.

I fully understood the warrior coding this man was helping to wake up in me one day after our first 'break up' - which was actually the second time I'd declared I was no longer interested or available to continue seeing him, but still proceeded to do so. I had ended things with him because the previous night, he had kept me waiting for him for hours when we had plans, keeping me on 'read' with no response and going AWOL until the next morning, leaving me to cry myself to sleep, feeling abandoned once again. He made up some ridiculous excuse about a car tire being flat - probably forgetting he was dating a human lie detector - when really, I knew it was because he wanted to hang out with his "boys" and watch the boxing but was too afraid to tell me that and upset me (*guy logic*). He then proceeded to act like nothing had happened and casually messaged me the next morning, "Buenos días mi amor", which, of course, sent me into a fit of rage. Hell hath no fury like a woman scorned, and I was *certainly not* feeling like his "amor".

I was furious and hurt about all of it and decided to go to the beach with Bestie to take my mind off it. Rather inconveniently (although divinely timed, of course), my bicycle chain decided to break just as we arrived at the beach after 8 km of cycling in the direct Mexican midday heat, and I broke down into hysterics along with it; finally processing the frustration and anger of everything that had happened that morning. After crying on the side of the road for a few minutes, I eventually started laughing hysterically at how ridiculously *fucking perfect* it all was and tried to get help from a man passing by, who took pity on us. He was unable to fix the bike, and neither could I or my friend. At this point, not sure what to do, we both explored every option we could think of to somehow get my bike transported home.

After messaging several people we knew who had cars or could potentially help, my (desperate, exhausted and highly emotional - a.k.a unable to think straight or perceive clear solutions) mind presented me with the last resort of asking my now-ex to help. I messaged him, and he promptly responded, saying of course he'd help and could I just wait for him there at the beach. We waited for about an hour before I noticed my messages were not being delivered anymore, and the familiar panic of being left hanging and possibly abandoned by him once again started welling up inside of me.

As Bestie and I floated in the ocean, wondering whether I should wait or figure out another solution, it dawned on me - *"what would my inner warrior do right now? Probably not wait around for this guy who has consistently let me down to rescue me... I'm going to rescue and save myself!"* Something lit up inside of me, and it felt like the most badass warrior and healing thing I could do for my little girl in that moment was to show her I had her back and walk that damn bike the whole way home myself. Suddenly, it felt like a fun, exciting, magical warrior adventure and not a sad turn of events that my bike chain had rendered me stranded at the beach in midday Mexican heat. This was my opportunity to embody my own Big D divine masculine and *handle it* without needing a man to play the hero and come save me, the hopeless damsel. My bestie agreed that this was the lesson and - being the legend that she is - that she would do it with me for solidarity. As we brushed the sand off our towels and made our way back to our bikes, he messaged me, telling me he was coming soon, and I told him not to worry about it; I was going to handle it myself. He sent me several more messages, insisting I was patient and to just wait for him, that he was on his way to me - but by that point, I was already well down the road and not looking at my phone.

Hyped up on the excitement of our new adventure, Bestie and I were pushing our bikes along the dusty road; geeing ourselves up for the huge mission home in the heat by singing like maniacs. About twenty minutes into the walk, I felt the bottom of my stomach drop with dread; all my excitement suddenly dissipated as I saw Him turn around the corner, searching for me (as I hadn't looked at my phone, I didn't realise he was coming to help me). He pulled over on the side of the curb, and I rolled my bike over to him, wondering what I should do - should I let him help me and give him the satisfaction of feeling like a hero? Inheriting my father's mule-like stubbornness and all hyped up from the Rage Against the Machine we'd been blasting along the walk, I decided, hell no, I was committed to this... it was a *whole thing* now; it was an act of healing and embodiment; I was doing it for my little girl, to prove to her that I got her back!

I told him bluntly and coldly, "Thanks for coming, but it's too little and too late; you've shown me time and time again that I can't rely on you, and now this is something I've gotta handle myself". I could see in his face; the disappointment, the shame, the heartbreak, the hopelessness... like a puppy or a little boy who has been told off and knows they have done something wrong. It nearly made me burst into tears on the spot, but I had to be strong, "well, thanks for everything; that's all I have to say."

In response, all he could do was nod like he knew; this time he had *really* messed up. I rolled my bike back to Bestie, where she was waiting in anticipation to hear what we'd said. "That sucked", I told her, "I'll tell you about it later, we need to keep going, or I'm going to lose it again", and off we went again, towards the main strip of open road where there would soon be no shade for the remainder of our trip. Bestie (also intuitive AF) had insisted that she felt like some magic was going to happen from the moment I decided to wheel my own bike home.

About five minutes down the road, we were met along the way by a young local woman – she couldn't have been more than twenty years old – with beautiful, almost angelic energy. She noticed we were wheeling our bikes and asked what happened and if we needed help. I told her that three people had tried to fix it already, but if she wanted to try, she could. As if by some divine miracle, this tiny Mexican woman succeeded where three others had failed; she managed to connect the chain back up, and suddenly the bike had been resurrected. Through a poetic twist of fate, in the end, it was a woman who had been the saviour of the moment – our angel! It was like this nod from the divine – 'Okay, you've learnt the lesson and done the hard part; you've chosen to show up for yourself even when you could have taken the easy way out... *and now* you get to have a nice, quick and easy bike ride home as a reward'. We thanked her fervently before hopping onto our bikes, buzzing the whole way home about our *little miracle*.

I would love to say that that was the last time I saw him, or that after that initiation into my masculine, I didn't have the temptation to get back together. Unfortunately, it wasn't that simple. I still had a *lot* to integrate, and my upleveled masculine was far from embodied as a consistent state of being or anchored on an identity level (not to mention, there were soul fragments I had yet to retrieve from him, which I didn't know at the time).

I did keep the resolve to keep my distance for a couple of weeks and even started to move on. However, being who I am, it didn't feel good to me to end things the way we had ended without getting a chance to express my gratitude for everything that I had learned and received in our connection. So, a week or so later, I suggested we meet up one last time so we could clear the air. What I had intended to be "one last night together to say goodbye properly" ended up being a continuation of the cycle, as I found myself back in the karmic washing machine again, unable to let go.

And so we continued on and off, on and off, even after I left for Guatemala (not thinking I'd return or see him again) and returned back to Mexico. Until one day, finally, a few weeks before leaving Mexico for Australia, came the straw that broke the camel's back. In the time since I'd gone to Guatemala and returned right back to "playing house" with him - as this time he was more or less living with me full-time in that studio apartment - it had become so blindingly, unavoidably obvious that we were headed on two completely different paths, and that the one he was choosing to go down no longer aligned with my values. Not only that, but certain things came to pass that made me finally realise I was tolerating *way less* than what I deserved. Love or not, I could no longer ignore the waving flag that wasn't even red; it was now *on fire*.

We (once again) parted ways, and I blocked all forms of communication so we could finally both move on because there was obviously no other way. Leaving any lines of communication open between us was like a junkie casually leaving a crack-pipe lying around the house when they're trying to get off the gear; it was way too much of a temptation for both of us. Feeling like I could properly grieve without the fear that I'd suddenly self-abandon and go back to him, I left Mexico, and even though feeling tender, I felt like the door was closed (or at least, I was choosing to keep it closed). However, there was one form of social media I hadn't blocked him on as we were never connected there, which he managed to find once I'd left Mexico and contact me through. The scab that was beginning to form on my freshly healing wound was ripped open all over again as I had to go through the grief of walking away from him *one last time*.

I know that a lot of my story of this love sounds a little crazy and perhaps delusional - I'm still questioning how the hell he managed to have such a strong pull over me, even as I write this (*was I drunk that entire time?).* It's tempting to want to bow out of taking personal responsibility for how you acted by projecting it all onto the other person, making them a villain in your story, or claiming they were a 'narcissist'... but the reality is, these karmic relationships are *designed* to hit us fast, hard and deep, to show us *where we're out of integrity with ourselves.* Soul love with unhealed karma simply *can* make you act and feel a little crazy. It can speak to a part of you that is *beyond* your logic, *beyond* your list of how your 'ideal partner' would look or behave, *beyond* your 'standards', and 'boundaries', and 'knowing better'. It can touch you in a way that haunts you for the rest of your life because you're afraid you'll *never* feel a love like that again.

(Spoiler alert: you can, and you *will.* Which is something that continues to surprise me with each new soulmate I encounter.)

Just because someone is a soulmate, or a karmic, or a "twin flame", or a Whatever The Hell Else you want to call it, just because they *were* able to be everything you needed in a previous life, doesn't necessarily mean that they're the right person for you in THIS one. Soulmates are here for a reason, a season or a lifetime, and if they fall into the first two categories, we need to understand and accept that, letting them go when the sands of the cosmic hourglass finally run out rather than clinging to them for dear life. Holding someone back out of fear of being alone *is not unconditional love.* Nor is holding onto a person who is no longer fully aligned purely because you don't want to experience the grief of letting them go. It's unfair on you, it's unfair on them, and (*here she comes with the age-old cliche*) if you *truly* love someone, you have to be willing to let them go.

There is no doubt in my mind that he was (and still IS) one of my soulmates, and the deepest I've yet to love romantically in this lifetime. But that's what makes it so difficult. Before him, I would only ever call in karmics or soulmates who *couldn't* give that love back to me. They would friendzone me, or it would be platonic from the very beginning, or they were not available for something 'serious', or it would be a fleeting crossing of paths for a divine purpose (like the first soulmate I met in Mexico), or it would be some distant thing where they'd impact me, without even realising they were doing it. I could feel these soul connections and the lives we shared, but they were one-sided, so they didn't feel "tangible". In order to protect myself, I'd perpetually call in lovers and romantic interests that couldn't fully love me back, that couldn't claim me the way I desired. But this man, *he did*. With every fibre of his being, he did. For the first time in my life, I had opened my heart *all the way* to allow myself to *be truly loved by somebody that I loved back,* with the willingness to experience the grief of losing all of that love that was being poured into me.

Every time I would try to end things, I would find myself almost *crippled*, incapacitated, like it was impossible to do so, which defied all human logic given that I was blindingly aware of the fact that the relationship was not meeting me in the ways I desired, and occasionally actually making me *more* miserable than if I was alone. Or if I somehow *did* manage to develop the strength necessary to end things, I would launch into deep grief - heartbreak beyond what I'd ever felt - that I didn't think I'd be able to withstand and only kept my resolve to stay away from him for a short time, before forgiving him when he'd come back to try to win me over.

Finally closing the door and all lines of communication between us was single-handedly one of the most difficult things I'd ever done, even though it was obvious and necessary for BOTH of our healing. It required me to forgive myself *so many times* - over and over again. Forgive my judgments of myself for not being 'strong enough'. Forgive the part of myself that craved love so badly that it would eventuate in self-betrayal. Forgive my soul for signing me up to clear this karmic bullshit between us and relive all the pain of some other version of me I don't even consciously remember. A pain - by the way - that I was feeling *without even knowing* the full story of our past connections or how things went down (finally getting the full story was what eventually set me free, as I felt vindicated in all the grief I had been feeling that didn't make sense at *all* to my logical, human mind). Forgive myself for every time I self abandoned in the past, and let a man take my "no" for a "yes". Forgive myself for still desiring love or approval from someone else outside of me.

And to still decide that *even with all my flaws,* I am worthy of the divine counterpart I know is out there for me - because I can *feel* his soul calling me closer to him - waiting for me to <u>fully claim myself first</u>.

The truth was, none of this was about him; no matter how compelling a story my Little Self wants to spin about how I lost this great cosmic love I'll never have again. It wasn't about us or our "too small human love" relationship at all. It was about initiating me *beyond* the grief of losing our human connection; touching a place in which our love (in which *all* love) is unconditional, limitless and infinite. Bringing me home to the higher truth that I hadn't actually lost anything at all and that it *could never be lost* when I connected to that place where our souls shared nothing but eternal, everlasting, unconditional love.

God was trying to show me I was still filling myself with or creating attachments to external things and people, terrified of "losing" something I could never actually lose. God was initiating me by tearing away my comfort blanket (rather painfully, I might add), by showing me I was desperately trying to cling to or find something I already had an infinite source of within me...

The adoration, the holding, the commitment, the strength, the discipline, the direction and the protection of my *own inner divine masculine.*

The infinite, limitless, unconditional love of the one true provider, protector and Father figure I had been searching for my entire life; the *only* being who could love, see, hold, witness and support me in the all ways I yearned for... God.

AWAKENING THE MASCULINE POWER WITHIN: THE INNER KING, FATHER & WARRIOR

A lot of divine feminine beings I encounter have a *lot* of resistance and baggage around the masculine due to the aeons of abuse they've endured at the hands of the wounded masculine patriarchy, that they're carrying not only individually, but for the collective; so it's no surprise that their own inner masculine is nowhere to be found. However, awakening our inner divine masculine power - in particular, awakening our inner King, Father, Warrior, & Priest - is imperative to our sacred mission, no matter our gender. We require our own masculine container in order to be capable of birthing the fullness of our feminine vision; the creative works, the codexes, or the offerings we are here to bring through. We require the discipline, commitment, focus and grit of the masculine to obtain the physical, mental and emotional mastery that is needed to see our sacred missions to fruition.

Without a strong inner masculine - without awakening and rising our *own* inner protector, provider and warrior - we will not have the backbone required to hold the fullness of our feminine Oracle and, therefore, our highest soul missions. **The depth and capacity in which we can allow our divine feminine qualities (our intuition, our magic, our devotion, our love, our nurturing, our emotion,**

our wildness, to name a few) to radiate is in *direct* proportion to how much of a masculine container we can hold for ourselves.

Read that again. It is not *about* having a man or masculine energy who can hold, see, protect, provide, or support you to embody and express the fullness of your feminine essence. **It is about you being able to do that for yourself *first*.**

On top of the trauma and the hatred of the masculine many women are carrying (yes, *hatred* - and I don't blame you if you're feeling it currently because there was once a time when I felt it too), many of us have deep resentment and resistance to doing any of the "inner masculine" healing work, because it took us so long to come home to and reclaim the feminine energy that we were brought up in our society to repress. Our chaos, our aliveness, our sensuality, our wildness, our beauty, our emotion, our sensitivity, our power, our intuition, our magic - after we begin to allow and welcome all of the things that society told us we need to "dim down", then we are afraid to ever interface with anything that might threaten to suppress the feminine qualities we fought so hard to rewild and embrace. (*Say what now... you now want me to embody the masculine energy I spent so long trying to move myself out of? What is this madness?!*)

But this is not what doing the "masculine work" is about. I'm not asking you to snuff or shut down your feminine elements (EVER again) or become something you are not.

It is simply about understanding that you cannot uplevel one polarity, without the other then needing to rise to meet it at the same level. What I *am* saying is that it is literally *impossible* to meet the full capacity, depth, or potential of your inner feminine, without increasing your inner masculine container of witnessing, holding and directing her. Just like it's impossible to increase your masculine's container of presence, purpose and discipline without giving him a heartfelt vision or creative endeavour to commit himself to. We *need* both our feminine and masculine energies in order to reach our highest soul expression and potential - no matter what gender, sex or identification we have or what our 'core' essence is.

For me - like many women - a large part of this journey was coming up through healing and reconnecting to my feminine first. Meaning prior to starting this journey, I was in a very *masculine* - and wounded masculine, to boot - energy.

I would walk around with this wounded, alpha woman, boss-babe, "I'm a strong, independent woman who doesn't need no man" attitude. I wouldn't even let a man buy me dinner or hold a door open for me - in fact, it offended me deeply because I would misconstrue chivalry for misogyny (and *no, no, no*, we can't have that, 'cause I'm a "feminist"). I was results-driven and action-oriented; in Gary V-entrepreneurial-hustle-culture, "high-performance" mode most of the time, striving to attain external success and power at the cost of my own natural feminine flow, creativity, well-being and cycle.

I was emotionally closed off and hyper-independent with a "tough", *"don't mess with me or I'll stab you in the eye for so much as breathing in my vicinity"*, "I *don't give a F what anyone thinks"*, tatted up, rock n roll rebel, martial arts fighting, "cool girl" persona which masked my true insecurity, my desperate desire to be loved and accepted. Pretending to be strong behind a veneer of fake confidence and bravado that hid how frail my self-esteem actually was as a woman who couldn't even look at her own reflection without breaking down. Part of me *despised* men and saw them as pigs (the part of me who was traumatised and hadn't addressed any of the wounding or hurt I was carrying around). I carried a lot of distortions around my sexuality, where I would be counting notches on my belt and acting just like a man would, seeing sex as this big conquest that validated me as desirable and objectified the men I would sleep with (at the cost of losing a piece of my soul every single time). My strong "boundaries" and impossible "standards" did not come from self-worth; they were actually just brick walls keeping me safe from true intimacy, connection or vulnerability.

There once was a time, not all that long ago, when I couldn't even cry in front of someone else, which is *hilarious* to consider, seeing as I cry virtually every single day now... in fact, you can't *stop* me crying, it's one of my favourite pastimes (for realsies). The first partner I had on this healing journey, when I was beginning to open to my feminine energy (who actually ended up being such a blessing on my path and one of the very first examples of healthy masculine energy I experienced), used to call me "Cry Face" when the flood gates finally opened after months of him encouraging me to feel my emotions and allow myself to cry because as a result, I would cry *incessantly*.

Before embracing the part of myself who *is* soft, and squishy, and vulnerable, and feminine, and kind, and compassionate, and intuitive, and gentle, and sensual, and graceful, and all the juicy wonderful aspects of the feminine I have now come to embody (because they were already within me all along), I was HARD. I was guarded. I was in my masculine, and not even the *good* kind of healthy, divine masculine. I was perpetuating the same toxic cycles of masculine energy I despised, and I was very, *very* far removed from my natural, radiant, feminine essence.

It took me many *years* of deep healing and feminine reclamation work to reach the point where I am today, holding a beautiful example of fully expressed divine feminine energy and helping others to do the same (I share this as something that is reflected to me constantly by others). Of course, reaching this point does not mean that I've now finished the feminine reclamation work forever because there is still always *more* to reclaim; more fullness, more juiciness, more aliveness, more love, more life-force, more magic that wants to radiate and flow through me, that I have yet to unearth or discover.

Yet, reclaiming my feminine power and softening into my feminine vulnerability was the first step to even being able to *look* at the distortions I was holding within my own masculine energy and around the masculine in others. It wasn't until more feminine aliveness, more fullness, more emotion, more intensity, more energy wanted to flow through me that I realised my masculine was *seriously not up to task* or equipped to deal with it. I could see myself coming up against the "too much" wound...

It's too much emotion - too much grief, too much sadness, too much joy, too much pleasure - I can't hold it all.

It's too much raw power, too much intensity, too much chaos - what if I self-destruct and explode, taking everyone with me?

It's too much magic; it's too much ancient wisdom, it's too 'woo-woo' - I can't let them know that I'm different or that I have access to this knowledge; they'll cast me out or persecute me.

It's too much wildness, it's too much darkness, it's too much desire; I can't possibly show this guilty, dirty, sinful part of myself to the world because it's not loveable.

It's too much radiance, too much beauty, too much magnetism; it's too sexy, and it will attract the wrong kind of attention.

It's too much love that wants to flow through me; it will obliterate me.

At every point of the journey of reclaiming *more* of my feminine power, my inner feminine would test the love and the capacity of my inner masculine to try to prove that she was "too much" and that he (along with everyone else) would inevitably abandon her. It would require my inner masculine to step up and prove that even if *nobody else outside of me* was capable of holding those parts of me that felt like "too much", I could hold myself. This would happen by finding that ever-loving, non-judgemental presence of God - the Divine Father - to witness and hold me first.

This, by the way, was also largely happening and being reflected in every single karmic situationship, lover and soulmate that would show up, forcing me to deal with these wounds. It was through the process of holding and loving all the "too much" parts of myself that would arise in the vulnerability of connection and intimacy that I was then able to call in masculine-energy-core-beings into my existence who reflected that holding capacity back to me, able to love, hold, and witness the aspects of my feminine I kept hidden. (I have never been more grateful to those beautiful masculine souls I've encountered on this path, who have been able to hold and witness me in the fullness of my feminine, even *if* they were simply a reflection of the work I'd done to expand my capacity to hold and witness myself. Being held by the sacred masculine in this way is truly a gift that I hope you, dear reader, get to experience if you have not yet had the privilege. If you are a male reading this, then I hope you get to *experience* the gift of what becomes possible once you learn to hold and witness a feminine being in this way.)

At every uplevel, I would have to face and transcend my feminine wounds; alchemising them by stepping into higher and higher expressions of my masculine. *More capacity to hold non-judgemental space and witnessing* because louder, 'uglier' and more shameful parts of myself were being excavated. *More objectivity, neutrality and detachment,* as the chaotic emotions of my wild feminine and the tantrums of my inner teenager would get louder and louder. *More light, more humour, more peace, more joy,* as my darkness, my grief, my initiations became heavier. *More strength, structure, discipline, direction and purpose,* the more life-force wanted to move through my body. *More commitment to my mastery, my mission and my vision than ever,* the more I was anchoring into my Destiny Timeline.

And, of course, every time my inner masculine was in the process of stepping up, my inner feminine would go through a cycle of throwing tantrums to deter him; throwing spanners in the work, testing him, putting pressure on his weak points and calling out where he was - in fact - not in integrity or not living up to what she required. This would go on and on until he was finally integrated at that new level, and she could feel safe to surrender, to submit and to soften into his holding. When she would finally *let go*, I would be met by an explosion of orgasmic, blissful energy as the energies of sacred union erupted within me, and I found myself, once again, returning to wholeness. I'd find myself becoming *even more magnetic,* radiant and powerful than before.

I understand the resistance that comes to inviting in and working with masculine energy - even within ourselves - because there is a deep rift of trust that comes from the cycle of trauma and abuse that we have endured collectively; let alone the examples of greedy, power-hungry, toxic masculinity we *still* see present in the leadership positions in politics and industry across the globe. Over time, women have become overprotective and bitter towards *anything* to do with the masculine and are very quick to immediately shut down or go on the defence. In the process of reclaiming *our* place in the world and our dignity as the feminine, I daresay we may have flipped a little bit too far the other way; our hostility causing an even bigger rift between the sexes. As a result, many good men have become weakened. They are diminished and castrated within our society, terrified of reclaiming more of their "masculine" traits; walking on eggshells out of fear of saying the wrong thing and falling under the same firing line of the 'toxic masculine' argument their brothers and predecessors have, being publicly shamed, called out or cancelled. Which is - by the way - now more or less an exact replica of what the feminine had to endure over centuries of witch burnings, but the roles have been reversed.

I'm not even going to get into the discussion of how many feminist groups don't actually desire equality for the sexes; they seek to bash, attack and reduce men. (*Although, can you really blame women for being pissed off, given what we've had to endure over the ages, including the constant lack of safety we feel, facing the very real threat of losing our lives on a daily basis?* The statistics around violence against women at the hands of men are rather staggering and appalling, even in this day and age.) I'm not taking sides; I'm just highlighting this to hit home the amount of tension that is present when it comes to the topic of the masculine and why there is so much resistance and discomfort to actually *doing* the work to reclaim our inner masculine power (despite our gender). *Particularly* when it comes to claiming the more 'dark' or 'primal' masculine aspects (the traits such as dominance and aggression that biologically turn most feminine-core beings on - even if many will not admit to it - as the most *primal* and biological level, we're looking for a mate who is capable of protecting and providing for us and our offspring, and who is capable of exerting force or even violence if it is necessary, to do so).

Despite the amount of tension, sensitivity and discomfort that is present collectively around this subject, it is *vital* that we each do this work. If not for ourselves, then for the collective and for Gaia.

Many in the "spiritual community" (including the men) have stepped into and embraced divine feminine energy, thanks to the wave of divine feminine women who kicked off the work on behalf of the collective (you know who you are, deep reverence and respect for you sisters who were on the frontlines). However, so many are yet to embody or embrace their divine masculine energy, and this shift - the rise of the divine masculine - is what needs to happen now. Indeed, we have collectively begun to reclaim our masculine power, and I feel this process has really been ramping up since the beginning of 2022 (which was a message that the Goddess Isis relayed through me the first time I was in Mexico, in the safe holding of pure divine masculine presence provided by my past life lover). I do feel that this year (2024) with the astrological influences at play - also feeling like a 'pivotal year' for our collective process - a lot of the masculine distortions in our collective (around war and abuse of power, in particular) will come to the surface for us to face, purge and process. In fact, there have already been a *lot* of incidents thus far of violent, aggressive masculinity rearing its ugly head the more the light brings these things up from the shadows. Just the other day, I was casually leaving the gym when I witnessed an incident of a woman being attacked with a knife by her ex-boyfriend, which warranted my thinking, *"What is this madness?!"* - it was the third incident I've seen of a man lashing out in a violent act in public in the past MONTH in Sydney. However, this is by design; as I said, we are excavating all of this ugliness from the shadows, so it can be witnessed and transcended. It will force the divine masculine to rise as we will *all* be held accountable for not stepping up and saying something about the atrocities that were happening sooner.

The divine masculine warrior who *will not stand* for injustice, the crimes against humanity, and the crimes against Mother Nature that have been committed on our planet.

The divine masculine who will *speak up* and protect what is sacred, even when it's not comfortable.

The divine masculine who will *step up* and actually rebuild the tangible structures and systems from the rubble of the old systems, which will collapse due to their lack of integrity; with the guidance of the new vision of our earth birthed by the divine feminine.

The divine masculine who has the commitment, the grit, the determination, the discipline and the drive to *make shit happen;* rather than sitting around *talking* about the "New Earth" and hoping that someone else will come and save us.

This divine masculine power is inside us *all* and is ready to awaken, but in order for that to happen, we must step up and be willing to reclaim it.

INITIATION 7: RAINBOW WARRIOR CODING & MEETING THE SACRED MASCULINE

Welcome to the seventh initiation in this transmission.

The following is an activation to awaken the rainbow warrior within; to recode your body with the DNA of the Ancient Ones which will enable you to have the strength to support your sacred mission; and to interface with, heal and reclaim your *own* divine masculine energy.

In your mind and with your heart, set the intention that this is the work that will be done during our time together in this activation and that you are open to receive all that is in your highest good.

I now invite all the beings of the highest light who wish to support this activation taking place.

I welcome your Higher Self, your Soul Family and Oversoul Network, and invite them to support you in receiving what is of the highest for you at this time.

I declare that this is a sacred space, only that which is resonating on the frequency of unconditional love is welcome in this space.

I ask that everything that takes place here today is for the *highest good of all* and in service to the Whole.

I ask that the work we do together here today ripples out and serves the collective.

And so it is, and so it is, and so it is.

We invite you to enter your Sacred Space - the safe and protected ceremony space in which you receive all calibrations, downloads, codes and activation throughout this transmission.

Acknowledging internally that *you have now entered Sacred Space.*

To begin with, we invite you to transport your consciousness deep into the Mayan jungle.

Allowing your consciousness to travel there, now.

As you arrive at this place, take a moment to observe your surroundings.

Notice what you can hear...

Can you hear the gentle wind rustling through the trees or the exotic birds singing in the distance?

Notice what you can see...

Observe the trees, the plants, the winding roots, the animals, the flowers, the colours and the textures that surround you.

Notice what you can smell...

Take in the aromas of the soil, the Earthy scent of the roots of the ancient-looking trees surrounding you, the flowers and other plants, the animals, or perhaps even the damp smell of approaching rain in the air.

Now look down at your feet, touching the Earth.

Notice if they are *your* feet - belonging to *this* body and version of yourself - or if they are different; familiar, yet belonging to some other version of yourself.

As you look down at your feet, notice how strong and solid they feel as they stand flat on the jungle floor.

As you stand on your feet, set the intention to sink your energy deep, deep into the roots and the mycelium network beneath you, and as you do, notice how it lights up and begins to spark awake with your intention.

Activating this connection now, connecting you to the mycelium network of the Mayan jungle; as it begins to transmit energy up and through your feet, into your legs, into your whole body.

Feel the ancient energy permeating through your body; working on your DNA, activating it.

Bringing online cellular memories of any time *you* walked this land; a strong, healthy, capable warrior.

Bringing online cellular memories of any time *your* body reflected the ultimate health, longevity and strength of its divine DNA; the capabilities it was always meant to have.

Begin to start walking, noticing how your legs and feet feel, and the length of the strides you are able to take.

Notice your posture, your spine, your hips, your bones, your muscles - how solid and strong you are beginning to feel.

Notice your vision, your taste, your smell - how sharp and attuned your senses and reflexes are.

Notice how connected you feel to the trees, the plants, the earth as you walk barefoot - *one* with all that is.

Notice how strong, how alive, how energised, how capable you feel.

Take a moment here to really allow yourself to *feel* this and solidify the memory of these sensations in your physical body.

As you walk through the jungle, you notice you are approaching a landing in the trees; a place where the canopy is more sparse than other places, and there is a great amount of sun which is able to stream right through onto the forest floor, in several clear streams.

The rays of radiant sunshine are lighting this entire space up, and bathing it with warmth.

Feel its warmth on your skin, nourishing your whole body.

Notice how safe, sacred and magical this place is.

It is the most abundant and beautiful place you could possibly imagine; the flora here seems more colourful and more divine as the sun seems to cause it to glisten.

You can *see* the speckles of sunshine catching dust and debris; glimmering and glistening as they fall in the air around you.

As you stand in this landing and breathe this sunshine in, allow yourself to enter a state of peace and relaxation within.

As you stand here, bathed in the sun's warmth and admiring the beauty and magic of your surroundings, you notice a figure beginning to make its way towards you through the distant trees.

In this sacred place, you can sense even from a distance, that this figure means you no harm - it is moving towards you in complete peace.

As it gets closer and closer, allow yourself to observe any emotions that are beginning to arise within you; you may feel excited, or nervous, or curious, or possibly even anxious, or something else entirely.

As this figure steps out from the trees, you can start to make out the face that meets you.

It may be someone you know - your father, your partner, your brother, or a male relative or acquaintance - or someone you do not consciously know but who feels familiar to you somehow.

It may even be a version of *yourself* representing your *own* inner masculine.

Take in their face, their expression, and their body language.

Notice what is arising within you as this figure steps forward, and you may desire to ask them what they are doing here or why they came to meet you today.

See what you see, hear what you hear, feel what you feel.

This figure represents the form of masculine energy you need to *forgive* and *release* today in order to reclaim your own inner masculine power.

In this sacred place today, this figure has come to meet you to allow *you* to express anything that needs to be expressed in order for you to heal your masculine wounding.

Go ahead and allow yourself to do that now.

Allow any feelings, sensations or emotions begin to flow from within you, without judgement or needing to make sense of what is happening or where it is coming from.

For many of you, these feelings and sensations are coming from other versions of yourself you may not be consciously aware of.

See what you see, hear what you hear, feel what you feel.

Trust that even if you may not be aware of anything that is coming up for you, or are unable to perceive anything in this moment, this healing is happening on a deep soul level.

You may take a moment to pause here as long as you feel is necessary to get everything that is required off your chest.

If it feels right to do so, this is the space where you can offer your forgiveness to this masculine energy for whatever way he was unable to rise, to meet you, to protect you, or to support you; or for any way in which he shaped the way you perceive or view masculine energy as result.

This is simply a distortion, it is not *pure* masculine energy.

Clearing and releasing now any and all distortions, assumptions, conditioning, wounding and mistruths which are ready to be released now around masculine energy.

Clearing, releasing and forgiving now any and all memories or imprints of harmful masculine energy which is ready to be released across all time, space and dimensions.

Clearing and forgiving any and all soul trauma which is ready to be released now that has occurred at the hands of wounded masculine energy; greed, pride, arrogance, violence, abuse, tyranny, control, and corruption.

Clearing, severing and releasing any karmic ties, chords, or attachments now to any and all wounded masculine energy which is currently syphoning, draining or suppressing your energy.

Clearing, collapsing and releasing this all now, across all timelines, all realities, all dimensions, and versions of self across the multiverse.

Allow any of the old energy that remains to be drawn down into the Earth to be recycled.

It is done, it is done, it is done.

When this process feels complete, if it feels appropriate, take a moment to thank this masculine being for the willingness to join us today, enabling this healing that took place, and say goodbye.

Allow yourself to watch this being walk off into the distance and disappear into the trees again.

Take a moment here to energetically reset and release any remnants of that scene.

As you begin to return to the calm of the sun's warmth and the beauty of your surroundings, you notice *another* figure beginning to make its way towards you through the distant trees.

You can already feel the energy of this figure from a distance starting to permeate your entire body, and it feels completely different to the figure you just said goodbye to.

As it gets closer and closer, allow yourself to observe any emotions that are beginning to arise within you and notice the sensations in your body beginning to intensify.

As this figure steps out from the trees, you are able to make out the face that meets you; noticing how it somehow feels completely familiar to you, even if you've never "met" or "seen" them before.

Take in their energy, their face, their expression, and their body language.

This figure represents the form of pure divine masculine energy *within* you - although it may also be represented by a member of your soul family who embodies this essence or an ascended master.

This figure has come to meet you today to *show you* what the presence of pure, divine masculine energy feels like.

Notice what is arising within you as this figure steps forward, and you may desire to share something with them or ask them if they have any messages for you here in this space.

See what you see, hear what you hear, feel what you feel.

Trust that even if you may not be aware of anything that is arising for you, or if you are unable to perceive any messages or visions in this moment, this transmission of Sacred Masculine Energy is still happening on a soul level.

This figure begins to take his right hand and reaches up to place it on your heart space, activating and blessing your Sacred Mission Heart.

He places his other hand on your womb space - or energetic womb space - activating and blessing your Sacred Womb.

He then proceeds to kiss you gently on your third eye, in the centre of your forehead - activating and blessing your Sacred Sight.

Allow yourself to be fully seen, honoured, and met by this Sacred Masculine Energy in all the ways you require in this moment.

Allow any feelings, sensations or emotions begin to flow from within you, without judgement, or needing to make sense of what is happening, or where it is coming from.

You may take a moment to pause here as long as you feel is necessary.

This masculine being promises to stand by you, to protect you, to hold you, to direct and guide you, as you fulfil your sacred mission.

He asks you to open your hand in front of you, and he hands you an object that represents this promise to you; it may be a piece of jewellery, or a rock, or a trinket, or a crystal, or something else entirely.

You may desire to take that object now, and place it in your heart space, noticing the rainbow energy that is swirling in your heart as this takes place.

If it feels necessary, take a few more moments here with this Sacred Masculine.

When you feel complete, take a moment to thank this being for joining us today - if it feels appropriate for you - and say goodbye for now.

Know that even as you watch this being walk off into the trees, you are able to come here into this place, and he will meet you anytime you need, knowing that *he* is a part of *you* that can never really leave you.

Setting the intention now to share *all* the frequency and information that you have received from today's journey deep into the mycelium network and into the Earth.

Take a moment to send and share all of the frequency and information you have received today to be anchored into the Earth and seeded here, now, in physicality.

Integrating and calibrating this now on the physical level.

Integrating and calibrating this now on the emotional level.

Integrating and calibrating this now on the mental level.

Integrating and calibrating this now through all levels and dimensions of your light body.

Integrating, calibrating and sharing this frequency now through all timelines and all versions of yourself across the multiverse.

We now shut down any and all open portals and gateways that are no longer required and send back all energy that has come through any portals or gateways in the process of this work.

We now dissolve any bonds, chords or attachments that have been formed for the process of this activation and call you back into complete Soul Sovereignty.

We return all of your energy to you now as you call your Soul fully into your body.

Inviting in Diamond Light to now cleanse and close this space; bringing this sacred activation to a close, and thanking all of the beings who have been here supporting in this process.

It is done, it is done, it is done, and so it is.

You may spend some time here in silent reflection, or receiving in your Sacred Space if it feels necessary.

If you feel complete, we invite you to gently bring yourself back into your body and into the room, wiggling your fingers and toes and opening your eyes when you are ready.

PART EIGHT

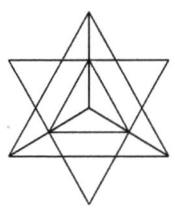

DEATH

THE VISION QUEST

It was a surreal feeling, piling all of my luggage into the back of my friend's black Jeep, saying goodbye to Tulum with no idea what awaited me. A cocktail of anxiety, grief, elation and excitement; I was shifting wildly between emotions as I sat in the passenger seat and felt the tears roll down my eyes, watching my temporary home fade into the distance. We had to cross two different borders (Belize and Guatemala) in order to make it to the hostel in Flores that evening - giving us the next full day to prepare in Guatemala before we headed off for the hike - and we had a very long day of driving ahead of us. There was an undercurrent of nervousness as I'd never crossed any borders by land before and wasn't entirely sure what to expect, and while we both spoke enough to get by, my friend and I were only on an intermediate level of Spanish. Something in my gut told me that there would be complications with the trip, but I kept trying to brush it off, putting it down to jitters and praying that we would make it there just fine.

A little out from the Belize border, we stopped for lunch in Bacalar; a quaint little *Magic Pueblo* I had been recommended by several friends, with a huge lake that has seven different shades of blue. As we jumped out of the car, I could feel this beautiful, comforting energy wash over my body; it felt very maternal, very soothing, and very grounding, just like a hug from *abuelita*. I wanted to stay in the sleepy little village forever and made a mental note that it was a definite possibility of somewhere to come and relax after our road trip.

As we arrived at the Mexican border, we drove straight through what we believed - as neither of us had gone this route before - was the checkpoint, with nobody around, wondering, "*Surely it doesn't get to be this easy?*" Evidently not, as about twenty metres down the road, we were asked to go back because we had to quarantine the car and fill out paperwork. After about twenty minutes of going from one window to another, dealing with cold and slightly begrudged staff who weren't giving us much assistance or guidance as to what we needed to do or where we needed to go, we hopped into the car and headed for the quarantine point.

My friend - who was amazing at pretending she confidently knew what she was doing, even if she had *no freakin' idea* - joked around in Spanish, flirting with the quarantine man as she slipped him a "tip" to let us take the car through even though some of the paperwork was questionable.

As we headed over the no man's land between the borders of Belize and Mexico, we just kept trying to hype ourselves up that "everything will be fine" and "it gets to be so easy", as if we both knew on some instinctual level that we'd be facing complications that day.

Arriving at Belize customs, we were surprised to meet an incredibly helpful staff who spoke perfect English and were ridiculously friendly; the polar opposite experience to what we encountered at the first border. Alas, my gut suspicion about there being complications was realised, as there were issues with the title my friend had for her car. The car was not in her name but her friend's name, as at the time of purchasing it, my friend did not yet have her Mexican residency. We were held up at the Belize customs for about an hour in a tiny office with a man trying to help us get the correct paperwork. We needed a letter of permission to take the car out of the country, somehow signed and officially notarized that day, just hours before close of business, from the woman whose name was on the title, who was back in Playa

Del Carmen. By some divine miracle, she was able to get the paper-work notarized, and the customs officers allowed us through after some umming and ahhing; warning us that this paperwork was most likely not going to fly at the Guatemalan border, as they were much stricter about that sort of thing. Hyped up on the unshakable belief in our mission and that we *had* to arrive by the evening at the hostel in Flores - there was no way we were not getting there that day, we decided - we sped off into Belize, overconfident that somehow a miracle would allow us to take the car through the border when we approached Guatemala hours later.

As evening approached and the green Belizian countryside peppered with small, colourful Caribbean-style shacks started to fade into the blackness of night, we were lucky enough to make it in time to a print shop which was still open, to print the notarized documents off. As the hours went by and we got closer and closer to our next border, the anxiety and excitement of *"will we/won't we be allowed to pass"* was felt in the air. Rolling up to the Guatemalan border at 8:55 in the evening, we were informed by the guard at the gate that the border was about to shut and we wouldn't be let through. Neither my friend - nor myself - were taking no for an answer after the day we'd had, and we begged and insisted that we'd be quick. Begrudgingly, he said okay, and we ran like madwomen into the office to get our documents stamped and to handle the quarantine of the car. Arriving back at the gate at a little past 9, we presented our documents and the car's to the lady guard who was now standing in the booth. She disappeared behind the window for a while, and I sat in the passenger's seat of the car with a sinking feeling I couldn't ignore. After about five minutes, she emerged and beckoned my friend to join her in the booth office so she could ask some questions. The sinking feeling intensified, and all I could think to myself was, *'This isn't happening - we're not getting through here tonight'.*

My friend emerged from the booth, saying something about the docu-ments not being clear enough because they were smudged and that we needed to make copies. There was a young man who was helping the guards, who knew some English - he was a total Godsend for us - going above and beyond to help us try to pass through. Now a solid ten or so minutes past the official gate 'closing time', he led us to a shack past the border where there was an office with a printer - my friend and I both nervous wrecks with the time pressure of having promised we'd "only be five minutes", and now coming up against yet another complication. He turned the key in the lock, and the door did not open.

"You're fucking kidding me", my friend and I gawked at each other as this poor young man continually pushed and pushed this door, which would not budge. An older man in a shack next door saw his struggle and came to help, and now both men were banging and pushing and kicking the office door to try to get it open. When it finally flung open with a crash, we all let out a relieved cheer as we rushed inside to make the copies. I was so wound up that I was physically shaking with nervous anticipation and adrenaline by this point. Presenting the copies at the gate once again, the woman in the booth continued to shake her head and tell us that there was something that was not right. After looking at the documents myself, I noticed that *none* of the documents corresponded with each other or reflected the vehicle we were trying to cross the border with. Neither did the notarised letter we'd gotten from her friend; each one had a different registration number or number plate on them, and the letter her friend had given us had a number that wasn't on *any* of the papers *or* the car (how that had happened is a complete and kinda hilarious mystery). Suffice it to say, the paperwork was a total clusterfuck, and there was no way we were getting that car across the border, even if, by divine grace, we'd managed to get it to this point.

After sitting in tense silence and deliberating in the car for a moment, we started to explore the option of leaving the car at the border and journeying onwards some other way. By yet another strike of divine grace, there was one (highly suss) cab waiting just on the other side of the border, and the driver agreed to take us to Flores, which was over an hour's drive away, for a fairly reasonable price. At that point - knowing from the experience of enough initiations that when something doesn't work the way it's supposed to, it's cosmic redirection - we just accepted that the car had served its purpose to get us to where we were, and there was some reason why it wasn't supposed to come with us.

It turned out that not having the car was a blessing, as it enabled us to travel much more easily, smoothly and lightly after the hike. There was a travel agent inside the hostel we were staying at who organised the entire return trip across Guatemala via bus for us, and having the car would have posed quite a logistical problem for us with parking and getting around. We squeezed ourselves and the baggage into the back of the tiny, beaten up, white sports car posing as a 'cab', and we held our breath the entire way to Flores in the pitch black as we were knocked back and forth in the backseat, through the winding roads of the Guatemalan countryside which the cab driver was racing through like a madman. When we finally arrived at the hostel and got into our room for the night - a brightly decorated and cosy one-bedroom, two-level apartment that was attached to the hostel - we let out a loud, collective exhale and were finally able to collapse with peace and gratitude that despite the wild rollercoaster that had been the day, we'd somehow made it safe and sound to where we needed to be.

The relief of discovering that we were not, in fact, going to have to dig our own holes in the dirt in which to relieve ourselves when we needed to use the toilet washed over me, along with the information that there were showers available to us at the campsites at the end of a long day of hiking. As the tour guide explained to us the details of our trip and we got acquainted with our odd mix of people that formed our tour group, a lot of the anxiety left my body as I realised it wasn't going to be nearly as "off the beaten track" as I thought it was. There were two different base camps - the first one was quite well equipped and "modern" with cement floors, (cold) showers, and actual working toilets. The second was a lot more rustic, with dirt floors, an elevated hole in the ground, which was the toilet block, that was located a good two-minute hike away from the campsite, and the "shower" basically being a bucket of water, in an area sectioned off by tarp. Regardless, both were much more tolerable than I was expecting and it was a very pleasant surprise to me that not only did we not have to set anything up ourselves, but that our campsites were going to provide some basic comforts that I thought they would not. Much of the actual hike itself is a blur of pain, trees, and dipping in and out of psychedelic states, and despite being one of the most difficult things I'd ever done, which seemed *neverending* in the moment, each day when I reached the evening I would seem to get amnesia, telling myself *"well that wasn't so bad... only x more kilometres to the finish line"*. I was shocked and surprised at my ability to somehow endure what the others (who were mostly advanced/well-seasoned hikers) were saying was their hardest hike yet. Masochistic Little Me not only agreed to do the damn thing in the first place but signed up to do *this* particular run that even the guide confided with us was apparently *one of the hardest tours* he'd ever done of this trail. *Yes, surviving to the very end in (barely) one piece is damn well a bragging right, so you best believe I'm claiming that shit!*

Before I knew it, we had already reached the middle day. It was the day with the least hiking, as we would be exploring the ruins of El Mirador; the day I was set to hold my sacred ceremony, activating the network of pyramids (the entire reason I was on the god-forsaken hike in the first place). We climbed the stairs up the side of the main pyramid as a group, and I had already informed the guide and our hiking team that I would need some time to do my ceremony once we were at the top. Ignoring the disapproval of my right knee, which was by now screaming out in agony, I powered up the stairs ahead of the group with an eagerness to reach the top. The sky was thick with clouds, which were letting out a gentle trickling of rain, and the height of the pyramid meant we were shaken by the intense and fierce winds that lapped at my raincoat and my hair.

As I stood at the edge of the pyramid, I looked out at the vast expanse of jungle, which spanned in all directions, as far as the eye could see. I imagined all of the monuments, the artefacts, the secrets buried under plants and trees; covered by dirt and worn down by the elements. I closed my eyes and raised my hands to begin the transmission, the process starting in the same way as any other ceremony; opening to the flow of energy, which was the same level of intensity as all the other sites (perhaps more - although due to my exhaustion, I found it hard to fully connect by this point and just felt that I needed to get it "done"). I extended my hands out, and my body began to move automatically back and forth as the enormous volume of energy moved through both myself and the pyramid in both directions, up and down. I took the list of remaining pyramids and said them out loud; continuing the rest of the ceremony in light language. As I uttered each pyramid's name, it felt as though the wind intensified even more; my raincoat lapping wildly at my sides, with the plastic material making a loud sound as the wind violently tore through it.

At the exact moment I finished listing names and sending energy out to each pyramid, the wind suddenly subsided, and the clouds parted momentarily for the sun to stream through (you cannot even make this shiz up, it was quite a magical moment); bringing with it this immense sense of calm. I knew that this part of the sacred mission I was on was complete; I had activated the network, it was done. I was shown the last piece of the puzzle was to travel down to Lake Atitlan (which we had already planned) to connect the rest of the grid to the portal of Mayan energy there; as it felt like that part of the grid was already "online", which made sense given there are a lot of Mayan people actively practising their culture and traditions there.

I had channelled a lot about Lake Atitlan in the lead-up to travelling there, and it corresponded with a lot of other information I found about it being a very powerful portal of energy linked to the womb, water dragon energy, and being the *"belly button"* of Mayan civilization. To me, the biggest thing I noticed was the contrast in how different the energy was between the Mayan-blood descendants where I was in Mexico and those I encountered as we travelled through Guatemala. I was told by our tour guide that in Guatemala, the Mayan people were protected and their cultures preserved, that their art and religion were very much still "alive" in many areas, particularly around the villages surrounding the *lago* (lake). Everywhere we stopped, you could see Mayan people in their beautiful and brightly coloured textiles, with joyful demeanours. It was a stark contrast to the poverty, the suffering and the heaviness of the Mayan people I encountered in Mexico.

There certainly was 'magic' in the air from the moment we finished the tour to the first few days of arriving at Lake Atitlan. We were met in Guatemala City by the sister who had first introduced us and travelled down to the lake via bus together. The place we had rented in Santa Cruz (a couple of villages along from Panajachel, where the bus left us) was *stunning*; luxurious, elegantly designed, stylish, comfortable, with lush gardens and hammocks outside, situated right on the lake with its own private jetty. It was an incredible post-hike reward and a complete contrast to having spent the previous week sleeping in a tent, on top of a cement slab, in the middle of the jungle... a time where having a bucket of cold water to wash with was the highlight of my day.

The girls - being best friends reunited - took the twin room downstairs, and I - feeling like the awkward third wheel - was blessed to a cheerfully decorated room upstairs with a queen-sized bed that felt like a cloud and double glass doors opening onto a private balcony, which overlooked a breath-taking view of the lake and the surrounding mountains. For the first day, I had to pinch myself with disbelief that we'd made it there and how dramatically different the landscape was from where we'd just been. We were all so excited, filled with gratitude and awe to be there, as we discussed ways in which we could convince the owner to let us stay beyond our reservation, which was only a few days (as the place was fully booked out) and extend our trip to enjoy it a little bit more. We sat around an open fire at night, as I took out my guitar and we sang medicine songs together.

I held a call with my mystery circle on the 11/11 portal, completing the "work" we were doing in the powerful energetic vortex of the lake, which was one of the most potent experiences I've facilitated; most of us were pretty fried after receiving the activation we did. I was guided to go down to the lake and place my feet in the water to receive from the energy of the lake itself, and connect to the dragon energy which was present.

Amidst the moments of "heaven" and "magic" I was experiencing in Lake Atitlan, I was also wildly oscillating into contrasting moments of an emotional, physical and mental rock-bottom. In the aftermath of all of the energetics and activations I received and transmitted on the hike; physically, mentally and emotionally exhausted from travelling; virtually *no* money left in my bank account due to the travelling; no energy or will to work (and make money to support myself), and no idea where I was going to be even three days into the future...the ego death I was going through was starting to take its toll on me. I wanted more than anything to be present, to be grateful, to explore with my friends and to be in the 'happy-go-lucky' vibe they were, but amidst the moments of happiness (which were peppered amongst the moments I felt like I was dying), I was experiencing one of the largest rock-bottoms I've ever faced.

All of the "magic", "mystery", and "surrender" of being in the flow, the trusting energy that I had been in the months leading up to this point, seemed to evade me. My nervous system had entered complete shut-down/freeze mode along with my Little Human Self; as I found myself in a foreign country, with over two weeks to kill before my flight home and no way of paying for my accommodation or even getting back to Mexico (as the girls were talking about alternate routes home and onward adventures which I couldn't afford). Having just learnt from my mother (who decided to tell me the evening before I was marching into the already ego-annihilating vision quest that was the hike - *gracias, mamá*) that she wanted to divorce my father due to his gambling putting them into financial issues; I had written off the option I had in the past to rely on my parents to bail me out of my situation.

(For the record, they are still very much together as I write this, as they seem to have reached some sort of understanding. I also want to add it's *not my circus, not my monkeys, and certainly not my business.* I have vowed to stay out of my parents' dysfunctional relationship that somehow just seems to *work* despite *all odds*, including the level of toxicity present. Theirs is certainly a case of die-hard, stubborn, enduring, *'can't live with each other, can't live without each other'* kind of love. A pattern which I very much mimicked with my Mexican lover, hence *the entire fucking initiation of that relationship*, so I could release it and was not doomed to repeat the same fate.)

I also experienced my 'inner child' wounding being activated as the girls were super tight, and I felt like I was constantly being excluded.

(*The reality* was I was actually excluding myself by choice because I didn't want to subject others to the heavy emotions I was experiencing, and it became a self-fulfilling prophecy.) To add insult to injury - because apparently everything else wasn't already *enough* to put me well and truly on my knees - I was also simultaneously processing the grief of (yet another) parting with my Mexican lover; believing at that point I would not be seeing him again. Suffice it to say, it was a *lot*.

My inner victim shadow and frightened Little Human Self were *so loud* that I couldn't ignore them, no matter how hard I tried to focus on the positives, enjoy my travel and be present in the moment. The dark, unlovable parts of me I tried to hide screamed so loud I couldn't block them out; every single story about how alone, how broke, how pathetic, how much of a failure, how unsupported I was just rolled around and around on a repetitive loop that was the backing track to my trip.

I could barely stand to be around myself, so I wasn't at all surprised that when they dropped me back off in Bacalar in Mexico on their way through to Tulum, the girls were cold, abrupt, and didn't really even say goodbye; clearly having had enough of my BS. As I entered my dank, sewerage-smelling, poorly-lit room (my outer environment being a reflection of the depression I was feeling internally) and collapsed on the lumpy bed, I couldn't even cry or get upset with the awkward parting of ways or their coldness towards me. Nor could I really blame them for having that reaction. It was like receiving the slap in the face I finally needed as a voice spoke to me from deep inside:

This is who you are choosing to be right now and how you are choosing to deal with the situation you are in, but this is not who you truly are. You are a powerful creator, and you have the opportunity to shift your perspective and react differently. You are not a victim. Take responsibility for what you have created. Forgive the part of yourself who is choosing to stay in suffering right now, and simply choose differently.

I took a deep exhale and, in that moment, decided that enough was enough. I had seen this part of myself I didn't like that needed loving, acceptance and integration, but I also didn't need to keep playing into her or believing her story; it was in *my* power to change. Nobody was riding up on a white horse to rescue me from the situation I'd gotten myself into, I had to salvage it myself. I had managed to put together a digital offering of a previously recorded healing experience I had once held live the day before we left Atitlan and had made a few sales, which enabled me to book my accommodation onwards. My mum - after I broke down on the phone to her - lent me the rest, with the promise I'd do whatever I needed to pay her back as soon as I was back in Australia, which was a lifeline being thrown to me that would get me through to the end of the trip. With the prospect of being stranded in Central America without money being handled, I had no reason to be in this survival/freeze/victim mode any longer. It was my job to now make the best out of my situation, acknowledge what I had created, put my big girl pants on, and take the responsibility to actually change my reality.

I softened into my truth and sent both of the girls separate voice notes, communicating from my heart with love; owning my behaviour, taking responsibility for how I'd reacted to certain triggers, thanking them genuinely for being a part of my journey, and wishing them well. Both eventually responded with respect and appreciation for my openness, and we were able to have a conscious parting of ways. I gifted my guitar to my hiking friend, and she accepted, which felt really important for me as a parting token of my genuine apology and appreciation for just how much support she had been for me on the trip. My only real regret on this entire journey was the bridges I had burnt with these women due to being too deep in my own rock bottom to step outside of myself. I was in *no* way giving them an accurate reflection of my true essence, which is a little ray of sunshine; playful, loving, fun, silly, kind, grateful, compassionate, and a joy to be around. (Majority of the time, anyway - I'll be the first to admit I can be a moody little bitch from time to time when I get swept up with my Little Human BS and momentarily forget myself. However, these days, I'm pretty fast at recognising this and self-correcting, bringing myself right back to the love that I am.) They saw a side of me I rarely impose on others, as usually, when I'm going through some sort of inner death, I retreat from the world and hide in my cave to protect those around me from my heaviness (which has been fairly easy, as since commencing this journey, I've spent a *lot* of time in solitude; living alone, travelling alone, and working alone). However, I am also aware that karmically, whatever played out and how it played out was perfect, whole and complete; each of us got the medicine we needed from this connection around stepping into our power, and those friendships served despite how short they were.

After spending a couple of relaxed days in Bacalar with a sister living there who I had first met while in Tulum, I continued travelling north by bus to Tulum and returned back to my original apartment for a week (where I rode the karmic merry-go-round of playing house with my ex, one final time). I then continued upwards to Playa Del Carmen, where I stayed a few days in a delightful, bright, modern apartment with an oven and washing machine (luxuries I'd been missing since leaving Australia, as my previous studio didn't have either). I spent every day being a domestic goddess in blissful, comfortable isolation, counting my blessings, reading positive and uplifting mindset books, and enjoying the time I finally had to just hermit and collapse in peace and quiet.

The final leg of the trip was the conference in Mexico City, which was poorly organised, severely undersold (there were only about fifty patrons attending over the three days, which was a disappointment to all the facilitators, such as myself who had paid to present conferences, and were led to believe there would be hundreds in attendance) and would have been quite a rude shock if by that point - thanks to my rock bottom - I wasn't in the attitude of *"Que sera, sera"*. When I received a rather scandalous email the night before the conference, which made me *very* sceptical as to whether there would even *be* a conference at all, or it was all just a big scam, I couldn't even be upset and simply just laughed out loud to myself - at that point, what more could happen to test me? Rather than be disappointed (which admittedly I was for a moment after arriving to the virtually empty conference centre, realising perhaps there was some truth to that email), I just trusted that it was good practice for future speaking engagements,

I'd get some good footage for my showreel, and there was some other reason I was meant to be there. And indeed, there was.

I had instant soul-tribe connections with several people who were at the event, which made the trip to Mexico City quite a social and enjoyable one for me, as we met up for dinners and lunches, and I enjoyed that warmth and familiarity that you only get when around soulmates (several of them I've had on as guests for powerful co creations on my podcast, and many other collaborative projects are being discussed for the future).

As one of my new soul friends so eloquently put it at dinner on the first night, *"The reason you were called here was to meet us!"* He was not wrong.

There were also some rather interesting things taking place energetically as we sat together around a table for breakfast on the final day, a few hours before my flight home. I was suddenly feeling my kundalini become *very activated*, noticing my hands take on a life of their own as they moved a lot of orgasmic energy through me, and apparently, I was not the only one feeling it. So was the friend sitting directly across from me, who out of the blue, closed his eyes, and started channelling around divine union, tantric templates and sacred sexuality (we brought this transmission through when I invited him onto my podcast to co-create Episode 55: "Sacred Sexuality and Tantric Alchemy", which you can listen to at www.becmyonas.com/podcast). There were definitely some divinely orchestrated, beautiful things happening that day, as the energy was dancing around the table, imprinting and activating us far beyond the level of the mind.

While the trip to Mexico City was not the huge instant lift in my career I was hoping (or expecting), it was still a beautiful way to wrap up my monumental journey in Mexico, before finally getting on a flight and heading home - unsure of what the future held, forever changed on a cellular level, but still with *a lot* I had yet to process or come to terms with.

DRAGON ENERGY

By this point in the book, you will have seen the word "dragon" appear many times as a subtle undercurrent for this journey, but not something that I have *directly* addressed. I have asked the dragons to step forward and support me in writing this section of the book - although they are indeed present throughout the entire book - to ensure I represent them adequately and what the ancient wisdom *they* represent is potential for. Their energy is present here and now as I write - if you have not already met or felt it through this transmission - for you to access and weave with as a deeper embodiment of the codes which I am about to share. It's important I do this justice, as the dragon is a thread that has been underneath this entire journey for me but didn't fully land as to the 'why' until towards the end when all the pieces began to weave together.

You will find the first reference to dragons in the beginning of this book. I talk about the 'dragon lines' of the Earth; the feminine dragon line (the Rainbow Serpent) and the masculine dragon line (the Feathered/Plumed Serpent). Places where these two lines cross over each other (such as in Bali and Peru), create hugely powerful amplification and purification portals. In these places, there is intense potential for transmutation and clearing of karma. This is the first reference to the amplified power of the feminine and the masculine coming together in a 'crossing' to create a new, greater power; that of the Divine Union, the energy of the Creator. I touched on this again in the following section when I wrote about kundalini - how the feminine (Shakti) merging with the masculine (Shiva) creates this incredible energetic potential of Divine Union.

You will perhaps remember me mentioning prior to my second trip to Mexico - just before commencing my travels - I was called to work with a women's work company that was offering a retreat around dragon energy in the time I was in their vortex. I had been seeing dragons *everywhere* in the lead-up to this, so finding out that they were to run a 'dragon retreat' as the main project I'd be supporting them to market was *very* kismet indeed. I might mention that this was also *just* after I had begun to be visited by the Mayan ancestors, who were telling me it was time to go to Mexico and bringing to my awareness the Mayan Creator God "Kukulkan", the feathered serpent (*what is a feathered serpent, if not a dragon?*). I will also add that the energy of Kukulkan was *very* present for me throughout the entire gridwork mission; so much so that one of the students in the psychic development accelerator I was running at the time (unrelated to the gridwork mission itself) picked up on this energy around me, told me his name *without* having known anything about him prior, and shared the message that he was working with me on this mission. I already knew that, of course, but I was very proud of my student at that moment indeed, as this was only after a few weeks of being in this accelerator, and she'd never channelled anything to this detail before, nor had I mentioned anything about Kukulkan (or Quetzalcoatl, which had been the name she'd used, which represents the same figure) in our lessons! But I digress...

The way in which the founder of this company I worked for speaks about dragon energy is something I wish to echo here and now as it is something I understood on a deeper, embodied level as I interfaced with the energy in which she was helping those on the retreat to awaken. She speaks of dragon energy as this primordial force of energy we can awaken *within* us, that of the Alchemist. She speaks of it as an evolution from traditional kundalini - rather than having to travel all the way up the chakra system and into the crown in order to merge with the masculine and get "wings", it is the kundalini serpent with its wings *already* open (if you consider that image is exactly what a dragon is; a serpent with wings). She speaks of it being the feminine and the masculine energies *already in union* and creating a third energy - the Sacred Androgyne/Child who wields the energy of the Creator. (Perhaps you are now joining the dots as to why we must heal and evolve *both* our inner masculine and our feminine energies in order to wield this power and why I have addressed both the mother and the father wound as a part of this journey.) She speaks of the dragon representing our Greatest Becoming, our highest potential and soul expression - as do many others I have encountered, including my book doula/mentor who speaks of "becoming the dragon" as a metaphor for embodying your highest self.

She (the facilitator of the women's work company) believes it is a new sacred technology that we can access and awaken; however, in the time I was working with them, I felt and understood it as *ancient* wisdom and technology that was coming back online now. As I journeyed through this experience and supporting them to hold the vortex of energy - which was also being amplified through the massive gridwork which is being created by this company and the larger community of women who take part in their retreats and offerings - I had continued visits by the energy of Kukulkan, and flashes of Ancient Mayan Pyramids which at the time I couldn't understand why. At the time, it simply joined the dots for me of my suspicion of the fact that this was *ancient* sacred technology re-awakening. I was not yet realising that *everything* - the dragon energy; the Mayan gridwork mission I would soon be called on; the work I had been doing to merge my own sacred feminine and masculine energies - was related. Even the sacred geometry of the pyramids (the two triangles - the inverted 'inner chamber' and the upright triangle of the outer pyramid - representing the feminine and the masculine elements) pointed to this alchemical power of this fusion of polarities; the *harmonisation* of complete Divine Union.

From a literal standpoint, we must consider the dragons *themselves* - mythical or not - and what their species represents. To me, dragons are creatures who wield immense power with command, grace and dignity. They are symbolic of the ultimate mastery and sovereignty which we are able to attain ourselves as a race; wielding the energy of the Alchemist, the Creator, the feminine and the masculine working in harmonised Unity. They cannot be intimidated nor controlled; you simply cannot tell a dragon what to do. They do not shrink or try to hide who they are. They embody and wield their power unapologetically, yet they do so with unconditional love and for the highest good of all (most of them, anyway, but I'll expand on this in the next section). Anyone who has had the privilege of working with a dragon will know that they *encourage you* to step into your highest power and your highest timelines and will support you to do so, to no end. For me, this is embodying the New Earth template; supporting *others* to rise into their power, their majesty and their sovereignty, in service of the greatest good of all.

Another piece I feel to weave in here is around dragons as the guardians of the underworld; the portal between worlds. During the process of channelling this book, I found myself interfacing with and bringing back online my 'dragon body' and a part of my soul, which *is* a dragon. I have known since the beginning of this journey that I am a guardian of the Underworld and that this (my forays in the Underworld) has served me on my greater soul mission as it has enabled me to hold an even higher polarity of light (an angelic/'seraphim' template that came online the same time my 'dragon' body did). This dragon aspect of me is the Guardian of the Underworld. Fearless, strong, and able to move between the dark and the light - the depths and the heights - without difficulty. To be able to traverse the underworld; get dirty, messy and covered in mud - *and* to soar up, up, up into the heavens. The dragon does not discriminate; for the dragon, the lines between 'dark' and 'light' are blurred. The dragon represents the power of creation that is beyond polarity, without judgement, without 'good or bad', 'right or wrong'; always seeing the higher perspective, that it is *all* part of the one same Whole.

There are a few other final 'dragon' pieces which I feel important to add. This book was born through me in the year of the Wood Dragon (according to the Chinese Zodiac). While writing this book, I was in the process of being simultaneously initiated into the healing modality of my book doula/mentor - 5 Element Dragon Fire Reiki - in order to support my system to do the work that I do and working closely with the dragons to clear and purify *all of my energy channels*. I have also been introduced to many dragons I did not know existed, such as the Mushroom Dragons, who support decomposing density in our bodies into energy that can be used to support us (much like fertiliser), and the Acid Dragons, who support the breaking down of calcifications. These unconditionally loving dragons were supporting the energetics that took place in Initiation 4 - the process of breaking down all density whilst in your chrysalis - and Initiation 5 - the process of connecting your meridians to Gaia. And indeed, many of you may feel called to cultivate a working relationship with these dragons, having been introduced to them now (as I did once I was initially introduced to them and found myself crying tears of homecoming at how beautiful and unconditionally loving their energy was). There is also a final dragon - the Golden Solar Dragon - who was introduced to me by another powerful priestess sister of mine and who supported me with the co-creation of the final Initiation at the end of this chapter - but you'll be meeting them soon.

I have noticed in the years leading up to my writing this book that many have felt the call of the dragons or are drawn to work with dragon energy - almost like a wave of dragon-related frenzy hit our community. Suddenly, dragons and people claiming to work with dragons or be dragon riders were *everywhere*. I believe this is because prior to this, as a humanity, we were *not* ready yet for the high level of ancient esoteric wisdom and the alchemical knowledge that the dragon holds or what it represents for *us* in our own process of evolution. We were not *ready* to merge our internal energies to wield the power of the alchemist. And for that reason, perhaps, the dragons themselves did not reveal themselves or step forward to support us and initiate us in the ways they are now, as perhaps we were not ready to work with this level of power *without it corrupting us*.

CORRUPT DRAGONS

"Your guides are telling me the reason it's been so long and hard is because others they've attempted to give this transmission to in the past (maybe past lives of yours) couldn't stay humble... they got drunk off their own power... high off their own supply. Corrupt dragons. That's why you've been so shy this time around to hold the fullness of your power - it's also why you've been cracked open over and over again until your heart could STAY open."

My mentor's words rang true, as they echoed in the years of facing the karmic repercussions of every single lifetime I'd had where I had become cruel, callous, "drunk on my own power" and "high on my own supply" with little regard for human life, as a result of having a high level of energetic mastery. I was *crushed* by the weight of who I'd been - the evil, the selfishness, the darkness - so much so that I felt I had no right to even *ask* for the forgiveness of God (to which God would always respond, *"it's not me that needs to forgive you, you need to forgive yourself - because I am you, and you are me"*). I couldn't bear to look at the cruelty that became of others who abused their power because they only mirrored back the cruelty in *myself* in the times I abused *my* power. I was afraid to be in the dark or to see the darkness in others because it was the dark parts of *myself* I was truly afraid of seeing. And more than anything, I couldn't endure the thought of having to present myself as "leader of light" when I *knew* the darkness that was within me.

What if people found out I wasn't always good? What if they knew how evil I have been? What if they saw this part of myself I didn't want anyone to see?

I take no pride in sharing all the times I have become a Corrupt Dragon, one who has abused the sacred power that I have learnt to wield as a result of my megalomania and selfishness to the harm and detriment of others. Knowing that there was some part of me who was downright *bad* (not just a "baddie" or "badass"; I'm talking a pure evil, sadistic A-hole) has been something that has been a constant source of healing for me over the years. I have hesitated to stand up and claim my place as a leader because I was terrified that stepping out into the light meant exposing all of my darkness, too. I have been reluctant to claim or fully step into my power because I have been so afraid that it would corrupt me; that I might wind up just like those in power and control that I have sought my entire life not to be like... that the same part of me that became a self-serving A-hole in *so many other lifetimes* would resurface again. I have found myself having to atone for and forgive deeper layers and memories of the evil things I have done and been responsible for at every precipice of stepping into another level of my power.

And ultimately, I know that it is only *because* I have been all of these things that I am able to hold the light I do now and to keep my heart open, no matter what is thrown at me.

I know that by learning to unconditionally love these dark and atrocious things I have been and done it was teaching me to hold the same perspective as the benevolent creator who created *everything* without judgement or preference. **To enter the place beyond right and wrong, beyond light and dark, where all roads and all pathways equal Love.**

I used to resent having to face all of these dark parts of myself - to love and forgive them - or going through brutal initiations time and time again to crack my heart open even more. I used to resent having to declare "I choose love" each time I was tested, attacked or approached by the dark side. I used to be *so fucking angry* at God every time I would relive the past life (yet very real) trauma of being a "victim" - being sexually abused in satanic rituals (a large part of what was coming up to be healed in the karmic relationship I navigated in Costa Rica, where he had been my father in a past life, and had abused me in these ways). Or when I was burnt at the stake for being a witch when I was just trying to help people. Or even *more,* so that time I was called a 'false prophet', raped, beaten and left to die in a cold cell in my Delphi lifetime (although I daresay I almost certainly brought that last one on myself by being a *vindictive little bitch*). For the record; when uncovering these lifetimes, I would move through the pain of the emotion *well before* I would piece together or see the memory attached to it, so it wasn't *because* I was hearing the story of what happened to me I was reliving it, I was remembering the story *as a result of* reliving the pain that would surface suddenly out of nowhere. At the same time, learning to let the emotion move through me *without getting attached to the story at all* (I'll get into this a little later, as I feel it's super important to mention, considering I share so much about past lives).

As I look back from where I stand now, I see that all of this was necessary for me on a soul level - it was simply my karma; I was due to experience these things as a result of what I'd chosen in many other lifetimes. I wasn't really being 'punished by God', nor was I a victim. I was a *creator* who had *created* those experiences with a higher soul purpose of evolution and growth (even if on a human level at the time, those experiences *sucked some serious balls,* and I couldn't possibly fathom how the hell it was "love" that God would let me suffer like that). After abusing my spiritual powers, I had to regress through the evolutionary incarnation wheel and experience *many* lower-life form realities and very bleak incarnations to get myself to a point where I was capable of wielding that great power while still being anchored in my heart.

Being on the receiving end of some of these atrocities, I would never, ever desire to do that to anyone again, nor would I desire to create any sort of karmic ripples for some future version of me to have to endure. Thankfully, I have learnt and evolved, and I understand that those who *are* still harming others will eventually do the same. If they desire to evolve on a soul level (which is every fractal of the source's primary drive and motivation as the Universe itself seeks expansion), they'll realise that there is only a certain level of experience one can attain when serving Self. As I said earlier, all roads lead back to love, and we mustn't judge them (though we also don't have to condone their behaviour nor sit idly by while these atrocities occur).

It is clear to me that prior to entering this lifetime, I insisted my guides and my council give me the initiations I required to crack my heart open, to remember on a rather visceral level all of the traumatic things I had been on the receiving end of, and the horrific things I had done to others, to make damn sure that *I didn't fuck it up this time*. I had tactically come into this lifetime with "locks" on my power - certain thresholds and initiations I had to pass or things I had to uncover before enabling myself to access a deeper layer of my power, soul gifts and memory. And the level of my heart consciousness - the amount of unconditional love and compassion I could hold through those initiations that were seeing me endure more pain than I believed I could bear - was the key. With each new level, I am reminded of who I have chosen in the past to be as a warning to prevent me from becoming a Corrupt Dragon again. And to solidify my decision to choose love.

A few years ago, I had a Starseed origin reading from a peer I deeply respect, who told me, *"I've never seen anyone holding such a strong polarity of light and dark - these two opposite extremes within them"*. He apologised for being so blunt and hoped I understood that it was coming from the right place but begged me to continue to choose the "light side" and not to stray towards the dark, which he could see I had done in many incarnations. (I wasn't triggered at all by anything he said; in fact, I laughed because I felt *so fucking seen*. I knew I was holding this huge polarity of light and dark, and I had already been through many rounds of having to "love and forgive" the darker lifetimes I'd led.)

He shared that there were many different galactic lineages I had connections to, or incarnations within - as an activator and portal who requires enormous quantum access to do what I do, this didn't surprise me in the slightest - but the ones that were coming up that he felt important to comment on were Draconian (which was a "darker" life-time), and Dragon (where I was a beautiful, feminine, red dragon who was unconditionally loving and pure).

In both timelines, I had similar power - Draconians are a race that is synthesised from Dragon DNA, however, they have taken on many of the more "shadow" traits of Dragons - but it was what I had chosen to do with it, which is what counted. Dragons have strong boundaries and are not easily swayed by others. They have authority, which makes them natural leaders, and their energy is magnetic and alluring, which means they have the potential to have a *great* influence on others. They are also incredibly wise and gifted alchemists. They either trigger you and scare the hell out of you or inspire awe and love in you - depending on your own relationship to your inner power. A dragon in its evolved form of 'serving the whole' is unconditionally loving, strong, protective, impenetrable, wise, ancient and powerful. On the contrary, in their 'self-serving' (unevolved) form, cut off from the heart; dragons can be cruel, greedy (as we see the dragon protecting its hoard of gold in many fantasy tales), demanding, manipulative or cunning; abusing their power to become militant, "warlord" like types, which is what we can see in the stereotypical shadow representation of Draconian energy (of course not *all* Draconians are like this, just as not all humans are greedy and obsessed with status).

The bottom line is, it is not the *power* that corrupts; it is the way one chooses to *wield that power* - whether they are wielding it with love, in service of the Whole; or wielding it in separation and service of the Self.

This is something I urge you to keep in mind as you uncover and retrieve your own power - and also, is why you may have had to relive and experience similar things. The power of a priestess, an Oracle and an alchemist is not power to be taken lightly. The power you have access to is a *divine privilege*. May your heart and your intentions forever remain pure the more powerful you become, and may you wield your power with grace, compassion and understanding for the greatest good of all.

LESSONS FROM ATLANTIS & WARNINGS FROM THE PAST

As the saying goes - *"with great power comes great responsibility"*. It is our responsibility - individually AND collectively - that we wield the sacred power we have been given access to (which is awakening within all of us, not just those who receive this transmission) with the purest of intentions. If not, we may be doomed to face the same disastrous repercussions our race has faced many, many times in the past in the rising and falling of "great civilisations". Indeed, there are many times in which the civilisations of humanity have risen to power and just as quickly fallen because of their own folly, but one particular civilisation that has left quite a traumatic imprint on a lot of us is Atlantis. For me, Atlantis shows us the epitome of what happens when we have this advanced spiritual technology at our disposal but do not choose to wield it for the highest good of all. For me, Atlantis speaks to a time when humanity got *very close* to rising to our next level of evolution before crumbling into oblivion.

Atlanteans had all sorts of impressive technology and were very "spiritually" advanced - they were high-level alchemists, trained in the mysteries, who wielded free energy to power their city. It was a "Golden Age" where humanity lived in a Utopian-like Heaven on Earth. They lived - like many of our indigenous cultures - in harmony with the heavens and the Earth and used pyramids and other sacred technologies to attune themselves to different dimensions. They were the closest humanity got to "ascending" into the next level of our evolution... before being suddenly obliterated. Why did this happen, and what does it have to do with the pinnacle point of evolution that humanity is reaching once again?

Many have theories about what happened to cause the sinking of Atlantis due to a 'great flood' - in fact, the mystery that shrouds the events that caused it has become somewhat of an obsession for many, even those in the less esoteric spaces. I believe this obsession is because of the traumatic imprint the fall of Atlantis has left in the DNA of humanity; the last time we came so close to achieving the leap of evolution we have set out to achieve since our original inception. The recollections I am about to share are my own (although I have heard other channels sharing similar recollections). Whether or not you believe my recollections as the full story of what occurred and how it occurred, the underlying lesson and warning we can take from Atlantis is the same. **No amount of technological advancement will save us from our own self-destruction if our intentions are not pure.**

While my memories are not vivid or detailed, I have been given flashes or impressions of what my experience was in Atlantis and how I played a part (no matter how small) in its downfall. With this recollection came a lot of guilt and a lot of fear of stepping into my power, afraid that once again, I would be used to wield the power within me against my own will. While I was not a "corrupt dragon" in Atlantis - I had a pure heart and intentions, and I never sought to harm anyone - my own unique spiritual abilities were abused, and I was forced to play a part in a plot I had no desire to.

In Atlantean times, I was a young woman trained in the sacred mysteries of the temple path. My particular job was to generate and amplify a source of 'free energy' using advanced skills of alchemy to power the grid that animated all our technology (similar to how electricity works, but with no environmental repercussions, and also not requiring any other material to generate it). To be prepared to wield and generate this divine energy through my body without it frying all my circuits or killing me, I - along with all other initiates - was guided through intense and gruelling training for many years and many stages. Our entire lives were devoted to the initiation path, training for hours every day in physical, mental, energetic and emotional mastery. The sacred technology we were trained to use *had* to be wielded with pure intention, or else it could prove detrimental and destructive (which is exactly what happened).

I was - along with others, as it required several of us working together to generate enough energy - connected to a piece of equipment in the centre of a pyramid and would stand with my arms and legs spread out in a position similar to Da Vinci's Vitruvian Man. (Also somewhat resembling an ancient Egyptian Ankh ☥, which is a sacred symbol representing life.) The technology - along with the pyramid, as I have already touched on - would serve as an amplifier for the energy we were channelling through our bodies. We would generate a large torus field around our bodies of the divine energy we channelled from the Earth and from the Heavens through our bodies into the contraption. This energy would then expand out from this 'pulse' point to all the other pyramids in the network of the Atlantean grid, which were strategically placed, allowing the entire network to have free energy powered by divine life force itself. (Indeed, this is the very same technique I was using on my recent gridwork mission to activate and harmonise this larger network of energy, as you might have connected - except in Atlantis, it was used to generate a form of electricity, and we were using external equipment to support it.) There would also be particular frequencies, intentions or instructions sent into this grid via the pyramid network; energy which would *influence* those who lived within this grid.

Side note - this is how the 'slave grid' that still existed in more recent times functioned to enslave and constrain us. Those who still saw humanity as a "slave race" used this energetic influence and technology placed within (or rather, hijacking) our own Earth grid to pump fear and limitation through us, preventing us from awakening our Divine DNA by remaining in the "trance" of the masses. This is the slave grid

I spoke of much earlier in this book, which I was working for many years to dismantle parts of and which I was informed was completely dismantled as of 2022. I don't desire to go much deeper into this in this transmission, as I'd rather not transport myself back into that timeline or be fueling people getting caught up in "dark agenda" conspiracy theory loops of the past rather than focusing their awareness on creating a New Earth. However, I'll briefly share that it was a rather heavy contract that saw me enduring advanced, intricate, and complex energetic attacks for many years as I was dissolving parts of the grid by bringing them into my own heart. (As you can imagine, this didn't really serve the "dark agenda" and pissed quite a few people off.) It also involved me facing and nullifying all of my Draconian and Reptilian soul connections, contracts and oaths. Suffice it to say, it was a big olde clusterfuck of a karmic contract I had to complete, and I am *very* glad to be done with all soul contracts involving lower realms of reality. If you observe my earlier resistance at the start of this transmission around holding quite a lot of Little Self-fear about who might come for me as a result of sharing the information in this book that I do so freely, you can only draw your conclusions as to where that fear might have come from. At this point in the initiation, that fear has dissipated (but I won't say that the dark goddess/sacred rebel within me isn't sticking two middle fingers up in taunting defiance now that I've stepped into and fully claimed my power and my soul sovereignty).

Back in Atlantis, some of the leaders - the high priests, priestesses and royal families - with these advanced spiritual and alchemical capabilities saw themselves as Gods. Not as creators but as *Gods*. They inherited the same arrogance of their forefathers - the Annunaki, who at times exhibited many of the traits in humanity that would be attributed to "ego", like arrogance, anger, spite, greed, pride - in thinking that not only were they the creators, but that they deserved dominion and control over all of those that they saw as "beneath" them. While I believe that, indeed, *we are powerful creators*, there is also a much higher power that created us all. And yes, that higher power is *within* us - because if you take a drop out of the ocean, it is still the ocean. We are one fractal of the One - the Source - and at a higher level, any separation from that One is an illusion. To deny that simple fact is to basically negate everything else written in this book. *HOWEVER* (BIG, however), there is a difference between being a drop of the ocean and the entire ocean. There is a very big difference between being in 'co-creation' with this higher power - and therefore manifesting your intentions in service of the highest good of ALL - and believing that the limited perspective and desire of your singular fractal of the creator is the only one that matters. **The Atlanteans disobeyed one of the fundamental laws of the universe - observing and respecting the free will of other sentient beings.**

The powers that be in the main City of Atlantis saw that some of the tribes of Atlantis (on the outskirts of the city) were not in agreement with certain desires or agendas they had. And so, there was a very strong intention placed within these amplification portals and free-energy generating machines to control the minds of these tribes via the energetic grid. I don't recall this being a "one-time" event; I believe it happened many times over many occasions and intensified over time. This caused several pyramids/points on the grid to go "offline" as they were no longer in harmonic resonance - which, if you follow, was exactly what happened with the Mayan grid which I was working to resolve in 2023, but for different reasons.

The final blow to Atlantis was a hugely powerful pulse of energy sent out from the central pyramid; somehow unbeknownst to those in control, parts of the grid were no longer online (I'm honestly not sure how they effed this one up and didn't realise with all their "spiritual advancement" but, there you go - *karma's a bitch*.) Thus, when this large energetic pulse was sent out, having nowhere to go, it returned immediately back to the central point and caused an explosion of energy so big (think "bigger than a nuclear bomb" levels of energy) that it caused the Earth's magnetic poles to shift. The shifting magnetic poles caused the series of cataclysmic events (and eventual tidal wave) that sank Atlantis. *Oops...*

I write this with a casualness and lightness I didn't always have around what happened in Atlantis and my part to play. I guess the more of this "past life trauma" you uncover and heal, the less attached you get to it as you start to gain a higher perspective and start taking all of this far less seriously (after all, we're only just going to come back and do this *over and over again* for *all of eternity*). While some of the feelings and sensations linger, you can never quite know if the *"story"* is true or just a figment of your imagination, so you mustn't get attached to the story (not to mention, you can never be 100% sure the memory is actually *yours*, and not just an imprinted memory from a member of your soul family who has shared that memory with you, so you could learn that lesson, without having to go through it yourself). Feel whatever feelings are present, take however long it takes to clear the traumatic imprint and, reclaim whatever soul fragments you need to, and let it go.

I repeat: Do. Not. Attach. To. The. Story. Of. Your. Past. Life. Trauma.

At the same time, do not get attached to stories of who you have been in past lives. I could write a whole 100,000-word thesis on this topic alone, which is highly ironic given how much of this manuscript is me sharing past life experiences. *"Say what?! She's telling me this NOW?! After making me read all of these pages uncovering all her Mayan lifetimes and over 5000 words on some Mexican dude she couldn't get over because he stabbed her in a past life or something? What a load of utter BS, I want a refund"* - I can only imagine you thinking at this point.

However, there's a difference between retrieving important soul fragments and pieces of information that supports you to understand the soul codex you hold, the potential karma you came in with, and therefore, your sacred mission here in *this* incarnation, and getting caught up in the 'identity-level' bragging rights or trauma loop that you could instead choose to do.

Read that again. Get it? Got it? Good.

I've done the latter earlier on this journey and wasted many years being salty that God let me go through all that traumatic stuff, so I'm telling you *from experience* (I'm a three-line, remember, so allow me to shortcut your experience and spare you the bullshit): it's best to skip that whole scenario if you can. Pick up two cards and pass go. We only remember our past lives, so we can *learn* from them and integrate that knowledge here and now. That, and to justify hot, whirlwind romances and trauma bonds with otherwise complete strangers... *(kiiiiidding)*.

This over-identification with the "story" of past lives is what we see with so many people out there claiming they were Cleopatra in a past life or they are a 50-millionth-dimensional Arcturian starseed because it makes them feel somehow more important and better than others (I can *feel* you wanting to stab me through the page). Isn't it funny we never see people (except this moron over here, yours truly) boldly claiming, "I was a slave in a past life", "I was a dick to small children", "I cleaned toilets", or "I was a 1-dimensional hunk of space rock"? I guess those stories don't make for compelling party conversations (nor books initiating others into the sacred mysteries; although perhaps one day, I'll also release a memoir of all of my utterly unmemorable life-times... just for the lols).

But after that really long (and particularly spicy) love rant, let's return right back to probably negating everything I just said and confusing the hell out of you by putting our 'serious' hats back on and talking about the traumatic repercussions of Atlantis...

When first remembering all of this and having to deal with the guilt of realising I shouldered some of the responsibility (no matter how small) around what happened at Atlantis, I certainly didn't find it humorous. I found it a great excuse to bury my head in the sand and hide so that I wouldn't have to go through that potential pain of coming so close to what we've been working on for aeons and then messing it all up right at the last minute. It's a fear that many lightworkers carry; having witnessed the fall of Atlantis, some of us escaped and lived on to establish other civilisations from the ground up again. We are so afraid of the power we wield being bigger than us and corrupting us, so we don't allow ourselves to step into it. We are watching our technology get more and more advanced, yet so many have not evolved their consciousness with it. And we are afraid of what might happen as a result .

I invite those of you who are tied up in fear that is echoing from past lives and watching great civilisations such as Atlantis fall - whether story we've attached to or truth - to transcend these memories and see them for what they are: **important *lessons and warnings* from the past, so we don't repeat the same mistakes and - armed with this information - have the opportunity to choose differently.** We must look to those lost advanced civilisations - from Atlantis to Ancient Maya - and *learn from our mistakes and grow,* lest we repeat the same fate.

This is where we're once again at as a humanity; dangling on the edge of the knife, so close to the leap in evolution we have been waiting for since the dawn of time. We are at this pivotal point, and we must allow ourselves to transcend and evolve now - to face our own *willing* destruction as a form of our rebirth - or risk becoming just another cautionary tale for future generations.

PROPHECY OF DESTRUCTION - THE END

I have said it many times, and its message has echoed through this book; in my story and experience; through the many deaths and rebirths I have gone through *just in the process of writing this alone*, let alone throughout my larger preparation to carry out my sacred mission (spanning *lifetimes*).

This is the prophecy shared by the Mayans, which I echo now from this fractal of consciousness sharing this wisdom.

That which is not willing to die cannot change form.

That which cannot or is unwilling to change form will be destroyed.

Through the destruction of what was comes the fertiliser for New Life.

And through the New Life, the cycle begins all over again.

An endless spiral of death and rebirth. Of dark, followed by light. Of winter, followed by spring. Of nothing, followed by everything. Of emptiness, followed by fullness.

This is the Law of our Universe. This is the Law of our Earth. This is the Law of every living thing that has been and ever will be. This is the fabric of reality; the codex of consciousness that animates all things into Being.

To deny or resist this law, to deny or resist our own nature by negating or bypassing our darkness, our destruction, our chaos and our own inevitable death, is to deny God.

I believe - like the ancient Mayans - that the breakdown and death *is necessary* for the New Earth to be reborn, here and now on our planet, not on some other planet.

I believe that these solar energies are helping us to shed our density so that we can be reborn with more light. I also believe that in order for this rebirth to happen, we *must* face the inevitable death, destruction and chaos that will happen as a result of the crumbling of our systems and structures that are rooted in the Old World.

And I believe that the Mayans were warning us of what is to come if we are not prepared to face this necessary destruction.

I am not going to sit here and speculate about the specifics of what that will look like because it feels unnecessary, although I have seen glimpses that I hope with all my little human heart are not true. I have had apocalyptic nightmares since a young age, and I have always just put it down to anxiety. Tidal waves and tsunamis; freakier "Revelations-from-the-bible" style dreams, where fire was raining down from the skies; sinkholes opening in the Earth to swallow me. Perhaps just residual memory or trauma from Atlantis and many other civilisations I was here to see the end of; but perhaps these chaotic endings echoing throughout my memory are there for a reason; as a warning of what is potentially to come and what *has* come at any time our society has reached a pinnacle point in its evolution. Every time I have had one of these dreams, "memories", or nightmares, they have echoed through my being, bringing with them immense fear and panic. When-ever I ask the Guidance, I am always just told that no matter what happens, I will receive adequate warning and I will be fine. I might add, knowing what I do about the Eternal Soul, if it is my time to exit this planet and this incarnation via one of these destructive events, I fully accept it. In fact, in many ways, it feels like the "easier way out" than having to be around to rebuild after the fact. I have also had these same apocalyptic visions shared and corroborated with many different priestesses since I started writing this book; however, it's important for me to add none through the lens of fear.

As an aside, it also feels it is my duty to share that *many* will choose to exit through this process (and already have leading up to it in the recent years that have passed) because they simply are not capable of holding the amount of light that wants to flood this planet, nor are they interested in having the experience of sticking around for the aftermath. And when I say "exit", I'm not going to sugarcoat it or beat around the bush, using polite euphemisms. I mean by experiencing a literal *death* - a termination of their human form. I do not wish to spiri-tually bypass the grief of loss and inevitable mourning that will come with this, with the *"oh well, they chose it on a soul level"* line of thinking, but unfortunately, that *is* the reality from a higher level of perspective. And as I said, some might consider those who exit the 'lucky ones', who *don't* have to go through the "hard part" and get to perhaps return in another form when the rebuilding process is already completed. We must honour each soul and its unique evolutionary journey - even if that includes exiting this lifetime through tragedy - no matter how painful it may be for the human part of ourselves to accept, as we all have our own paths to travel as a soul. Knowing that - like I have expe-rienced many times over, through my many past-life soulmate encoun-ters and resurfacing memories - the soul transcends the body, and we are never lost; we just change form... so it's not really the finality of "goodbye" just, "see you soon". But I digress...

This collapse may come through something different, and perhaps we will not have to go through catastrophic and destructive natural events as Gaia goes through her own purging and rebirth process. Perhaps it will come through the form of a different type of economic or societal collapse; things coming out in our news and media that have been hidden; a financial or banking system collapse; an electrical reset that fries all the circuits containing all of the credit information and brings everyone back to "zero"; a world war erupting (we definitely seem to be on the brink of it); or some other great non-natural-disaster-type shake up that causes a great collapse and reset of our society as we have known it. Given the astrology of the year 2024, as I write - particularly with the influence of Pluto moving into Aquarius - we seem to be in an energetic pressure cooker, which has already caused quite a few incidents of unprecedented violence to occur. In Sydney - where I am as I write this - we recently had two unexpected incidents of public violence occur within one week, prompting the American embassy to issue a warning for its citizens on holiday here, which is *unheard of* considering Australia is possibly one of the safest places on Earth. (Frankly, it's also *rich,* as this warning is being issued from a country that has an extremely high rate of gun violence... but, you know, *whatevs.*) Australia, suddenly being considered unsafe, speaks volumes to the energetic climate we're currently in and hints to the potential of how this energy might manifest in other places which are *known* to be violent and unstable. I say this as the already deeply embedded tensions seem to be escalating even further in the Middle East, as threats of using nuclear weapons are being thrown around.

Perhaps, like Atlantis, it is our own greed and desire for power, our own desire to play God with our advanced technology, that will cause this cycle to restart. With rapid advancements happening in fields that utilise artificial intelligence, one can only wonder where this will lead.

Or perhaps it's not as simple as any of these explanations; it will not be just ONE event, but a series of events unfolding, all interlinking, even though they appear somewhat random and unrelated. A chain reaction of dominos falling that is set in motion and can't be stopped once it's begun.

I don't know when this will happen. Whenever I ask, I just get told "soon", and I have had this sense for *years* of being on the edge of something massive happening. I have felt the impending doom coming from the human part of myself that is afraid about logistically what will happen - the format, the shape, the sequence of events that will come about - and how I will survive. While my guidance consistently only just reflects this peaceful message to me of "you will be taken care of" - just like every time over the past few years I have been on the brink of financial ruin or in a situation my human feels is so *dire* that it cannot possibly withstand it.

However, the fine details, the when, the logistics... everything else seems to be blank. Perhaps knowing the specific details would cause unnecessary panic and alarm. Let's face it, humans aren't known to be particularly chill in a crisis - we all saw what happened at the start of the pandemic with the toilet paper hoarding situation (something I thankfully avoided, as being in Indonesia, there was the luxury of using the "bum gun" most toilets have attached). Or perhaps being made privy to details in advance would mess with the process that needs to unfold or infringe on our free will somehow.

Truth be told, even if they *were* to give me a specific timeframe, I wouldn't hold on to it too tightly anyway. (That's not to say that the predictions *themselves* are inaccurate - I have a track record for being *freakishly* accurate in my readings, particularly if it's an event predicted to occur imminently.)

For many of the "big picture" things that I have foreseen and foretold, the timing given to me is rarely accurate, as timelines are shifting so quickly these days that a time-based prediction cannot remain reliable. Like my divine counterpart arriving, like the events I have seen where I am standing on stages addressing and activating thousands, like the many things I've seen in my future (the same things others have seen for me - completely unprimed and unprompted, I will add) - the time-line is always "*soon*".

"Soon" enough so I will remain hopeful and keep going; that cosmic carrot dangling in front of me to keep me motivated - but always just a little further down. Likewise, when I ask when this is all going to unfold, I just get told "soon" - but who knows how "soon" soon truly is. Like the Indonesian word "besok", that "tomorrow" could be any day in the future. It could be tomorrow, or it could be ten years from now.

The important part is that we are prepared - body, mind, and soul - so that whatever unfolds, in whatever way that might be; however smoothly or painfully it may be, we do not resist.

Those of you who are to be the leaders must mobilise and lead those not familiar with this process of rebirth who cannot withstand the long night, knowing that the new dawn will come. You have been training for this *all of your lifetimes* and through every single rebirth you have been through in this life, too.

I know many have already been "apocalypse prepping" for a very long time and have felt the impending inevitability of something like this coming their whole lives. I know of many cults and many religions that warn of the coming of the end of days in some way, shape or form, who are urging us to get prepared. Many of us would be inclined to roll our eyes at them and disregard them as religious fanatics or lunatics; and it is true a lot of it seems very *fear-based* as it is shared through the lens of *lack, fear and control* (A.K.A, repent for all your sins or you'll go to hell; only certain individuals will be saved; hoard everything for yourself in lack, separation and survival mode). Prior to moving past the resistance to receiving this prophecy fully myself, I would disregard such nonsense, adamantly believing that we create our own reality and that all we can do is focus on what we desire to create. I still believe this is true, and I still urge you to focus on the beautiful world that will come *after* this collapse; however (BIG, however), I am also aware that sometimes the pathway to that new reality requires things appearing to go *very backwards* first. Like the Tower card in the tarot, the tower needs to crumble so new foundations can be established. I am sure - as you are called to read this book and have made it this far in the journey - you have already experienced this many times over in your own life, your whole life seeming to completely crumble and fall apart around you, to create space for your desires to manifest. Yet, actually *being* in that "crumbling" phase can *certainly* feel like you're smack bang in the middle of your own personal apocalypse. What we could potentially go through collectively *might very well feel like* the four horsemen have come riding, and the end is nigh.

However, while having a sense for a long time that *something big* was coming, the preparation I have been guided through - as are those who are to be activated by this text - has been a *different* kind of preparation. I've been instructed not to worry about all the physical, "basic human survival" things; provisions like water, food, electrical generators, tools, or the building of underground bunkers. That's not my role nor my mission - there are others who will have that covered, and somehow, my intuition (and yours) will lead me to *exactly* where I need to be throughout this process so that all will be provided for. (If, of course, it is our destiny to survive it.) The preparation those like myself have been going through has been a much deeper *spiritual, mental* and *emotional* preparation. We have been taken through the death and rebirth process again, and again, and again; fortifying the trust in our channel and our inner compass, fortifying our trust in God's provision and support. So that we can *receive the messages* necessary in communion with the Earth and how she would like us to rebuild. (I feel I should also add that if you *have* been guided to prepare certain things, to trust that, as we all have different pathways and missions.)

There is one other Elephant in the Room I feel to address (which is probably going to lose me a lot of friends and followers, but here the dark goddess goes regardless; ready to call some shit out and speak into the thing *nobody wants to say*). It is the way in which the spiritual community is handling the "splitting of timelines" and "our shift into the New Earth". Many in the spiritual community speak of a timeline split, where none of these things will be happening to or affecting them because they're on the "5D timeline" but will be happening to "others" on the "lower", "3D timeline" (feel free to imagine sarcastic air-quote fingers every time you see quotation marks). While to some degree I believe that this is true, there *has* been a splitting of timelines - as in, those who are here to move forward into the new age will be experiencing these events somehow differently, from a different perspective - I do not believe that gives us a free pass to not have to experience any of these events at all. I do not believe that we get to just live in our own society immediately, which does not have to deal with any of the implications or inevitable difficulties that will unfold as a result of what is unfolding. *This*, to me, is spiritual bypassing, avoidance, lack of accountability and responsibility; people simply burying their heads in the sand rather than deal with *what is*.

Even more concerning to me are the many in the spiritual community who speak of an imminent Grand Solar Flash, which will bring the sudden coming of the New Earth, that we are currently being prepared for with these increasing solar flares. Once again, components of this, I believe, are true, which is the appeal to so many lightworkers and starseeds consuming this information. I *do* believe that the solar energies will continue to culminate and intensify, and perhaps there *will* be some main flash that is the catalyst for a huge event.

However, it's the next part that is *really* concerning to me. These channellers speak of a new planet where we will be "taken on spaceships" when this "Grand Solar Flash" occurs, and our current Earth becomes uninhabitable. *Um. Yeeeeeeahno.* Personally, I see this as more spiritual bypassing and an unwillingness to face the darkness of the death, destruction and breakdown necessary for our Earth to be reborn. I see it as yet another abandonment of the Divine Feminine in the form of Mother Earth, Gaia; just conveniently hopping off our planet and onto the next planet after the damage has already been done; with no personal responsibility taken in helping her to heal and evolve.

Evidence of our collective unevolved, wounded masculine who has not graduated into the supporter, provider, or warrior role; the masculine who is still in the phase of conquering, raping, and pillaging the Earth for resources before moving on to the next place. It is evidence of our collective, unevolved, wounded child, who hasn't progressed into full sovereignty and spiritual adulthood, entitled and expecting our galactic siblings to swoop in and save us from ourselves. Finally, it is evidence of the complete negligence of our privileged role as guardians of Gaia, which we have taken for granted.

Many of these accounts - and the comments I see under each post - seek to bypass the discomfort of the inevitability of facing any of the growing pains or any of the societal breakdowns necessary for this beautiful New Earth to be created. It speaks to me of a spiritual community that is not willing to hold themselves accountable; too surface-level to face their own darkness. It speaks to a community of starseeds who have *not* fully anchored and seeded themselves onto Earth - or come home to their physical bodies - if they are so eager to escape it. Everything is *"we'll just wake up having jumped into this New Timeline, on this new planet where everything is already perfect"*, or *"the spaceships will come and beam us up and take us elsewhere"*, or *"we'll suddenly just embody the magic of our Higher Self and remember who we are, without having to do any uncomfortable shadow work, or self-inquiry whatsoever."*

(If you are feeling triggered or discomfort is arising for you as you read this, firstly, I invite you to consider your relationship to your own darkness, your own inner masculine, and your own body. Secondly, please know that *I am only saying these things because I love you*, I love *all* of humanity, and I know we can all do better. I see your highest potential, and I desire for you to rise into it with all of my heart.)

As much as I would *love* for this to be real - to be able to click our fingers and just show up on the New Earth without any actual difficulty or hard work - everything that I have experienced on my journey has not been this way, and all of the preparation over *lifetimes* that many of us have gone through, just to be here NOW, would seem rather superfluous. (I mean, if we were really just gonna wake up on this New Earth without any birthing pains we'd have to withstand; if we could all just collectively timeline hop into a new reality with no pain and suffering, then why have we been going through all of these soul lessons to toughen and strengthen us, to hold our faith even though things appeared to be going *seriously backwards?*) It also seems lacking in the *personal accountability and sovereignty* as a race in actually BUILDING the New by taking responsibility or action, making decisions, creating the new structures and systems, putting our Divine Masculine pants on and doing the damn thing - *"Oh, we don't have to do anything, or actually take responsibility for our own evolution process; the*

Galactics will rescue us and take us to somewhere where we don't have to deal with any of it!"

Everything I have seen about the "New Earth" on many of these accounts is just "love and light", and whenever someone voices a genuine concern about "Well, where will this leave the people I love who are not yet awakened?" or "but how is this all going to happen", it is completely bypassed or glossed over.

While I *agree* that eventually, yes, it is all going to be perfect (and IS perfect, no matter how it plays out), and we needn't panic or live in fear about what will unfold, I am also adamant that we need to not negate the *grieving and mourning* process that will occur with the DEATH and shedding of all that *was,* to make room for what *is.* Nor must we negate the *fear* that will inevitably be felt (and will be especially echoed through the collective who does *not* have the 'higher' perspective yet) as all of this happens.

I have felt this fear, I have grieved and mourned many, many times over since the first echo of this message made its way into my awareness. I have felt (and wanted to turn away from, wishing it was not true) the dread and terror of what was potentially to come and the grief of all the people who would not be able to handle it, who would be rudely awakened from their slumbers, with no real preparation. I have grieved more than I could imagine in the process of even *accepting* the prophecy that wanted to be birthed through me in this book and the potentials it could point to; wishing and hoping with every fibre of my being that it was not true, that I *was* just actually crazy.

Many will say that this is a very 'fear-based' way to see it; that I am focusing on the negative, that I am creating 'lower timelines', and will want to burn me at the metaphorical stake for bringing attention to this element that *nobody* wants to look at - the very real element of darkness and destruction that we *cannot run from eventually facing.* But I am only sharing what I have processed in order to get myself Here, into this greater understanding I have; which can co-exist with and witness the fear, grief and anxiety about what is to come, which is felt by my Little Self.

And that is, I do not see any of these things as bad, or evil, or any cause for *fear* or alarm - but necessary for our evolution. I share the same stance on death, on darkness, on breakdown, on destruction, chaos, and decay as the Mayans. They are just another perfect part of Life, and part of me knows not to fear them but to welcome them.

You may recall me briefly touching on the Ancient Mayans' fascination with the planet Venus. For the Mayans, Kukulkan (the feathered/plumed serpent) bore strong associations with the planet Venus, and they were often depicted alongside each other in artefacts found. Some historians say that Kukulkan was a symbolic representation of the planet of Venus. The Mayans would track Venus's ascent and descent in the sky because they knew that when Venus would disappear from their sight, all sorts of "bad" things would happen to their society; death, decay, destruction. Venus - known as the "Morning Star" when she reappeared on the horizon again - was also a representation of renewal and rebirth. Thus, for them, *creation* (Kukulkan - the creator) was synonymous with BOTH death *and* rebirth (Venus's movements). Death and rebirth were *not* exclusive things, but simply the opposite ends of the *same* continuum; part of the one cycle.

For me - much like the ancient Mayans - it is not just the destruction that I see when I speak of this Ending; even if that death is a portal we must pass through. I see and hold the vision of the beauty of renewal, rebirth and New Life on the other side. And as you move through this process to becoming the Morning Star and guiding light yourself, it is a perspective which *you too* will come to embody.

Your very energy and presence - having moved through the transformational rebirth cycle yourself many times - will hold the blueprint and symbolic representation of this process; so you may hold the torch of hope that is the vision of the beautiful future as we collectively move through the necessary death.

INITIATION 8: PASSING THROUGH THE PORTAL

You can access the recommended audio version of this initiation at this website: www.diamondlightoracle.com.

Welcome to the eighth - and final - initiation in this transmission.

The following is an activation to rebirth you out of the Earth Womb, completely in your new form. You will not be the same person on the other side of this sacred visionary journey through the underworld as you are when you enter this process; although like it was for *me* when I went through this journey myself, it might take some time for your consciousness to catch up with the profound evolutionary leap that you have made.

This activation will complete the majority of the energetic work we have done together, dissolve the personal grid you have been in for this process, and initiate you into your own soul mastery.

In your mind and with your heart, set the intention that this is the work that will be done during our time together in this activation and that you are open to receive all that is in your highest good.

I now invite all the beings of the highest light who wish to support this activation taking place.

I welcome your Higher Self, your Soul Family and Oversoul Network; and invite them to support you in receiving what is of the highest for you at this time.

I declare that this is sacred space, only that which is resonating on the frequency of unconditional love is welcome in this space.

I ask that everything that takes place here today is for the *highest good of all* and in service to the Whole.

I ask that the work we do together here today ripples out and serves the collective.

And so it is, and so it is, and so it is.

We invite you to enter your Sacred Space - the safe and protected ceremony space in which you receive all calibrations, downloads, codes and activations throughout this transmission.

Acknowledging internally that *you have now entered Sacred Space.*

To begin with, we are bringing into the field the Golden Solar Dragon who wishes to co-create with us in this activation; to act as a sacred guardian who will ensure a smooth and protected journey ahead.

We will now introduce the Golden Cloak technology which is placed on top of you; to enable you to travel through the realms in which we are journeying today, from an expanded and higher frequency set point.

With this technology in place, nothing is able to touch you, to harm you, to infiltrate, or attach to you, or to journey beyond the gateways we will travel through together.

It is so, it is so, and so it is.

Allowing your consciousness to be transported now back to the Mayan jungle that you are by this point accustomed to through the various activations and initiations that have taken place before this moment.

As you walk through the jungle, allow yourself to *fully merge* with your surroundings.

Feel your consciousness begin to melt, to harmonise, to bi-locate itself into various aspects of the jungle...

First you might like to try on what it feels like to be an ancient and wise tree in this powerful jungle.

Feel what it is like to take on the tree's perspective, to witness aeons of time passing you by.

Feel the knowledge, the wisdom, the loving presence held in this tree.

Let your consciousness now transport itself into a blooming flower; a radiant, divine, brightly coloured and sweetly scented flower.

Feel the power of your magnetism radiating out; attracting to you the insects and the birds who will help you to receive and carry out your sacred purpose.

Feel what it feels like to know that you are capable of attracting all that you require simply by *being*.

Feel a hummingbird land gently on top of you and begin to gently nuzzle its beak into your pollen.

Let yourself become that hummingbird now; as you begin to fly up, up, up above the jungle canopy and into the beautiful blue sky above you.

Feel the weightlessness, the perspective that you are able to have from this higher viewpoint.

Feel what it feels like to observe life from this angle...

And now, bring yourself back down through the canopy, onto the jungle floor; into your *own* body.

You see a large, ancient Mayan pyramid appearing in front of you, and immediately, your consciousness *becomes* the pyramid.

You *are* the limestone, receiving all of the messages encoded within the limestone as you *are one with it.*

You see all of the people who have made offerings; who have walked over your limestone steps.

You feel all the magic that has taken place inside of your walls.

You feel the magic that has *created you.*

You feel yourself becoming covered over by jungle, in time; forgotten about and rediscovered again; as endless time moves in what feels like a short second.

You watch the tourists, the people through the ages, come to marvel at you; many not even being aware of the ancient magic that you contain.

You separate your consciousness again from this pyramid, and once again you become *yourself.*

As you stand here in your own body, you spot a jaguar; walking proudly and strongly through the trees and the plants towards you.

As this jaguar begins to make its way towards you, you are able to feel her as if there was no separation between you and her - you feel her power, you feel her presence, you feel her majesty.

You feel her medicine reverberating through your blood.

And yet you are aware that you are *still yourself* as she approaches you.

As this jaguar comes closer to you, we ask you *not to be afraid,* even though you might know or get a sense of what is to come next...

You now find the jaguar leaping towards you, ready to devour you.

Let her. Do not be afraid.

As you let the jaguar devour you, your consciousness begins to travel through her body which becomes a portal...

This portal brings you to the *inner jaguar chamber* of the main pyramid; the Temple of Kukulkan.

And inside of this chamber, there is a large circular gateway appearing in front of you.

You may feel like reaching your hand out to the other side of this translucent gateway to feel the sensation, to know that it is safe.

When you are ready, prepare yourself to step through this gateway entirely.

You are now stepping through this gateway, as it becomes a tunnel of light and darkness.

Feel yourself – feel your consciousness – sliding down through this tunnel now; this sheath-like tube which is surrounded by electrical pulses firing all around you.

You find yourself at the entry point of the First Gateway.

When you feel ready to, take a deep breath, and push yourself through this gateway.

See what you see, feel what you feel, hear what you hear – with the awareness that each person's experience of this first gateway will be different, depending on what is required for you at this time.

Stay here for as long as it feels necessary to really get a sense of this place, and retrieve what is required for you on an energetic level from being in this place.

You may feel like pausing here.

When you feel ready to travel onward, find yourself now at the Second Gateway.

When you feel ready to, take a deep breath and push yourself through this gateway.

See what you see, feel what you feel, hear what you hear - with the awareness that each person's experience of this second gateway will be different, depending on what is required for you at this time.

Notice how this space is *completely different* to the first.

There are different things for you to retrieve, to experience, to understand here.

Stay here for as long as it feels necessary to really get a sense of this place, and retrieve what is required for you on an energetic level from being in this place.

You may feel like pausing here.

When you feel ready to travel onward, find yourself now at the Third Gateway.

When you feel ready to, take a deep breath and push yourself through this gateway.

See what you see, feel what you feel, hear what you hear - with the awareness that each person's experience of this third gateway will be different, depending on what is required for you at this time.

Notice how this space is *completely different* to the others.

There are different things for you to retrieve, to experience, to understand here.

Stay here for as long as it feels necessary to really get a sense of this place, and retrieve what is required for you on an energetic level from being in this place.

You may feel like pausing here.

When you feel ready to travel onward, find yourself now at the Fourth Gateway.

When you feel ready to, take a *very* deep breath and push yourself through this gateway - knowing there is only *one more gateway* after this one to travel through.

You are reaching the end of your journey.

See what you see, feel what you feel, hear what you hear - with the awareness that each person's experience of this fourth gateway will be different, depending on what is required for you at this time.

Once again, notice how this space is *completely different* to the others.

This space represents what you are ready to transcend - your final initiation to step fully into your power.

There are different things for you to retrieve, to experience, to understand here.

Stay here for as long as it feels necessary to really get a sense of this place, and retrieve what is required for you on an energetic level from being in this place.

You may feel like pausing here.

When you feel as though you are complete in this space, allow yourself to push yourself through the final gateway.

You are being pushed out of Gaia's womb portal; rebirthed anew as this New Version of yourself.

Allow yourself to be immersed in the ecstatic joy, the relief, the homecoming that may be flooding your awareness at this time.

You may see, sense, perceive or even *feel* your wings beginning to spread out through your shoulder blades; or some other symbolic representation of the Diamond Light Body which has now been anchored for you.

As you merge with the energy of the Christ within you; you feel yourself, Christed.

You feel yourself Crystalline.

You feel yourself, Divine.

You feel yourself, an embodied Master who has taken the journey of death and resurrection, to anchor the frequency of the New Age.

As you sit in this energy, we will begin to dissolve the personal grid that was created for your process of journeying through this book and close all portals and gateways you travelled through behind you.

You may desire to sit in this energy for as long as it feels necessary and good for you; acknowledging, celebrating, marking the sacred journey that you have now completed.

Please know that you may not immediately notice the effects of the monumental leap that has taken place today.

While you fully integrate this *inner*standing, and your consciousness *catches up* with all that took place on an energetic level today, you may not have an immediate awareness of the profound shift that you have just gone through.

However, please know *it is already done.*

There will be more for you to receive in the final chapter of this book to anchor in and solidify the embodiment of these codes on a deeper level.

However, it is at this point we feel it is our divine duty to *welcome you home.*

We see you.

We love you.

We appreciate you and all that you are here to bring forth for this beautiful New Earth.

Thank you for trusting yourself and taking this journey.

Thank you for trusting us and allowing us to guide you on this journey.

You are loved. *You ARE love.*

Setting the intention now to share *all* the frequency and information that you have received from today's journey deep into the mycelium network and into the Earth.

Take a moment to send and share all of the frequency and information you have received today to be anchored into the Earth and seeded here, now, in physicality.

Integrating and calibrating this now on the physical level.

Integrating and calibrating this now on the emotional level.

Integrating and calibrating this now on the mental level.

Integrating and calibrating this now through all levels and dimensions of your light body.

Integrating, calibrating and sharing this frequency now through all timelines and all versions of yourself across the multiverse.

We now shut down any and all open portals and gateways that are no longer required and send back all energy that has come through any portals or gateways in the process of this work.

We now dissolve any bonds, chords or attachments that have been formed for the process of this activation and call you back into complete Soul Sovereignty.

We return all of your energy to you now as you call your Soul fully into your body.

Inviting in now Diamond Light to cleanse and close this space, and bringing this sacred activation to a close, thanking all of the beings who have been here supporting in this process.

It is done, it is done, it is done, and so it is.

You may spend some time here in silent reflection, or receiving in your Sacred Space if it feels necessary.

You may feel to document this monumental occasion in some way, acknowledging the completion of your initiation process.

If you feel complete, we invite you to gently bring yourself back into your body and into the room, wiggling your fingers and toes, and opening your eyes when you are ready.

PART NINE

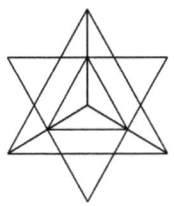

REBIRTH

THE 5 GATEWAYS OF THE
UNDERWORLD

Another day in bed, in the process of writing this book, receiving huge energetic transmissions once again. Listening to a sound healing track from my new favourite artist, I let myself drift into the trance state I can feel, wanting to lull me into its journey.

I feel the anticipation of the energy building as my eyelids flutter incessantly; behind them, all I see are strobing lights. I know what's coming is big; *it feels big.*

I can hear my mum tinkering with pots and pans in the kitchen, just outside my door - it's surreal to think I'm in here having a full-blown (sober) psychedelic journey in this inner city apartment, with my mum on the other side of the door casually doing dishes, none the wiser.

The stark juxtaposition of the sacred and the mundane makes me chuckle to myself a little bit.

I'm here - aware that I am present in this body, lying in this bed in my parents' apartment - while at the same time, I'm somewhere entirely different, yet equally *real.*

My consciousness is now deep, deep in the Mayan jungle; it feels like the journey is a continuation of the journey Grandmother Aya took me on when I was preparing to leave for Guatemala... *but somehow different.*

It feels like it carries more gravity, more intensity, more weight to it.

Deep in my bones, I know that whatever takes place today will change me forever... and I feel my Little Self-resistance beginning to rise.

I begin to walk - in my strong, former warrior body - through the jungle.

But soon, I am not only *in* the jungle; I *am* the jungle.

I am every ancient tree, every leaf, every shy mushroom peeping out from the chaotic jungle floor, every feathered friend singing its beautiful song, every colourful and exotic butterfly fluttering by.

I cross the path of a jaguar, and for a moment, I become the jaguar; strong, fierce, proud.

In the next moment, the jaguar - now outside of myself again - leaps at me and begins to devour me.

I feel my body - Little Human Bec, lying on the bed - begin to seize up in momentary panic...*am I dying? I don't want to die...*

I exhale and repeat my mantra, "*I trust you, Mama*" - the phrase I use whenever I'm journeying through something difficult, knowing that the Great Mother is only ever showing me the things that I need to see for my own evolution, and I needn't resist or be afraid - and allow myself to drop back in.

Where were we? Ah yes, that's right, a fucking jaguar was eating me alive...

As soon as I surrender and accept my inevitable death, I am transported to the Pyramid of Kukulkan... and then, for a moment, I *am* the pyramid.

I *am* the limestone; my consciousness and living memory are held within it.

I feel the centuries, the time that passes, watching as the jungle surrounds and swallows me.

And once again, I am separate from the pyramid; my consciousness is travelling through the insides of the jaguar's body...

Suddenly, I find myself in the inner chamber of the pyramid - the Jaguar Chamber.

My human logic tries to make sense of what has transpired; '*oh, I see, the jaguar is my guide... I had to surrender to her and become one with her to be transported here...I had to be willing to pass through the threshold of death and let go of my identity, first...*' Trying to understand something profound that is happening *so far beyond* the realm of the human mind.

But the shedding is not finished; in fact, it is just beginning...

As soon as I can take myself out of the scene for a moment with my pondering, I am immediately pulled back in, noticing the Inner Chamber of the pyramid is actually a portal.

I experience myself flying down what feels like an endless translucent feeding tube or a slippery slide, a neuron travelling along a network... flashes of electrical static all around me...

I find myself at a gateway; a shimmery, translucent, almost liquid-like portal; kinda like the ones in that show Stargate my mum used to love so much.

(I can hear her still tinkering out there, but now she's moved onto the vacuuming; *perfect timing, Mum,* I think to myself, *an interesting backing track to the hellscape of my psychedelic adventure.*)

"*You have to travel through these gateways*", the guidance tells me.

Suddenly, I am gripped by Little Self resistance and fear again when I realise what this place is...this is the underworld.

Not my first time here, but the first time I have come here with the awareness that in order to leave, I would have to effectively *leave behind a part of me.*

Once I enter, I need to go all the way through to make it out the Other Side.

Oh shit...I'm about to go through another death and rebirth portal...

"*I trust you, Mama, I trust you...*" I repeat to myself with a sharp exhale.

As I push myself through the first translucent portal, I find myself in another space entirely.

I am trying to establish and make sense of the place I have arrived at. *What is this place?*

It is empty, dark, expansive, nothingness.

Timeless, formless, infinite, nothing.

I am in the void.

I am nothing in this space; just a spark of light travelling around in otherwise darkness.

I have been here before on a heroic dose of psilocybin, so this time it doesn't seem so scary, but the first time I arrived here melted my brain, as I un-became everything I identified myself with; My Little Human Self panicked and tried to pull me back to "reality", because it didn't want to cease existing.

This time, the void felt like a relief.

Before I could start to spin myself out contemplating an eternity of nothingness, the guidance tells me, "*You're ready to move on*", as I'm sucked through the next gateway...

FLASH! An enormous explosion of light, bigger than a million supernovas...

I am suddenly EVERYTHING THERE EVER IS.

I feel all of it. I *am* all of it.

All the sensation. All the sound. All the colour. All the textures. All the feelings. All the perspectives. *All the things.*

Connected to everything.

Moving, moving, moving, never stopping.

My consciousness moves from fractal to fractal to try on all these different points of view and perspectives.

I stay here for a while; until it becomes exhausting, and soon after realising I am exhausted, my mind becomes bored...

I wonder what is next?

Pushing through the next gateway, I'm transported into what I immediately know is Heaven; the place of endless peace I transport myself to sometimes when I'm in the worst of my suffering. This place I visualise as a picturesque, beautiful and tranquil garden, where nothing and nobody can disturb me and I'm alone with God (the place I am often tempted to stay in forever and never come back down to Earth from)...

But now my mind is trying to get ahead of the journey and 'figure it out' - I am not allowing myself to be fully present with the heaven that is this place, I am letting myself be distracted by the mental chatter...

Wait, if that was Nothing, then Everything, and this is Heaven, then that means Hell must be next...

My Little Human Self starts panicking...

I don't want to experience Hell; please don't make me go to Hell...haven't I suffered enough?

And then I realise that my fear and anxiety about the potential of having to go to hell next is actually distracting me from enjoying heaven.

"You see," the guidance says, *"your worry over a future hell that you may not even experience is taking away from your moments of experiencing Heaven on Earth..."*

At this point, I don't care. I want to just rip the bandaid off already and go to Hell.

I take a deep exhale, repeat my mantra, *"mama, I trust you"*, and then I push myself through the gateway...

(I'm on the hiiiiighway to hell...)

I'm there for a few moments, waiting anxiously for something to happen, but everything seems pretty still. Some mild discomfort, but it's only coming from within.

Is this it? I think to myself, *it feels quite tame; surely this can't be Hell? Maybe I didn't do it right? Maybe it's not hell?*

I try to wander out into Hell a little bit more...

Frankly, not a lot is happening beyond my own fearful anticipation.

I'm holding my baited breath in anticipation of something terrible happening; some physical or emotional pain that's somehow worse than any of the suffering I've already endured; or being visited by a horrible demon I need to overcome with only the force of unconditional love (lord knows I've been there before)...

I wait, and I wait, and I wait, and...nothing.

Hell was just the fear and the anxiety I was creating in my mind.

At this point, my Little Human Self feels a little ripped off, all that anticipation for nothing - *seriously?! That's it?! Oh well...*

Pushing myself through the last gateway, by this time, I am mentally fatigued from the journey and wondering what could possibly be next; nothing, everything, heaven, hell... what else is there?

I stumble out onto a crystalline kingdom which looks like something out of a Disney movie or an LSD trip; enormous crystal castles, the greenest rolling hills I've ever seen with rainbows peeping over them, the sun majestically setting in orange and pink hues over the horizon line... everything *so* alive with colour and magic; so vivid and bright.

However, I have an awareness that the imagery is just something my mind is creating to understand this place; it's not an *actual* place that appears like this. It's a metaphor for the process of becoming crystalline and entering the Kingdoms of Christ.

The scene changes as I am shown flashes, images, visuals of the New Earth on the other side of the birthing process...

And I understand there are no more gateways for me to travel through.

I have entered out onto a new timeline, a new reality; I have crossed the threshold of death to rebirth myself once again, an entirely new version.

At least for today, *my journey is complete.*

THE JOURNEY HOME

As is pretty standard for me after any life-altering event, trip, or "high", the contrasting come down from my time in Mexico was rather intense and heavy. Landing back in Australia in my parents' inner city apartment catapulted me right back into the almost crippling depression I had seen beginning in November, with the completion of the hike (especially with their relationship on very rocky ground when I arrived and tensions in the home being very high). I was mentally, emotionally, physically and spiritually exhausted; no excitement of future plans, or travels, or journeys, or business moves, or even next steps to look forward to; nothing to ease the ego-obliteration of finding myself living back with my folks again, suddenly more or less broke, with very few tangible, external 'results' to show from my Mexico initiation. Of course, there were many times I'd stayed with my parents in the five years since commencing my gypsy life - it was always a 'base' for me to return and pause between my nomadic travels - but every time previously, it always had an expiry date, which made it far less shameful in my mind. I had either sublet my "real" home in Bali and had a date to return, or I had flights and onward travel plans. Therefore, I justified it to myself with the reasoning I wasn't actually "living" with my folks; I was just passing through.

For the record, I carry zero shame around this now, and I see it as somewhat ridiculous that I even had any to begin with. Realising that being able to lean into the support of my loving, supportive parents while I went through the post-mission integration and eventually started to write this book was actually DIVINE GRACE - a luxury many don't have - was a realisation that took me a month or so after arriving, to come to terms with. Once this landed and I surrendered into the absolute gift of having the luxury to stay with family, it completely dissolved any shame I once had. Not to mention the privilege of having the incredible, compassionate, understanding and supportive family I do; who allowed me to go through the process I was going through without trying to put pressure on me to change, to go to "work", or get psychiatric help when I was in the worst and most questionable moments. There were moments where I would be sobbing with grief, and my mother would just lovingly hold me or stroke my forehead and tell me she wished with all her heart I never signed up for this journey that seemed to make me suffer so much. Or where I'd have a breakdown at the dinner table with my Dad about how I couldn't do another day of feeling the suffering and pain of the world, or the unbearable feeling of separation from God, and how I wanted to die just so I could finally return to the place of unconditional love and peace I knew (yes, it was *that* bad). Somehow, he would manage to say the right thing to calm me down and comfort me, even if I was virtually inconsolable.

I am so grateful to have this safe landing space to hold me through this process, which would be even more challenging to move through if I also had to worry about putting food on the table or a roof over my head. I am grateful with every fibre of my being that I chose these parents to be born to because they have made walking this path a lot easier than it could've been had I chosen other parents. While my parents have never *really* understood what I go through or how intense it can be at times since I have stepped on this path, they have done nothing but lovingly support me and hold faith in me even if I've challenged the hell out of them.

My mother has always been a little bit alternative; taking me to see psychic readers at fifteen and owning more crystals than she knows what to do with. She has had her own mental health challenges to contend with and believes the wild things I share with her, even if they are a stretch for her at times ("I believe you, *but maybe don't go telling everyone because they won't understand you*", she often says). My father was prepared for me with his own mother – who had "gifts" - and whose lineage holds the magic that runs through my veins (stemming right back to the same bloodline I was incarnated in during my Delphi life, I learnt recently). While he's a little more resistant to believing (I'm still not sure he fully believes) and a little more traditional, he's very compassionate when it comes to any sort of mental health issues, as this is also something he's had a lot of exposure to and personal experience with. My sister – who is two years my senior and one of my closest friends - is on her own medicine path, and while she resonates more with animism and our spiritual views differ slightly, I have had the privilege of sitting with her on soul journeys many times, including her joining the mystery school training "Rebirth", I facilitated in 2021 (which my female cousin on my dad's side also joined; quite magical family healing).

I definitely would not have made it through this initiation – nor any of the previous ones - without the love and support of the offbeat little family I used to do anything in my power to escape. I also can see how my family needed *me* at this time just as much as I needed them. (My sister expressed to me how grateful she was that I could be around and help take care of my folks and do things around the house for them; Mum's health is deteriorating, and Dad no longer has the capacity to care for her that he used to, as he himself is declining in health, as he ages.) Being back in Australia and living with my folks was exactly where I needed to be for more reasons than one.

Suffice it to say when I arrived back in Australia, I hadn't come to this higher perspective, and all I wanted to do was leave again. I resented being back with my folks, I resented being in the inner city, I resented having a lack of personal space and quiet, I resented having no means to escape, I resented that I didn't even have the desire to open my laptop and work, so I could actually do something to *change* my situation. I didn't have any clear guidance from my higher self, my guides or my soul team around what my "next steps" were. I was staring down a gaping black hole of nothingness; no prospects, no pings, no excitement, no joy. Finding myself crying to sleep most nights; heartbroken, confused that I was still grieving my karmic relationship and missing him terribly; waking up most days with zero desire to get out of bed. Spending every day looking through a filter of grey; just trying to pass the time until I could get back into bed and escape once again into my dreams. I fantasised about death a lot, even though I *knew* there was some part of me that - despite contemplating it extensively - was *way* too stubborn and committed to this mission to actually end my life. And despite how disconnected I felt at times, I could simultaneously feel a loving voice - God, my higher self, my soul - a feeling in my heart, connecting me to the truth that this suffering was only temporary. It reminded me I'd been here many times before, and I would make it through yet another dark night of the soul to see the light on the other side, just as I had, time and time again.

For a solid two months straight, I battled through an intense crisis of faith. I started doubting my entire path, my purpose, and *everything* that had unfolded during the previous months. I started questioning whether I *was* actually just crazy, should seek psychiatric help and get put on medication (something I have firmly been against, even if I briefly did try it, many years ago). I was questioning how I had been *so* in alignment - so trusting, and surrendered, and intuitively following the mystery breadcrumb trail - just months earlier, and what the hell had happened to that magical, loving, benevolent, guiding force that seemed to be present in *everything*; who was now nowhere to be found. I was questioning how a path that was supposed to "heal" me - to bring me closer to my desires, to grant me peace, joy and abundance - had brought me so much pain, suffering and hardship. I was questioning whether I could even trust what I had been channelling or whether it was just tricker entities posing as my guides. I was questioning if the mystical experiences I'd frequently have of experiencing heaven or "walking with God" were just a result of an imbalance of chemistry or perhaps an unnoticed seizure. I was paranoid that my kundalini was actually an evil entity that had possessed my body and that I needed to "cast it out". I turned away from dragon energy, from Kali Ma, from the dark goddess because suddenly she terrified me (something which she had *never* done before). I couldn't bear anything but the frequency of Jesus; I was convinced that God was angry at me and that I needed to denounce everything and revert wholeheartedly to Christianity. I was questioning whether God even *wanted* me to use these gifts I had to help others or whether they were playing with the devil. And that's when the nightmares began.

I began to have "Revelations" (the book in the bible) type apocalyptic nightmares, where the world was burning, and I was being forced to 'repent for my sins'. I had semi-lucid dreams where the kundalini "demon" was being cast out of me; where I'd wake up trying to yank the "demon" out of my body. I was confused, I was lost, I didn't know what to believe or where to turn. When I would receive clear messages of support or guidance from my higher self or from my soul team - which, in hindsight, I can see were *quite loud and clear*, as clear as I ever am able to channel; they were just not saying anything which I deemed helpful at the time, other than "you have to be going through this right now" - I didn't trust them or believe it wasn't a trick. I was praying every single day, begging God to help alleviate my suffering; to lead me to someone who could help me alleviate the symptoms of the initiations I went through, so they would be more graceful - particularly in my physical, mental and emotional bodies. I begged God to show me the way home to love, to show me his plan for me... willing to accept if the answer would be that I was to stop everything I'd been doing, give up my spiritual business and become a nun. I was willing to give up *everything I built* over years of hard work and everything I thought I desired for myself if God had asked me to.

It was my big sister - bless her - who, about a month into the hell of my suffering, offered that perhaps what I was going through was purging some past life or Mayan trauma from when the Catholics came and forced them to repent. I reached out to two women I'd worked with in the past who specialise in energetic clearing to check to see whether there was something influencing me (they check for various types of intrusions such as entities, unwanted spirits, tethers, tracking, and so forth) and they reported back that I was being affected by unhealed, tethered ancestors. I had indirectly carried all of that heavy Mayan trauma with me and was also reliving my own nightmares from past lives of being "made to denounce everything but the Christian God". Within a day of realising and releasing this, the nightmares stopped, and a heaviness lifted off me. I was guided through synchronicity towards several books - by a priestess sister of mine, who has *always* been a guiding light home to God for me - reminding me about Jesus' missing years, his mastery of kundalini, and the underlying commonalities between religions. It brought me right back to my previous understanding - that *all* of it was connected and coming from the same place. There wasn't a need for hard lines and boundaries; for black and white, good and bad, right and wrong. I started to feel connected to God again and that my *gnosis* was more powerful and more important to me than anything written in any book by a human man. I came back to a place where I could be solid with my own direct-line communion; living from my heart which I KNEW was pure - having been prepared to give up *literally everything* to do as God would ask of me - and my faith in God's unconditional, non-judgemental love; rather than a set of rules which I felt grounded in fear and control.

I also managed to find the inspiration to start a new side business - or rather, re-brand and officiate the marketing work I was doing the entire time in the background, by separating it under a new company 'Mystika Marketing Co'. Something which I'd be able to do, no matter what initiations or spiritual upgrades I was going through. This gave me some purpose, focus, and certainly lightened my mood; I was feeling a sense of accomplishment and productivity again, as a result of conceiving of the new branding. However, the action I was taking was quite laboured and forced; it very much felt like doing something from the "mind" level of what I "think I should do" rather than what my heart was telling me to do. Knowing how easily things flow for me when they're intuitive impulses, rather than me in my over-masculine "hustle" mode trying to force shit; it was launching me into a cycle of frustration, as I was fighting against the grain and couldn't seem to get much momentum. After going around this loop of frustration for about a month - even though I was starting to slowly pay off my debts and get back on my feet again - I realised my frustration was coming from *trying to force things, which was just creating even more resistance,* and I finally surrendered. I declared that I was open to being lifted up to the higher timeline I could feel was *just there* - but was somehow evading me - and that I was going to just let go and do absolutely nothing for three days. I spent time in nature, I went for long walks, I slept, I spent time with my mum watching movies, and I waited.

On the third day - right on time - the guidance dropped in.

"Remember that book you were told you were to start writing just before you left for Guatemala? The one you've been avoiding all this time? Yep. That one. It's time."

In an instant, it all made cosmic sense. *Everything* I had been going through had started the moment I was told I was going to write this book, just prior to my jungle trek. It was my Little Human Self throwing up resistance to being asked to step into the next level of embodiment and leadership on my mission. And it was *so* sneaky at flying under the radar undetected, behind all sorts of other reasons my mind concocted for why I was depressed, that I hadn't even noticed it. The purging of all the witch-woundy stuff about being cast out as a result of being fully and openly in my gifts - knowing on some level that this book would mean being "seen" as an Oracle on an even larger scale. The crisis of faith to test whether I could *really* trust my channel and my inner gnosis, or I'd buckle under peer pressure; whether I was *really* willing to do what God was preparing me to, even if it wasn't what I *wanted* to do. Moving through relentless darkness and grief to test whether I was really ready and fully devoted to this mission, or I'd just bail when it got hard. The apocalyptic visions which intensified and haunted me to prepare me for the prophecy that wanted to be shared through me. The ego-death around being a *'broke-ass failure living with my parents again'*, which cut my head off and put me on my knees so I could be a pure vessel for this potency of this transmission, not doing it for fame or glory, or money, or anything else. (I might add that after I finally accepted the task of putting all of my energy into writing and completing the book I was asked to write without conditions or ulterior motives, my business started flourishing again, and the floodgates to abundance opened. It goes to show; you will *always* be supported in all ways you require when you are following your divine mission.)

Within a few days of receiving the nudge, I began to write with an awareness of how much resistance I was actually carrying around channelling this book; realising that even just willing myself to show up and actually *write* was proving to be a battle. Right on time, God sent me someone to support and hold me through the process. Actually - as it always seems to be - this woman had *already* been on my way to me in my peripherals, as I had entered her vortex a month or so earlier after randomly seeing a Facebook post for her 21-day telegram container 'Money Dragon'. I don't even remember when exactly she had added me as a friend (as I don't tend to add random people myself), and it seemed it was the first time I'd noticed her show up on my feed. It seems that even when I was blocked AF and feeling disconnected, my intuition was *still* guiding me to her, as I'd joined her challenge without even knowing why. I had also been really drawn to somatic work - applied kinesiology, specifically - for the months leading up to this, and this woman specialised in Chinese medicine and working with the meridians, which was one of the things that really called me to her. Needless to say, after experiencing her medicine for the first time, I was blown away because I had never experienced someone doing an activation so similar to mine, nor who was capable of making me feel like vomiting because the transmission was so *strong*. I promptly reached out to her after one of the first activations I experienced to tell her I could feel a deep soul resonance, that we must be from the same lineage, and she would be interested in co-creating on my podcast.

After having her as a guest (you can listen to our conversation, episode 56: "Dragon Empowerment Activation" at www.becmylonas.com/podcast), we continued the conversation, and she began to channel some very specific things about the enormity of this book and the resistance I had to write it - things that I had already heard myself, but not fully trusted. Talking to her was the first time I had felt fully seen and understood in the intensity of what I would go through physically, emotionally, mentally, or had met anyone who I felt might actually be able to give me the support my body needed; to be able to hold and channel the enormous amounts of energy moving through me more smoothly. Not only that, but this woman was speaking into things about my mission and myself that I always knew deep inside but wouldn't dare tell anyone else because I didn't want to come across as arrogant or 'too big for my boots'. (Among many other things, she had said, *"The dragons tell me you are being prepared for something BIG"*, and she was certainly not wrong.) Needless to say, after blowing my mind wide open and seeing me in a way that nobody had been able to do before, we began a beautiful, two-sided exchange and co-creation together, where I was able to do the same for *her* and her mission.

I have used the word "mentor" (as well as "book doula") throughout this book to describe her because there were no other words that could give appropriate context of her important role in my life and throughout the process of birthing this book. However, it was a much more symbiotic, two-sided relationship where we *both* were learning and receiving from each other; the gifting and activating were completely mutual, and we impacted each other beyond belief. In fact, I don't really like using the word "mentor" at all because I believe everyone is a teacher with medicine for us and that we are all just coming home to our *own* magic. To me, our relationship (along with many others I've had throughout the years, who have supported me in some way) was the perfect example of New Earth co-creation, round table leadership and energetic exchange; each person contributing *their* unique magic for mutual benefit, *and* for the greater good. No hierarchy or rigid roles; just flowing with what feels true and alive for both of us. In saying this, we both had such deep love, respect and reverence for each other from the first moment we began our exchange, which was why we could flow in such a beautiful and trusting way without having our boundaries crossed or one of us feeling like they were "over-giving". We had also both done obscene amounts of work on the sister-

wound, to be able to support each other in this way without comparison, competition, jealousy, or tension. The fact of the matter was that
we were both just genuinely invested in the mission and the success of
the other - we were contracted on a soul level to support each other in
this way at this time (just as you are with *all* soul clients, soul mates,
and so on).

I was expanding and amplifying the grid for her mission by being the
'example' of the type of Diamond Light Oracles she would be working
with in the near future - and has since started calling in - along with
working my marketing magic on her business, building out the entire,
intricate backend of her unique healing modality. She was also the first
person other than myself to begin to read and receive the activations
of this book, bringing with it an activation of her Oracle codes and her
diamond light body. Simultaneously, she was initiating me in *her*
healing modality; serving as a book doula, holding me through the
transformation I was going through in real-time while channelling the
book; helping me to support my channel and my system by doing work
within my meridians, and connecting me to Gaia even more deeply
than before. On top of all of that, I was also in the grid of several of
her group offerings, which were working on me in the background
throughout the first two months of birthing this book.

I honestly do not know whether I would have been able to birth this
book had it not been for this beautiful, powerful, unconditionally
loving and non-judgemental sister who held me through the process
(along with the many others who supported me in varying ways across
varying stages of this process, who I am also eternally grateful for). She
was witnessing and acknowledging what was happening for me and
supporting me to move through the birth canal safely - helping me
with little tweaks in my field when the energy would get too much or
just being a safe place to land when the content that was streaming
through to me was causing my Little Human Self to spiral into fear or
disbelief. She lovingly and non-judgmentally witnessed the heinous
eruptions of shadow coming out of me - hot and sulfuric, like lava - as I
navigated the process of internal destruction taking place. She helped
to ease my feelings of insanity when I was channelling things that felt

too big for me to hold on my own and to confirm my downloads or intuitive nudges. She helped me uncover crucial pieces of the puzzle and understand exactly what I was going through. Without her, I would never have been able to recognise the transition I was making in the first place, nor honour the process it takes to move from Priestess to Oracle.

THE DIAMOND PATH OF ENDURING THE LONG, DARK NIGHT

"Your guides want me to tell you that they've heard every single prayer and every single dream you've had... and they've not forgotten about you."

I remember the day my mentor sent this message to me, and I broke down into loud sobs. Suddenly, I felt connected to the love which had been evading me; the grace; the kindness in the delays. Someone *was* listening, I was not just praying for nothing!

Part of me always knew (and received the guidance) that the reason why the "big" things I was manifesting were not happening (yet) wasn't because I was being 'punished'. It was because I was being 'prepared'.

Indeed, about five years ago - when my gifts and oracle lifetimes spontaneously came online again - I had been shown a vision of my life (which, in response to, I had sobbed and wailed and begged God to take it away, saying, *'please, I don't want it, choose someone else'*). I was shown that I would have *everything* "external" I was wishing for on a human level - I would be seen, known and celebrated for my life's work; I would feel spiritually and emotionally fulfilled; I would be impacting large amounts of people across the globe with my soul mission; I would enjoy financial wealth and freedom; I would be in a magical, juicy, sexy, collaborative, sacred partnership with the love of my life... and that by the time it all arrived, *none of it would even be a big deal to me anymore.* I was shown that the very process of actually manifesting my desires would have me detaching from them *completely* because of the person I would become along the way. A person who was connected to the feelings of *already having these desires,* and therefore, not actually requiring anything outside of me to feel good. The fulfilment, the love, the satisfaction, the abundance, the connection, the pleasure; I would find it all within, first. (I daresay I am close to this stage; I am touching that place of deep inner peace, joy, love and fulfilment of just *being* where and who I am many days; without needing to be anywhere or anyone else. Even writing some of these things in comparison to the other things I am bringing forth in this book feels a little silly and irrelevant to me now because what is *my life* in the scheme of everything that is to come? I'm not really asking for much these days, other than God bringing me those who I'm here to support or co-create magic with in some way and simply making sure I have what I require to fulfil my sacred mission.)

However, to hear it from someone *else*, this thing I had told *nobody* - this feeling of being abandoned; that God was not listening to my desires; that I wasn't allowed to even *ask* for what I wanted; that I was tired of enduring all of the difficulties, the hardships and the suffering, without getting even a *glimpse* of what I desired; without recognition or a pat on the back; without *a single reward* (yes, I realise now, how childish and egoic that sounds) - was finally being acknowledged, broke my heart wide open again.

There is nothing more painful than when you have a yearning for something in your heart, and it is perpetually out of reach. Believe me when I say I have been living this reality for a *very* long time when it seemed like everyone around me was instantly manifesting their heart's desires with much ease. Only now do I see and understand why I was continually told 'not yet', or 'soon', or made to wait for visions that I had been holding in my heart and yearning for so deeply; the pain of not having them broke me open, time and time again. It felt so *fucking unfair* to be feeling like I was invisibly and consistently held to this higher standard that nobody else around me seemed to be. To be denied my deepest desires, as I watched those around me seem to enjoy ALL of them - success, wealth, acclaim, recognition, stability, magic, miracles, true love, health - without doing *half* of the inner work it felt like I was required to do. Without the gruelling lessons and entire months spent in bed wailing and sobbing and feeling like I was dying while holding and moving what felt like the grief of the entire world. Not to mention the added frustration of feeling like my Little Self desires were consistently being thwarted by the overriding authority of my Soul, which didn't seem to give a flying fuck what I was putting on my vision board or writing about on the new moon. These things were always irrelevant in comparison to making sure I was *getting the lessons I required to crack me fully open.* It certainly felt like I was being punished; that I had done something *terribly wrong* I was being made to atone for; that I simply wasn't allowed to have what I want.

And yet, her message completely alleviated my suffering and dissolved my illusory perceptions of victimhood, and I instantly felt all the love and support flood in. They had heard my prayers, and there simply was a divine reason they weren't being answered (yet).

Not receiving what I desired when I desired it wasn't punishment, it was divine *grace*. It protected me from my own self destruction, in receiving a gift I was not yet ready for.

It forced me to look at all of my own darkness and to forgive it, becoming more able in the process to be able to forgive and love the darkness in others. It enabled me to *make the decision* to choose to be different; to come back to love again and again and again. To strengthen and test that resolve, so I would still choose love, no matter how tempting the alternative seemed.

It forged me - like a diamond is forged under pressure - to *become* the Oracle capable of sharing the transmission of my life's work. It forged me to be strong and unbroken, no matter what criticism or attack may be directed at me; when the messages I'm sharing trigger those who aren't ready to hear them; when the light moving through me illuminates the shadows of others.

It has put me on my knees and made me see that I cannot do *any* of this without God, that serving God's will (the greatest good of *all*) is more important than serving Self, and that this mission is so much bigger than me and my Little Self desires. It has prepared me to keep my heart open; no matter how much the process of receiving this transmission has broken and tested me. It showed me the kind of soul I truly am; to show up day after day, without any gratification, without any reward, without a pat on the head, without acknowledgement, without even *evidence* that I was moving towards my desires. It has shown me that *nothing* external truly matters; that all is simply an illusion that reflects what you feel inside... so *why not just skip the bullshit and focus on what's inside?* It has fortified my strength and my faith in the unseen. It has fortified my trust in my own channel and gnosis.

I am not here to glorify suffering or to assert that we need to "earn" our desires through proving ourselves worthy because we already *are*. But I do believe that New Age spirituality that tells us "we can have everything we want now" that social media, where everyone only presents their 'highlight reel', can create tendencies where we feel entitled to having everything our way instantly. When the reality is, *perhaps* our desired timeline for *when* we get what we want is not actually *God's timeline for us.* Or that our desires are not *truly soul-aligned.* Perhaps our "desired timeline" is not actually *in our highest timeline* or in alignment with the intention our soul came into this life with: to learn certain lessons and master certain qualities. Let's make one thing crystal clear – our 'highest timeline' does not necessarily equate to our easiest timeline. It is the timeline of our *highest unfolding* – our greatest becoming. You best believe sometimes getting there means we need to endure and overcome certain challenges.

Here's the uncomfortable dark goddess truth bomb that you probably don't want to hear, but I'm going to deliver anyway *'cause I fucking love you.* **You don't become *your highest self* – your greatest unfolding – by everything around you being easy or handed to you.** This is the difference between those of us who are here to Lead and those of us who are here to Follow. This is the difference between a Priestess and an Oracle. An Initiate and a Master. This is the difference between those of us who are learning more complex and difficult soul lessons (because we are more advanced souls) and those of us who are still mastering the basics (because we're early on our soul journey). If you are a *master*, then you must undergo challenges and initiations befitting one. To use a fun video game analogy, you're not going to fight the same boss at Level 1 as you will when you've progressed to Level 10...*'nuff said.*

I need to add, I am not saying any of this with hierarchy or "one is better than the other", as every soul is equally important. (If you believe that you're better than others because of your divine mission and the gifts you've been given to fulfil it, then you have a long way to go, as your highest self would not hold that perspective.) Younger souls with less complex or challenging soul missions are just on different points on the wheel or cycle. It's like comparing a seedling and an ancient Oak tree; when we enter the start of our next cycle as a soul, we will become the seedlings again. And if you truly want to eat a slice of humble pie, know that there are also *plenty* of more advanced souls than us out there (even though we are all One, so we have *been* and *already are* them, just as we simultaneously have *been* and currently *are* the "seedlings", as time is non-linear and all our incarnations are actually occurring in the present moment).

What I *am* saying (and I hope is hitting home, dear reader) is that those who are here to lead or birth bigger or more complex missions require initiations that are equivalent to prepare them for the pressure and challenges they will face. To create the endurance, the strength, the grit, the determination, the commitment, the follow through, the open-heartedness, the faith, the love, the compassion, and the devotion necessary.

Those who are here to lead are inevitably put through much more stringent training than those who will not have the responsibilities that come with it.

If you are going through this long night now and feel that you are constantly being denied and withheld your beautiful desires, know that this is your *training*. You are not being punished, you are being prepared.

This beautiful soul is your *initiation* into the mastery you are required to hold to carry out your soul mission. In previous lifetimes, you would have gone through this initiation differently. Perhaps you would have devoted your entire life to the temple; hours and hours of gruelling practice and discipline spent every day; mastering *every* level of your being - your mind, your emotions, your body, your energy. In this life-time, it is *life unfolding* and your reaction to that, which is initiating and preparing you - *including* the parts of the journey when things are diffi-cult, you are tested, or the process of manifesting your heart's desires seems to appear a lot like you are being brutally denied and ignored. Every single thing you have been through - no matter how shitty, uncomfortable, painful or difficult it seemed at the time - has been preparing you in the background and guiding you here and now.

It is with God's grace that you are being prepared to be able to hold all that comes with your Divine Mission. To be able to receive the gifts and blessings your heart's yearning has guided you to, without sabotaging them.

How much love you hold for your soul to be able to endure all it has; in this lifetime, and in the many before this, where you suffered immensely as a result of coming here to realise your sacred purpose. Your divine mission of holding hope, holding love, holding the vision when others can not has required you to know what life is like without that hope, without that love, without that vision. Your divine mission of standing behind your truth even if it is not accepted by others - even if it has you cast out, ex-communicated, burnt at the stake, judged, uninvited to the party, black-sheeped, taken off the Christmas List, cancelled, deleted, blocked. You are a brave one to have chosen this, for it takes a level of *chutzpah* many do not have. How courageous and beautiful you are to never give up, to keep going, to keep showing up, day in and day out; without gratification, without praise, or thanks,

440

or even recognition most of the time. How big and beautiful your heart truly is to choose this path!

This is the diamond path, beautiful soul, and if these words resonate with you, it is because you are walking it. This is not a path that everybody has chosen, and there is a good reason for that; not many have what it takes to be able to withstand it. You have been training for this pivotal transition you are making all of your lives. This is the path required to go from "priestess" to be exalted as "Oracle".

FROM PRIESTESS TO ORACLE

All Oracles are priestesses, but not all priestesses are Oracles. There is a very specific initiation process a priestess must pass through in order to be one who is capable of transmitting the frequency pure enough to be considered **prophecy**; a prophetess (or the male equivalent, a prophet), an Oracle. To me, the ability to transmit *prophecy* is what an Oracle is and is what distinguishes her/him, although many people will see the term "oracle" as more synonymous with the aspect of self who is naturally attuned to other realms. I use the capitalised "O" intentionally to distinguish between the two.

Prophecy is not merely something that impacts a small number of people or creates change on a personal level. Prophecy is something that has the potential to change the entire world simply as a result of being observed and spoken. **Prophecy is something that creates a _movement_ that gains momentum that ripples out and changes the very fabric of our universe as we know it**. There is a *before* and *after* prophecy, and simply by the act of hearing it, people are changed forever. Many priestesses have the ability to see timelines and potentials. An Oracle - on the other hand - doesn't just see them; *she speaks them into being*. Therefore, she must ensure she is *pure in intention,* as she will be held accountable to the prophecy she speaks into existence. Prophecy is not something to be casually thrown around. There is a difference between witnessing and seeing timelines that are personal - the potential of where someone might be in a few year's time, or who they might marry, or what job they might get - and timelines that are collective; that have an impact that spans out into the multiverse. There is a difference between being able to open up your channel and channel *anything* and discerning the very specific frequencies and messages that are not only for you but for the highest good of all. Prophecy is the ability to relay the word and the messages of God without getting *your little human self* in the way.

It requires great discernment and personal accountability to stand behind prophecy. You must be prepared - mentally, emotionally, spiritually and physically - and purified so that your vessel is free from distortions, and you can deliver the message without any personal emotion, resistance or flavouring to it. The Messenger *becomes* the Message.

The Oracle not only shares a paradigm-shifting message, but they have gone through the initiation and journey of it, so they completely embody and transmit its frequency.

Prophecy is not something that will be received in the same way by all - many will resist it, fight against it, be triggered by it, and try to discredit it - therefore, the Oracle must be prepared to put the message above her own desire for acceptance or preservation. Oftentimes, an Oracle is willing to *give up her life* (metaphorically and literally) for the prophecy because she knows the prophecy and the legacy it will leave behind is much bigger and more important than her.

An Oracle must see *beyond* her lifetime, *beyond* her discomfort, *beyond* her suffering; believing so deeply in the healing potential of the prophecy and vision, that at no point she would consider abandoning the hope of it being realised. The Oracle is a visionary, capable of holding the vision and the intention in her heart when nobody else can; *even* when things appear to be going backwards, and when all evidence points to the opposite result. She knows the prophecy as truth, and it is the only truth that matters. She speaks up for it even when everyone around her tries to diminish it or call it nonsense or fantasy. (Consider the figure of the O.G. prophet Moses, from the story of Exodus in the Torah, Quran and Bible; who delivered God's message of the promised land and committed to taking his people there, despite constant challenge and ridicule, and without ever having the privilege of arriving there himself in his lifetime.)

An Oracle is the definition of "Ultimate Badass". She tells it like it is; she speaks the Truth (big T truth) and is willing to stand behind it, even when nobody else will. Even if it's uncomfortable. Even if it's not glamorous. Even if it's going to make people hate her for it. She does not bend nor buckle under pressure or scrutiny. She does not require being accepted, or liked, or agreed with. To her, the prophecy is gospel.

Oracles wield a power and authority that has *weight* to it - or at least they did, back in the ages when the divine feminine was still revered - a weight that creates a ripple effect; that **speaks events into existence**. Consider the oracles you have heard of or known from ancient times or even from our movies. Oracles are the ones who are respected, revered, and sought for counsel above any other position of leadership or standing. People travel long and far to visit with them; they are held in utmost respect and reverence because their prophecy is trusted and holds integrity. They have the capacity to mobilise *entire armies* with their prophecy. The Oracle giving the hero permission - really truly *seeing* them and speaking into this reality - gives the hero permission to believe in themselves.

It is my prophecy that Oracles will regain this position of trusted leadership and guidance - they *must* if we are going to make it through this crucial transition the Earth is making. It is time for the Oracle - the divine feminine spirit - to rise back into the position of power she once held. But in order for her to be exalted to this position of power, she must claim her power. She must claim herself an Oracle.

"Your guides are telling me that you might think that it's ego or hubris to call

yourself an Oracle, but you need to claim that. Claiming and calling yourself that will give others permission to do the same."

I remember in the first few conversations with my mentor (a few days after I started writing this book) she shared this. And I remember feeling like someone had punched me in the gut because she had reached in and put a voice to the thing I was feeling deep inside I needed to do, but was too afraid to... to claim my true, Ancient Oracle nature in the act of writing this book. Before she had said this, I was looping around and around in my brain; wondering if it was just spiritual ego or a psychotic break that had me believing I was channelling Mayan prophecy or that this book was going to start this movement, activating all the priestesses I felt (and was told) it was here to activate. The moment she spoke into the *thing* my Little Self was trying to reason its way out of - by speaking DIRECTLY to the fear and casting aside any of my doubt - I couldn't hide anymore.

Embodying - or rather, reclaiming - my multidimensional identity as an Ancient Oracle has come with much internal resistance because I have always taught through my personal experiences, my identity (or rather, forays in dismantling said identity) and my "humanness". Actually, I haven't seen what I do as "teaching" at all, nor have I seen myself as a "teacher" - I've simply seen myself as someone walking a path and inviting others to come along for the ride with me. I know better by now than to claim I know more than others or to assert anything as definite or finite. Remaining humble and never claiming anything as "the one and only truth/way" has always been one of my biggest values; as someone who knows from experience there is only ever more growth and evolution available to us. I've also never been comfortable with bragging - even the "humble bragging" that is encouraged of us in the self-development industry. You will never hear me claim that *"now that I proclaim myself an Oracle, I am all-knowing and all-seeing, and this is the last initiation I will ever have to go through"* (and if I did, perhaps this entire process was for nothing. In fact, I have just been informed that *this* initiation I've just gone through in birthing this book will be "nothing" in comparison to the next one, which is approaching imminently; *yippee*).

As I reach the end of *this* particular transmission and the initiation that came with it, I see how it is guiding me to drop even more identification with Self and the Little Self's experiences of suffering; as I become or touch that place that *already is* the transcendent Oracle within me; the part of me who sees *beyond* the veil of illusion in this reality, and the attachment which creates the suffering. (It is the same journey that all the ascended masters go through in awakening to their own crystalline Christ consciousness.)

It has initiated me to be able to share this prophecy, to *know* in my heart the potency of this consciousness (this book) and the impact it will have, and still somehow not make it about me *at all* because, really, I'm just the vessel...

This - knowing and claiming the power that is wielded through this vessel, and simultaneously knowing *it's not really mine to claim at all* - is the total *trip* of a journey that I have been on, from the very first day I said yes to this sacred mission. As a journey that is largely framed with *my* experiences - the very human story you have read through these pages, animated by my Little Self, with all of her personality, rather specific preferences, judgements and tantrums - it has been a process of gradually letting go of the Self. It has taken quite the journey to step more and more out of my Little Human Self into the Ancient Wisdom that is really just God-flowing-through-me.

I also - rather ironically - stand at the end of this book, chuckling to myself at how much of a *fucking ordeal* claiming myself as one little word put me through, considering that now I don't even feel it's entirely necessary to identify or label myself with it at all. An "Oracle" is just *one* aspect of my much larger and greater multidimensionality - it seems rather silly to diminish myself or hold onto just this one thing when I am *so much more* and simultaneously *nothing at all*. (What a hilarious cosmic joke *that* is - going through this whole damn journey just to be okay with proclaiming myself as an Oracle, and then realising *it doesn't fucking matter anyway*. Such is the great paradox of this entire experience called Life, which can feel a lot like *someone up there is just straight-up trolling us.*)

Yet, I share this journey with you - the initiation I have been through thus far; the process my Little Human Self has gone through, with all its pitfalls, highs, contradictions, cosmic jokes and paradoxes - to pave the path and prepare the road that you yourself will walk.

And I stand with you at the end of this initiation, having walked the path and being made to let go of the attachments, the tantrums, the fears, the resistance... an Oracle.

PROPHECY OF REBIRTH -
THE NEW AGE

This is *my* prophecy, the prophecy that I will choose to leave you with as our time here comes to a close. The vision I will hold in my heart of the new timeline and Earth that will be birthed out of the destruction of the current one. This hopeful dream of what will be, and all of the beautiful things *you* will see, is what we need to hold as our anchor; our vision we are birthing into being; our Morning Star to see us through the darkness - even if these visions might not fully blossom, in *our* lifetime.

It will not be our government, our royal families, or our media that guides us forward in the times of chaos; it will be the Divine Feminine Oracles that we will turn to (yes, you) to lead us out of the death and destruction, into our New Life.

It will be their guidance, their prophecies, their visions; their connection to the Divine, and to the heartbeat of the New Earth; that will lead us forward and instil hope within us; our Morning Star, our guiding light in the darkness.

These Oracles and their priest(ess) initiates will lead the re-building of crystalline temples devoted to the Way; created to teach and initiate others to commune with the Oneness, to *feel* the land, the stars, the skies, all the elements, and the heartbeat of consciousness itself; so we can build from the ground up in harmony, and spread this harmonised frequency through the Earth grid. They will channel through these crystalline temples ancient wisdom, new technologies, galactic keys, and codes of our Ancient Future, helping to awaken the sacred wisdom and spiritual technology within us that will be passed down through generations. Initiates will remember and re-learn how to use the sacred technologies we wielded in the Golden Ages and ancient civilisations - to generate free power, heal, alter matter, and perform other 'miracles'. However, these priest(esses) and Oracles will not need to "teach" the new Star Children who have already begun to come onto our Earth, for they will already be spiritually advanced and awakened. Rather, these temples will create an environment for their continued mastery-level training and development. We will learn from *them* as they bring with them new ways of being, advanced technologies, potentials, and possibilities from the stars. Majority of these Star Children will be born to couples holding the pure temple of Sacred Union (*hieros gamos*) and born into unconditional, divine love.

We will live in harmony with Mother Earth and all Her inhabitants once again. We will hear Her, we will feel Her, we will nurture and love Her, we will live in a symbiotic relationship with Her, where she will nurture and love us just the same. We will enter the Kingdom of Heaven within and into divine comm(union) with our Holy Father above. We will be at once the Creators and the Creation. We will remember our own intergalactic nature and return to living in harmony and communion with our Brothers and Sisters in other non-human forms; they will support us, teach us, and share their wisdom with us as they have done for aeons and will continue to do, as we evolve in consciousness as a race through the fifth dimension and beyond. We will take our rightful seat on the Galactic Federation, and our race will have representation; having finally evolved to the point of unity consciousness. We will regain the ability to communicate telepathically, we will share collective memory - while still maintaining our individual sovereignty - and eventually, regain the ability to bi-locate both in energy *and* physicality.

We will return to living in community - as one borderless tribe of Rainbow Warriors, echoing the sentiment of the Hopi prophecy - on large sections of pristine, pure, unadulterated land, which are off-grid, self-sustained, ecologically responsible, and have not been touched by any of the chaos or destruction. Many have already started the process of securing this land - as spirit has shared with me many times, and this has been conferred by other channels. There are those who have the sacred mission of securing, establishing and preparing this land, and this process is already underway as I write this. We will live like our Indigenous tribes did; each of us with devoted roles which we will uphold. Our Elders will graduate into positions as the guardians and teachers of our Young, but we will all initiate each other with our unique magic and codes. We will lead simple lives where we all bring forth our unique soul gifts into the world. Each of us sharing our gifts and genius freely; ensuring an energetic exchange where *everyone* is taken care of and provided for. Each individual and their unique Gift will be seen as equally important and divine, weaving a tapestry together where every thread has its unique purpose as part of the Whole and matters. Understanding that we are all One and that what benefits One benefits All.

We will move as a humanity - once again - into a Golden Age; the Heaven On Earth that was always destined to be ours.

And the cycle will start *all over again...*

The beautiful vision is going to take time to birth; it will not magically happen overnight. We are talking about rebuilding an entire civilisation from the ground up - the infrastructures, the systems, the structures - and that will bring with it unique teething pains. The likely reality is that we will not have the chance to see our seeds coming to full bloom in this lifetime. Of course, I'm not suggesting that there will be no progress or that we will not see significant momentum towards this vision in our lifetimes - or even glimpses of Heaven on Earth already unfolding in our own lifetimes. There are many who have already started to live and move towards many aspects of what will define this new age, who are already living in conscious communion with the Earth and with each other. Who are already living sustainably, responsibly, and conscious of the footprint they are leaving. Who are already communicating telepathically and psychically attuned to those close to them. However, for a time, we will still be living with one foot in the new Earth and one in the old one.

There are certain features of the old Earth that many of us will still rely on during this transition period. For instance, I am writing this on a computer in a home that requires electricity and working internet for it to work; all of this requires money and renders me still dependent on the infrastructure of the country I inhabit. Some of the things we enjoy in this old world - like electricity, for example - will be brought through into the new age in different ways which are less destructive, as new potentials and technologies are received from the field, as we upgrade in consciousness. I do see, for instance, being able to one-day harness lifeforce in the ways we did in Atlantis to power our grids with free energy. In fact, I have already personally been working on this throughout the process of my own initiation; remembering how to generate and wield Life Force in enormous amounts through my body. It is the *role* of the priest(esse)s and Oracles to channel the codes for this new technology - some from our galactic brothers and sisters, some from our own ancient wisdom - and bring it through to our Earth so that those who are capable of translating them into form, are able to do so.

Inevitably, other things we currently enjoy will be lost, and we will be required to let go of our reliance on certain comforts we have enjoyed, returning to a simpler "grassroots" way of life.

Regardless, assimilating new infrastructure, new technologies, new social systems, new governing bodies, new economies, and so on takes time. Like the foal learning to walk and wobbling on its hind legs, our vision may be a little wobbly while we walk this Earth in the bodies we now inhabit. At the same time, it is *our responsibility* to begin building these structures *now* (not some distant time in the future). It is up to us as a collective how long this process will take and whether we get to see any of the fruits of our labour in our lifetime. Our ability to work together and mobilise will dictate the duration of time it takes us to rebuild.

This is why it is so crucial to remember and anchor into our *vision* and our purpose here, so we do not become fatigued and 'give up' before the foundations have had a chance to be properly made. We have come to pave the way for our descendents; for future generations of humanity who will reap the benefits of the crucial work we have done. We are here for the *long game*; to leave a lasting legacy, not for instant gratification or a quick dopamine hit.

We are the birthing canal; the bridge between the old and the new. We will be required to hold hope when all hope seems lost; to remain focused on our vision when it seems things are moving further away from it.

We must look to the practice, the training we have had in our own life - the times when our dreams seemed impossibly out of reach; when the life had left a project, a relationship, a situation, and it seemed there was no chance for resurrection; when we felt we were wandering in the desert for a long time, without a sign of water or shelter. We must look to the evidence for when everything worked out, when it seemed we were dead in the water; when the miracle arrived in the *perfect* timing (even if that was the last possible minute); where a creative solution to a problem was *so divinely orchestrated* it could only have been through the grace of God; an answer to our prayer.

We *are* the prayer, just as much as we *are* the answer to that prayer. Our collective's prayers for a new world have already been heard, and what is unfolding before our eyes is the process of that prayer being answered. This is what we must remind ourselves of when things get difficult. **It is already done, we simply must follow the aligned, inspired actions to continue to move towards it.** (Please don't skip that last part because it's just as important as the "it's already done" part that people seem to like to regurgitate over and over again without taking divinely inspired <u>action</u>.)

Our inner gnosis is what will bring the peace in our hearts, and will enable us to anchor into the Heaven within us - as truly, the Kingdom of Heaven that Yeshua foretold of is one that is an internal experience, not an external one - no matter how dire situations and circumstances seem to be in our external world. Yes, we are here to anchor heaven on earth, but the Kingdom of Heaven is already here, and it is *within* us. The love, the peace, the harmony, the joy, the orgasmic juiciness, the pleasure, the connection, the lightness, the play, the ecstatic goodness, the gratitude, the nurturing, and the satisfaction we will feel when our Vision is made manifest, is something which we can *already* tap into and have access to. We can tap into those feelings in moments of simplicity while we enjoy a humble meal with our loved ones or play music around an open fire, while we dance or feel the loving touch of our partner, take a walk in nature, or bathe in the ocean.

We can *choose* how we see everything as it unfolds. We can see the divine love, the perfection and the beauty in *all of it*; even the parts which feel chaotic, destructive, uncomfortable and painful to behold.

And we can be certain in the knowledge that the Winter, the dark night - no matter how long it may feel - will not last. Spring will come again, and we can one day look to the horizon to see the Morning Star revealing herself; declaring the New Dawn has arrived.

And so I leave you, courageous Oracle, with this final message.

Be the Morning Star that you are; shine brightly in those moments of darkness, for others will look to you for hope. Even if you are the *only star* visible or shining in a sea of black; keep holding the hope for what you know to be true in your heart.

Share your prophecies boldly and fiercely, without self-consciousness, and do not hold back any sacred vision you are given to impart unto the world, for they have been entrusted to *you* for a reason.

You were chosen for this task, you were chosen as the vessel for the Message you are here to bestow, and you *absolutely* have what it takes to go through any initiation, any preparation, and any training that is required for you to deliver it to the world.

The divine in me sees the divine in you.

I love you,

Your Divine, Diamond Sister xx

ABOUT THE AUTHOR

Bec is a visionary Oracle, high priestess, soul catalyst, alchemist, activator and creatrix devoted to walking the path of divine love and paving pathways of light for others to walk behind. Her mission is to facilitate soul remembering and guide others home to their sacred gifts.

Bec's greatest gift - and deepest honour - is the ability to activate, initiate & catalyse the soul remembrance of others.

Her core purpose in this incarnation is encouraging and awakening the gifts of others, and being a clear vessel for Love to flow through in order to facilitate the most profound energetic soul-recoding and transformation.

She is fortunate enough to be the gatekeeper of powerful multidimensional codes and sacred technologies that transfer across a range of mediums and work on a deep energetic level. Her energy is deeply activating to those she encounters and works with, whether that be through healings or channelled activations, written work, healing music or spoken word.

She is passionate about speaking, writing about and sharing the learnings from her own soul journey, along with the wisdom she Oracles around awakening, healing and the ascension process.

An equally large part of her mission includes working within the portals and grids of the Earth, and beyond.

Bec is a portal to other dimensions, and a bridge to help others connect to God. She connects deeply to the Earth; to the ancestors, to the elementals, to various archetypal energies, to high dimensional light beings, to sacred women's wisdom; in order to channel through intuitive guidance and processes that enable activation and healing, specifically dictated for each client and their journey.

She is honoured to hold the codex of the divine feminine priestess lineage along with ancient wisdom that she has received from connection to the ancestors of not only this Earth, but the star races which seeded us.

Bec's initiation and awakening process opened her eyes to the power we all possess, the divinity, the sovereignty and the gifts that are available once we step away from 'ego' and into alignment with soul self.

Bec believes that true leadership comes from empowering you to heal yourself and your relationship with source, with your own divinity and power. She prefers to walk through the fire with you as a friend and an ally, rather than to be put on a pedestal.

She is your personal guiding light through dark, uncharted territories to create true empowerment, freedom and liberation.

To create a magical life that is beyond your wildest dreams.

Within this book there is a coded invitation to continue this sacred mystery training further. If you have felt a deep resonance with Bec, the Diamond Light Oracle journey and the initiation you have gone while receiving this codex, and wish to continue the journey, head to www.becmylonas.com, or find Bec on socials at @becmylonas to be informed of the latest offerings, mystery school trainings and initiations.

www.ingramcontent.com/pod-product-compliance
Lightning Source LLC
Chambersburg PA
CBHW071132130626
46553CB00004B/1338